**W9-BVE-844**

Checklists

Throughout this book, you'll find Checklists that offer helpful questions to assist you in preparing more effective, more usable documents in technical communication.

A Concise Guide to
Technical
Communication

Laura J. Gurak
University of Minnesota

John M. Lannon
University of Massachusetts–Dartmouth

PEARSON
Longman

New York   San Francisco   Boston
London   Toronto   Sydney   Tokyo   Singapore   Madrid
Mexico City   Munich   Paris   Cape Town   Hong Kong   Montreal

Executive Editor: Lynn M. Huddon
Development Editor: Michael Greer
Marketing Manager: Thomas DeMarco
Senior Supplements Editor: Donna Campion
Media Supplements Editor: Jenna Egan
Production Manager: Ellen MacElree
Project Coordination, Text Design, and Electronic Page Makeup: Nesbitt Graphics, Inc.
Cover Design Manager: Wendy Ann Fredericks
Cover Designer: Nancy Sacks
Cover Photos: Clockwise from top left: Mason Morfit/Taxi/Getty Images, Inc.; Johner Images/Getty Images, Inc.; Digital Vision/Getty Images, Inc.; and Fisher/Thatcher/Stone/Getty Images, Inc.
Senior Manufacturing Buyer: Alfred C. Dorsey
Printer and Binder: Quebecor World–Taunton
Cover Printer: Coral Graphic Services

For permission to use copyrighted material, grateful acknowledgment is made to the copyright holders on pp. 343–344, which are hereby made part of this copyright page.

Between the time Web site information is gathered and published, some sites may have closed. Also, the transcription of URLs can result in typographical errors. The publisher would appreciate notification where these occur so that they may be corrected in subsequent editions.

Many of the designations used by manufacturers and sellers to distinguish their products are claimed as trademarks. Where these designations appear in this book, and Longman Publishers was aware of a trademark claim, the designations have been printed in initial caps.

Library of Congress Catalog on file with the Library of Congress.

Please visit our Web site at http://www.ablongman.com/gurak

ISBN 0-321-39168-3

1 2 3 4 5 6 7 8 9 10—QWT—09 08 07 06

Brief Contents

Detailed Contents

CHAPTER 9
Graphics and Visual Information   154

Part Two   Technical Communication Situations and Applications   183

CHAPTER 10
Everyday Communication Situations   185

APPENDIX B
Documenting Sources   311

Preface

Even the most casual observer can see the powerful, compelling relationships between technology and communication. The growing number and complexity of new technologies, from personal computers to medical devices to Internet applications, require accurate information on how to operate and maintain these devices. The use of technologies—HTML coding, Web applications, online help screens—to communicate information across global boundaries means that every professional needs to understand technology.

To meet this need, institutions offer technical communication degrees or certificates through a combination of face-to-face, interactive television, and Web-based classes. Some students major or minor in technical communication, whereas others take technical writing and communication courses to fulfill humanities requirements and enhance their skills as engineers, scientists, or other specialists. In addition, writing-intensive programs, especially in engineering or science institutions, often focus on technical writing. Even high schools are now adding technical writing to their list of elective classes.

Whatever its context, technical communication is rarely a value-neutral exercise in "information transfer." It is a rhetorical, social transaction comprising interpersonal, cultural, ethical, legal, and technological components. In today's global environment, a one-size-fits-all approach simply does not work. Effective technical communication must be clear, accurate, and organized, and must be tailored for specific audiences and purposes.

With those requirements in mind we have created this Third Edition of *A Concise Guide to Technical Communication*. This book draws on the strengths of John M. Lannon's best-selling *Technical Communication* (now in its Tenth Edition)—accessible style, clear examples, and time-tested approaches—but in a streamlined version focusing on critical topics such as copyright, document design, usability, information technologies (including the Internet), and communication in cyberspace. The book retains key qualities of the larger text but in a smaller, concise, technology-centered volume. Students and faculty alike will appreciate its trim size, content, and direct access to information.

Audience for This Book

Most technical communication texts have dual audiences. One audience is instructors, who use textbooks to plan a syllabus, design assignments, and create lectures and discussions. This *Concise Guide* is suitable for a range of instructors, from experienced to novice. All instructors will find this text easy to digest, streamlined in its use of features, and relevant to current technology topics. Novice instructors will find useful examples, exercises, and checklists; in addition, the Companion Website offers online tutorials, additional exercises, teaching tips, and other teaching resources. Experienced instructors will find that the concise format allows for enhancements within their classrooms without restricting them to one perspective or set of examples.

The student audience for this text is also varied. Students in introductory technical communication will find that the text and Web site contain fundamental concepts, situational strategies, and other supporting features. Advanced students will be able to move quickly into issues of audience, purpose, and design. All students will appreciate the emphasis on the Internet, visual communication, and usability. Examples throughout this text reflect a variety of majors. Students from engineering, science, health care, and other disciplines will find this book useful and relevant, whether in a traditional technical writing class or in a writing-intensive section of their major.

How This Book Is Organized

This book is organized into two parts. Part One, Technical Communication Techniques and Considerations, covers issues of central importance to today's technical communicator: audience, purpose, usability, research, the Internet, ethics, copyright, document design, and graphics. Part Two, Technical Communication Situations and Applications, incorporates the considerations from Part One in treating various types of workplace communication (email, memos, reports, specifications, oral reports, Web pages, and the like).

Hallmarks of the Third Edition

Layered approach.   Instructors can use this *Concise Guide* alone or in combination with their own materials. Instructors may wish to teach the chapters in order, which allows for a logical teaching sequence, especially for an introductory course with students from mixed disciplines. Yet the chapters, and the modules within each chapter, can be taught in virtually any sequence.

Range of skill levels.   Students in technical communication courses often span a wide range of writing skills. Although this book contains a solid section on grammar and style (Chapter 3 plus Appendix A), certain features of the Companion Website will be particularly useful for students who need help in this area. The Companion Website offers intensive exercises, links to style guides, and links to online writing centers.

Compact format.   For instructors and students alike, a shorter, more compact text is extremely appealing. Instructors will appreciate the small size, because it allows them to use supplementary material without overloading the student. Students will value a concise text, because material is easy to look up, access, and carry in a backpack.

In addition to its compact size, the *Concise Guide* offers a unique combination of features:

- real examples taken from industry, government, and high technology, reproduced to look like the originals
- sections on copyright, ethics, and social issues
- sections on usability, document design, and page layout from a human factors perspective
- a thorough chapter on visual communication
- a cutting-edge chapter on technical communication in cyberspace
- end-of-chapter items including checklists and exercises titled Focus on Writing, The Collaboration Window, and The Global Window.

New to the Third Edition

In developing *A Concise Guide to Technical Communication*, Third Edition, we have included new and updated examples throughout the text. Most of the Web pages and many of the sample documents have been updated. Each chapter in this Third Edition emphasizes usability, with revised examples, discussions, and guidelines.

A sampling of new material:

- **An updated and thoroughly revised Chapter 8 (Page Layout and Document Design)** features new discussion of templates, new model documents, inclusion of "before" and "after" documents to demonstrate effective document design, and new checklists for layout and design.
- **New coverage of project management** includes the new sections "Teamwork, Virtual Teams, and Project Management" in Chapter 1 and "Telecommuting and Virtual Teams" in Chapter 5.
- **A new complete, annotated model long report** is included in Chapter 12.
- **Chapter 10 includes new coverage and models of résumés and cover letters**, and the use of PowerPoint in oral presentations.
- **Chapter 4** features updated coverage of Web research and the use of other electronic research tools (databases, for example), and new tips for evaluating sources.
- **Chapter 5** offers new coverage of corresponding with others using email, blogs, and instant messaging.

- **New CSE documentation models** have been added to Appendix B.
- **New strategic usability Checklists** have been added throughout most chapters, in place of the former "Review Checklists."

Instructional Supplements

These ancillary materials are available to accompany *A Concise Guide to Technical Communication,* Third Edition:

- An *Instructor's Manual* includes chapter overviews, learning objectives, teaching tips, suggested exercises, Web resources, and chapter quizzes, with answers. The manual also offers an appendix with additional grammar exercises.
- A dedicated Companion Website provides activities that take students and instructors beyond the textbook. The site includes chapter overviews and objectives, Internet exercises, Web icons, individual and sample documents, and links to resources for both students and instructors. For more information, visit http://www.ablongman.com/gurak.
- *MyTechCommLab* is a comprehensive resource for students in technical communication. It offers the best multimedia resources for technical writing in one, easy-to-use place. Students will find guidelines, tutorials, and exercises for grammar, writing, and research, as well as a gallery of model documents, an online reference library, and Pearson's unique Research Navigator and Avoiding Plagiarism programs. Visit http://www.mytechcommlab.com for information about how to access this remarkable site.
- *The Literacy Library Series*—*Workplace Literacy* by Rachel Spilka, *Public Literacy* by Elizabeth Ervin, and *Academic Literacy* by Stacia Neeley offer additional models and instruction for writing for each of these three different contexts.

Acknowledgments

We are grateful for the insight and ideas contributed by reviewers for the Third Edition: Renee Barstack, Glendale Community College; Jerry DeNuccio, Graceland University; Daniel Ding, Ferris State University; Jo Mackiewicz, University of Minnesota, Duluth; Becky Jo McShane, Weber State University; Neil Plakcy, Broward Community College; and Pat Scanlon, Rochester Institute of Technology.

Thank you to the teachers and scholars who reviewed earlier versions of the text: Christine Abbott, Northern Illinois University; Susan G. Baack, Montana State University—Billings; Roger Bacon, Northern Arizona University; Marck Beggs, Henderson State University; Lee Brasseur, Illinois State University; Linda Breslin, Texas Tech University; Eva Brumberger, University of Wyoming; Patricia Cearley, South Plains College; Dave Clark, Iowa State University; Daryl Davis,

Northern Michigan University; Ray Dumont, University of Massachusetts; Patrick Ellingham, Broward Community College; Julie Freeman, Indiana University–Purdue University; Lucy Graca, Arapahoe Community College; Howard Graves, DeVry University; Kay Harley, Saginaw Valley State University; Joyce Harlow, Rogue Community College; William Wade Harrell, Howard University; Kathy Hurley, Minnesota State University, Mankato; Mitchell Jarosz, Delta College; Robert Johnson, Miami University of Ohio; Dan Jones, University of Central Florida; Charles Kemnitz, Pennsylvania College of Technology; Karla Kitalong, Michigan Technological University; Elaine Kleiner, Indiana State University; George D. Knox, Portland Community College; Renee Kupperman, University of Arizona; Eleanor Latham, Central Oregon Community College; Mary Massirer, Baylor University; Robert McEachern, Southern Connecticut University; Brad Mehlenbacher, North Carolina State University; Yvonne Merrill, University of Arizona; Dennis Minor, Louisiana Tech University; Paul Morris, Pittsburgh State University; Joe Moxley, University of South Florida; B. Keith Murphy, Fort Valley State University; Roland Nord, Minnesota State University; Alice Philbin, James Madison University; Carolyn Rude, Texas Tech University; David Alan Sapp, New Mexico State University; Carol Senf, Georgia Institute of Technology; Katherine Staples, Austin Community College; Tom Stuckert, University of Findlay; Zacharias Thundy, Northern Michigan University; Janice Tovey, East Carolina University; Alex Wang, Normandale Community College; Martin Wood, University of Wisconsin–Eau Claire; Judith Wooten, Kent State University.

Thank you to Lynn Huddon of Longman Publishers for her editorial support of this book. A special thanks to Erin Wais for her editorial assistance, Lee Scholder for her work on the Instructor's Manual, and David Kmiec and Erin Gurak for their assistance with copyediting. Also, heartfelt thanks to Michael Greer for his insight and assistance with this Third Edition including his work on the Companion Website. We especially appreciate Janet Nuciforo's expertise in all aspects of production. Finally, we wish to thank our colleagues and families for their ongoing support.

Laura J. Gurak

John M. Lannon

Technical Communication Techniques and Considerations

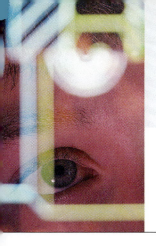

CHAPTER 1

An Introduction to Technical Communication

Communicating About Technology
Main Characteristics of Technical Communication
Types of Technical Communication
Technical Communication in the Workplace
Teamwork, Virtual Teams, and Project Management
Societal Dimensions of Technical Communication
Ethical Dimensions of Technical Communication
Checklist for Quality in Technical Communication
Exercises
The Collaboration Window
The Global Window

Communicating About Technology

We live in a world in which many of our everyday actions depend on complex but important technical information. When you purchase a wallet-sized calculator, for example, the instruction manual is often larger than the calculator itself. When you install any new device, from a VCR to a microwave oven to a cable modem or new computer, it's the setup information that you look for as soon as you open the box. Household appliances, banking systems, online courses, business negotiations, government correspondence and affairs, and almost every other aspect of your daily life are affected by technologies and technical information.

Technical communication has existed since the very earliest times of human writing. The Sumerians, in 3200 BCE, used a stylus and a block of wet clay to record information (Wilford, 1999). Most people trace the rise of modern technical communication as a profession to the United States after World War II. The rapid development of new technologies during this time created a need for accompanying technical information, such as instructions, manuals, and documentation. And in the 1970s, when the personal computer was invented, well-designed technical communication became vital as more and more nontechnical people began using computers, software, and related devices. Today, with a large percentage of the population using the Internet, banking via the telephone or the computer, and interacting with technology in so many other ways, we all recognize the importance of well-designed technical information.

Main Characteristics of Technical Communication

1.1

Recognize the characteristics of technical communication

Technical communication is the art and science of making complex technical information *accessible, usable,* and *relevant* to a variety of people in a variety of settings. To some extent, effective technical communication is an art, because it requires an instinct for clear writing and good visual design. Even more important, technical communication is also a science, a systematic process that involves certain key principles and guidelines. The following principles characterize effective technical communication.

Accessibility

Information is accessible if people can actually get to it and understand it. If documentation for a help system is included on a CD-ROM, the people using this information must access a CD-ROM drive in order to use the information. If a set of instructions is being distributed across the globe, these instructions must be written in various languages in order to be accessible to international users.

A group of technical editors at IBM has developed a list of "quality characteristics" that help them determine if their technical documents meet high standards and are of superior quality. These characteristics suggest specific ways in which communication can be made accessible (Hargis, Hernandez, Hughes, & Ramaker, 1997, p. 2):

- Accuracy—has no mistakes or errors
- Clarity—avoids ambiguity
- Completeness—includes all necessary information
- Concreteness—uses concrete examples and language
- Organization—follows sequences that make sense for the situation
- Visual effectiveness—uses layout, screen design, color, and other graphical elements effectively

Usability

Usable information is *efficient,* because it allows people to perform the task or retrieve the information they need as quickly and easily as possible. Usability is often measured by studying the design of the table of contents, index, headings, and page layout, as well as determining if the language is written at the appropriate technical level. When technical communicators assess a document's usability, they may want to know how long it took a person using the document to find specific information and whether this information could be located using the index or table of contents. For instance, a manager may consult the company's employee handbook for information about vacation time. If the manager cannot find this information and cannot do so quickly, the document would not be considered usable and would need to be revised. (Learn more about usability in Chapter 3.)

Relevance

Relevant information maintains a focus on the specific *audience*—the readers, listeners, or viewers—who need information, not piles of useless data. Information is relevant if the audience can apply it to the task at hand. For instance, if a person is interested in how to use Internet service provider (ISP) software to connect to the Internet, the documentation should explain how to install the software and dial up the ISP and not digress into a history of how the Internet developed. Similarly, for an audience of general computer users who want to install a sound card, overly technical language is inappropriate. Relevant information also maintains a focus on the *purpose* of the communication. Although the history of sound cards might be interesting to some engineers, the purpose of the communication (how to install the sound card) dictates that this history is not relevant.

Often technical communication is thought of in relation to the documents and technologies we have just described; that is, technical communication is designed to teach a general audience how to perform a specific task involving a common sort of technology—how to set up a VCR, install a new sound card in a PC, or install the mulching blade on a lawn mower. But technical information is also used by technical specialists, managers, and others. A surgeon performing heart surgery must have clear information about how to install a pacemaker. A government research scientist must have accurate instructions about how to write a grant or how to perform a particular experiment. An engineer must have access to the right specifications for designing a bridge or configuring an application. In all settings in which people must understand complex information, there is a need for technical communication.

Consider the following example, which illustrates just one of these ideas: how technical information is made *accessible* by the writer's use of consistent terminology. Unlike some forms of writing, in which authors are often told to vary their choice of words, technical communication strives for accuracy by using consistent terminology when referring to the same item or task.

For example, assume that you have just purchased a new children's toy that needs assembling. In one case, the writer of the instructions decided that she would vary the terminology. Here is her first draft:

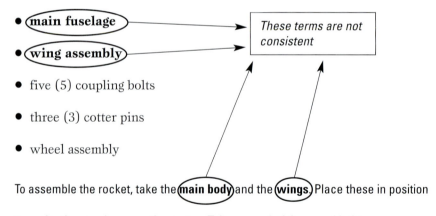

Your new RetroRocket comes with the following parts:

- main fuselage
- wing assembly

These terms are not consistent

- five (5) coupling bolts
- three (3) cotter pins
- wheel assembly

To assemble the rocket, take the **main body** and the **wings.** Place these in position to each other as shown on the carton. Take several of the round bolts . . .

The list of parts says "main fuselage" and "wing assembly," but the instructions say "main body" and "wings." Likewise for "coupling bolts" versus "round bolts." Are these the same pieces? If you don't use the same terms, how will your reader know for sure?

No list of technical communication characteristics can address all possible situations and decisions you will encounter. Wherever you work, you will face challenges that ultimately require your best analytical and social skills. For instance, "clarity" is a typical characteristic of technical communication. But in some cases, being crystal-clear may be impossible, because you can't get enough information.

In other situations, clarity and directness may be seen as overly blunt and offensive to some readers. As you read this book, remember that communication ultimately takes place in the workplace, among people, in situations that change, and often under time and budget pressures.

Types of Technical Communication

Some common forms of technical communication are listed here. Although these categories can overlap considerably, they should give you a feel for the kinds of documents technical communicators produce.

- **Manuals.** Almost every technology product or service is accompanied by a manual. Manuals may include information on how to use a product, along with background information, such as technical specifications or lists of materials. You have certainly used such manuals—to connect the components of your sound system, to do routine maintenance on your bicycle or inline skates, or to set up your answering machine. Most manuals are also available in electronic form: as help files, on CD, or as PDF documents on the company Web site.
- **Procedures.** Procedures are an important form of technical communication. Procedures explain how to perform a task or how a particular process happens. Many companies maintain standard operating procedures (SOPs) for tasks such as how to test soil samples or how to access corporate databases.
- **Instructions.** Instructions resemble manuals and procedures in that they explain how to do something. However, instructions are often very specific, systematic lists of the actual steps involved in using a product or performing a procedure. For instance, if you purchase a memory upgrade for your computer, you will probably receive a list of instructions on how to install this upgrade. This list may be a separate document or part of a manual or larger set of instructions.
- **Quick reference cards.** In some situations, a long list of procedures or instructions is inappropriate, because the user is already familiar with the "big picture." For instance, you may regularly call home to access your voice mail, and you may have the primary commands memorized. But there are certain tasks you may perform infrequently, such as changing your outgoing message from another phone. For tasks that users perform on a limited basis, a short summary of the keypad commands may be all that is needed. These commands can often fit on a quick reference card designed to fit in a wallet or fit in with the actual device (over the telephone keypad, for instance).
- **Reports.** There are many types of reports, including recommendation reports and analytical reports. Reports generally focus on a specific problem, issue, or topic. They may recommend a course of action or analyze a particular technology or situation. For example, a task force in your community may be studying plans for highway expansion or a new shopping center. After completing an

initial study, task forces often present reports to the city council or other decision makers, and written copies of these reports are available for public review. Reports can be made available in hard copy or on the Web.

- **Proposals.** Proposals make specific recommendations and propose solutions to technical problems. A proposal's purpose is usually to persuade readers to improve conditions, accept a service or product, or otherwise support a plan of action. Proposals are sometimes written in response to calls for proposals (CFPs) or requests for proposals (RFPs). For example, a nonprofit child care facility may seek safer playground equipment, or a pharmaceutical company may wish to develop a new Web-based education program for its employees. These organizations would issue RFPs, and each interested vendor would prepare a proposal that examines the problem, presents a solution, and defines the process and fees associated with implementing the solution.
- **Memos.** A vital form of technical communication, memos serve various purposes: to inform, to persuade, to document, or to encourage discussion. Memos are usually brief and follow a format that includes a header ("to," "from," "date," "re") and a page or two of body text. An employee might write a memo to his manager requesting a pay raise; an engineer might write a memo to her design team explaining a technical problem and offering a solution; a team of students might write a memo to their instructor explaining their progress on a class project.
- **Email.** Email is, essentially, the electronic version of a memo. In fact, most email is patterned after the memo, with a header containing fields for "to," "from," "date," and "re" already built in. Yet email messages are more common than paper memos. In most work settings, people use email to relay scheduling, policy, procedure, and miscellaneous information. They communicate via email with clients, customers, and suppliers, as well as with associates worldwide. People are more inclined to forward email messages and tend to be more casual and write more hastily than they would with paper memos.

Although these forms are common, many others exist, depending on the company or profession. Nursing, for example, requires specific forms for documenting a patient's medical condition; engineering has its own types of technical communication. In addition, the specific audience and purpose in each situation will determine the appropriate type of communication.

Various types of communication can also be formatted and packaged in various media:

- CD-ROM
- Internet Web pages (the entire worldwide Internet)
- Intranet Web pages (an internal network)
- Electronic text, including email or attachments
- Online help
- Printed matter, including books, paper memos, bound reports, and brochures
- Training sessions or oral presentations

Technical Communication in the Workplace

1.2
Resources on
the profession
of technical
communication

People who make technical information accessible to different audiences are called "technical communicators." In more and more organizations, this position is a full-time job, with titles including the following:

- Technical writer or editor
- User experience engineer
- Web designer
- Online documentation specialist
- Information developer
- Instructional developer

Technical communicators write and design documentation, online information, software interfaces, and other documents and materials for users of high technology. Technical communicators also write technical memos, reports, grant applications, and other specialized documents.

Virtually all technical professionals, at one time or another, function as part-time technical communicators. These technical experts are often required to present their knowledge to nonexpert audiences. For instance, a nuclear engineer testifying before Congress would need to explain nuclear science to nonscientists and to address the concerns of policymakers. People from many other walks of life (lawyers, health care professionals, historians, managers, and so on) communicate specialized information to nonexpert audiences:

- Medical professionals discuss health matters with patients.
- Attorneys interpret the law for clients.
- Historians describe complex historical events for people who did not experience those events.
- Managers interpret business objectives for the people they supervise.

Teamwork, Virtual Teams, and Project Management

Technical communication in workplace settings is rarely done by one lone writer or editor; instead, most projects are done in teams made up of writers, Web designers, engineers or scientists, managers, legal or regulations experts, and other members of the organization who are part of the project. Teams may be made up of people from one site or location, but increasingly, teams are distributed across different job sites, time zones, and countries. The Internet—via email, streamed video, instant messaging, blogs, and other digital communication tools—provides the primary means for distributed teams to do their work. In addition, tools such as computer-supported cooperative work (CSCW) software and project management software (like Microsoft Project; see Chapter 5) allow complex projects to be discussed, planned, and implemented among virtual teams (also known as distributed teams). In the end, teams, whether entirely on-site or entirely distributed, are made up of people and personalities; team members need to be able to work together, and the digital tools they use should be supportive of their communication, collaborations, and key tasks to complete the project successfully.

There are two important issues to consider for technical communication team projects: *teamwork* and *tools*.

Teamwork: How to Manage a Collaborative Project

1.3
Collaboration
software and
tools

Teamwork is successful only when there is strong cooperation, a recognized team structure, and clear communication. The TIPS box provides some guidelines for managing a team project—on-site, virtual, or a combination (Debs, 1991; Hill-Duin, 1990, pp. 45–50; Hulbert, 1994, pp. 53–54; McGuire, 1992, pp. 467–68; Morgan, 1991, pp. 540–41).

TIPS FOR MANAGING A TEAM PROJECT

- **Appoint a group manager.** The manager assigns tasks, enforces deadlines, conducts meetings and keeps them on track, consults with supervisors, and generally "runs the show."
- **Define a clear and definite goal.** Spell out the project's goal and the group's plan for achieving it.
- **Identify the type of document required.** Is this a report, a proposal, a manual, a brochure, a pamphlet? Are graphics and supplements (abstract, appendixes, and so on) needed? Will the document be in hard copy or digital form or both?
- **Divide the tasks.** Who will be responsible for which parts of the document or which phases of the project? Who is best at doing what (writing early or final drafts, editing, layout, design and graphics, oral presentation)? Which tasks will be done individually and which collectively? Keep in mind that the final version should display one consistent style throughout, as if written by one person only.

  Note: Be sure to spell out, *in writing,* clear expectations for each team member.
- **Establish a timetable.** Gantt charts (see pages 164 and 167) help the team visualize the whole project as well as each part, along with start-up and completion dates for each phase.
- **Decide on a meeting schedule and format.** How often will the group meet? Where and for how long? Who will take notes or minutes? Set a strict time limit for each meeting and for each discussion topic. Distribute copies of the meeting agenda and timetable to each member

beforehand, and stick to this plan. A meeting works best when each member prepares a specific contribution ahead of time.

- **Establish a procedure for responding to the work of other members.** Will reviewing and editing be done in writing, face to face, as a group, one on one, or online?
- **Develop a file-naming system for various drafts.** It's often too easy to save over a previous version and lose something important.
- **Establish procedures for dealing with interpersonal problems.** How will gripes and disputes be aired and resolved (by vote, the manager, other)? How will irrelevant discussion be curtailed?
- **Select a group decision-making style.** To focus group effort, Intel Corporation requires every group to decide on a specific decision-making style before each meeting. Some possible styles:

    Authoritative—the group leader makes the decisions.
    Consultative—the leader makes decisions on the basis of group input.
    Voting—decisions are made by majority vote.

- **Appoint a different "observer" for each meeting.** At Charles Schwab & Co., the designated observer keeps a list of what worked well during the meeting and what didn't. The list is added to that meeting's minutes.
- **Decide how to evaluate each member's contribution.** Will the manager assess each member's performance and in turn be evaluated by each member? Will members evaluate each other? What are the criteria? (Members might keep a journal of personal observations for overall evaluation of the project.)
- **Prepare a project management plan.** Figure 1.1 shows a sample planning form. Distribute completed copies to members.
- **Submit regular progress reports.** These reports (see page 208) track activities, problems, and progress.

Tools: How to Use Digital Technology to the Best Advantage of the Team

Digital technology is key to teamwork. The following tools are commonly used in most workplace settings:

- **Email.** Probably the most commonly used tool, email is great for short messages and as a way to include many people and to keep track of what was agreed to. And it's easy to add attachments to email.
- **Project management software.** Most large organizations use some type of software, such as Microsoft Project, to manage large, complex team projects.
- **Instant messaging.** IM is a fast and easy way to get an answer to a quick question.

- **Conference calls.** Use conference calls to connect with your team in real time.
- **Track changes and attachments.** Microsoft Word and other tools have features that let you insert comments and changes in a way that everyone on the team can see. More sophisticated systems use something called "version control."
- **Blogs.** Blogs (Web logs) allow you to post material in reverse chronological order and are a very good way for the entire team to share ideas and link to each other's ideas, too.

Project Planning Form

Project title:
Audience:
Project manager:
Team members:
Purpose of the project:
Type of document required:

Specific Assignments	**Due Dates**
Research:	Research due:
Planning:	Plan and outline due:
Drafting:	First draft due:
Revising:	Reviews due:
Preparing final document:	Revision due:
Presenting oral briefing:	Progress report(s) due:
	Final document due:

Work Schedule

Team meetings:	*Date*	*Place*	*Time*	*Note taker*
#1				
#2				
#3				
etc.				

Mtgs. w/instructor
   #1
   #2
   etc.

Miscellaneous

How will disputes and grievances be resolved?
How will performances be evaluated?
Other matters (Internet searches, email routing, computer conferences, etc.)?

Figure 1.1 Sample Project Planning Form for Managing a Collaborative Project.

Societal Dimensions of Technical Communication

Good technical communication has a societal component, because it can make important topics in science and technology (such as genetically modified organisms, cloning, or computers that diagnose disease) understandable to the general public. Such communication opens doors to new information—doors that might otherwise remain shut if the information were hard to read, too technical, or impossible to interpret. If the general public tried to learn about these topics by reading technical journals, people would come away scratching their heads, because the language and presentation would be too technical for general readers. But if this information is written to match the reader's level of knowledge, readers can understand these important topics. In a world in which science and technology play major roles in our everyday lives, technical communication becomes increasingly important. When you create effective technical communication, you not only help others use the information but also help people learn about important ideas.

Ethical Dimensions of Technical Communication

Technical communication involves an ethical stance as well, because the words, fonts, graphics, and colors that convey the information may influence your audience's perception, interpretation, and understanding. For example, think of the many advertising claims hinting that certain herbal remedies may cure diseases. These claims, technical in nature, often have no basis in traditional scientific methods. Yet some technical communicator chose (or was instructed) to write these words. The workplace pressures of communicating what the boss wants or what will make more money for the company are often at odds with the ethical pressures to present information fairly and accurately. Visual communication, such as charts and graphs, can also be misused. Later chapters address the ethical issues involved in technical communication. In the end, you will need to balance your own ethical stance against the interests of others, including your company and your customers or end users.

Checklist for Quality in Technical Communication

Accessibility
- Is the information *accurate?*
- Is the language *clear* and unambiguous?
- Is the information *complete?*
- Are the examples *concrete?*

(continued)

- Is the material appropriately organized?
- Is visual information (layout, screen design, color) used effectively?

Usability
- Can users find what they need *efficiently?*
- Is language at an appropriate *technical level?*
- Does the document contain a *table of contents*, index, or other such device?

Relevance
- Is the material appropriate for this *audience?*
- Is the material appropriate for and relevant to the *purpose* at hand?

Exercises

1. Find an effective technical document and bring it to class. Use the above checklist to explain to other students why your selection can be called "technical communication." Explain the ways in which your selection is accessible, usable, and relevant.

2. **FOCUS ON WRITING.** Research the kinds of writing you will do in your career. (Begin with the *Dictionary of Occupational Titles* in your library or on the Web.) Interview a member of your chosen profession or a technical communicator in a related field or industry. What types of writing can you expect to do on the job? For what audiences will you be writing? How much of your writing will be transmitted or published in electronic forms (Web sites, intranets)? Summarize your findings in a memo to your instructor or in a brief oral report to your class.

3. **FOCUS ON RESEARCH.** Gather examples of different kinds of technical documents on the Web. Use the Web pages listed here as starting points; then expand your search by using a search engine to locate Web pages related to your career and interests. Bring printed copies of at least three sample pages to class, and work in a small group to compare the examples you have collected. Identify key features of both good and bad technical communication, based on the criteria (accessibility, usability, and relevance) presented in this chapter.

    - **http://locatorplus.gov**
      The National Library of Medicine's Web catalog of over 5 million books and other materials. The NLM, the world's largest medical library, collects materials and provides information and research services in all areas of biomedicine and health care.
    - **http://elib.cs.berkeley.edu/photos**
      The CalPhotos project at the University of California, Berkeley. This project houses over 90,000 images of plants, animals, fossils, people, and landscapes.

- **http://www.lanl.gov**
  The main site for the Los Alamos National Laboratory, with photos and descriptions of the lab's ongoing research projects in national security and strategic science.

The Collaboration Window

Most writing and communicating, especially in the workplace, is done collaboratively, that is, it is done by and among many people and takes numerous ideas and suggestions into account. In class, form teams of students who have the same or similar majors or interests.

Create a list of technical terms and concepts, with short explanations, that you feel are important for people to understand your major or career interest; in other words, create a miniature "dictionary" for your major or field. Your list may consist of only ten terms and must fit on a single page. Collaborate on forming this list as follows:

- Each person in the group should create an individual list.
- When everyone is done, compile these lists into one master list. You will need to negotiate among members of your group about what ten terms to keep and how to define these terms. Share your list with the other groups in class.

The Global Window

Technical communication is an international activity. Technical products and services are used around the world, and communicators need to create information that is attentive to international needs. For example, if a company is shipping portable MP3 players to several countries, the documentation must be written in clear English that can be easily translated and contains internationally recognized symbols or visual information.

Find technical documentation that is written in English plus several other languages (instructions for household appliances, tools, or stereo equipment is often written in several languages). How many languages were used? Why did this company select these languages? Compare your findings with those of other students.

To learn more about global communication, use a Web search engine to locate information about the International Standards Organization (ISO). This group specializes in creating technical and communication standards for worldwide use. Identify a particular aspect of this site that you find interesting or that is related to your major, and share this information in class.

CHAPTER 2

A World of People and Purposes

People, Purposes, and Communities

All forms of technical communication are ultimately intended for an *audience:* the readers, listeners, viewers, and users who need information to make decisions or perform tasks. A good technical communicator always designs information with an audience in mind, carefully reviewing a vast array of information, selecting what is important, and crafting the information into a useful tool for a specific group of people. The technical communicator's audience, made up of a specific group of people, can also be thought of as a *community.* In other words, technical communicators must always take into account the needs of the community for whom they design information. Furthermore, technical communicators themselves are members of the community in which they work, and often the communities of both technical communicators and the audiences for whom they design information overlap.

Identify Discourse Communities

The notion of community, and of *discourse community* in particular, has recently gained attention in organizational and professional settings, as well as in academic disciplines. A discourse community is "a group of people who share certain language-using practices. . . . The key term *discourse* suggests a community bound together primarily by its uses of language, although bound perhaps by other ties as well, geographical, socioeconomic, ethnic, professional, and so on" (Bizzell, 1992, p. 222). Discourse communities have the power to influence and shape the way that information gets communicated within and outside of a group. Different types of discourse communities use language unique to themselves; for instance, a community of medical researchers uses technical or scientific language that is different from the language used by a community of software programmers. Ultimately, technical communicators need to carefully analyze the audiences they are writing for, in order to better understand their needs.

2.1
Communicating with multiple audiences

A technical communicator can belong to multiple discourse communities. For example, a technical communicator might be a member of a workplace project team; however, because a good technical communicator should be an advocate of the needs of her audience or users, she might also feel a sense of connectedness to the community for which she designs information. The presence of common stylistic conventions (see Chapter 3) may help create a sense of community and interconnectedness among technical communicators and their collaborative teams in the workplace; however, the technical communicator's external audience can also influence and shape stylistic conventions and language.

For example, the brochure in Figure 2.1 is designed by a biomedical device company to inform a specific community of physicians and other health care professionals who treat patients with heart conditions. Knowing how this audience of doctors and nurses feels about meeting individual patient needs, the writers begin

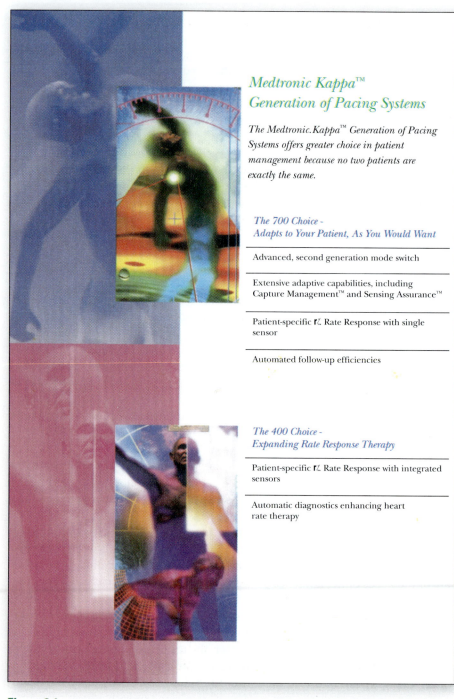

Medtronic Kappa™
Generation of Pacing Systems

The Medtronic.Kappa™ *Generation of Pacing Systems offers greater choice in patient management because no two patients are exactly the same.*

The 700 Choice -
Adapts to Your Patient, As You Would Want

Advanced, second generation mode switch

Extensive adaptive capabilities, including Capture Management™ and Sensing Assurance™

Patient-specific r⌐ Rate Response with single sensor

Automated follow-up efficiencies

The 400 Choice -
Expanding Rate Response Therapy

Patient-specific r⌐ Rate Response with integrated sensors

Automatic diagnostics enhancing heart rate therapy

Figure 2.1 A Technical Brochure. This brochure about a heart pacemaker system is designed to speak to a specific audience and to address its primary concerns.
Source: Medtronic Kappa™ Generation of Pacing Systems. Reproduced with permission of Medtronic, Inc.

with the following sentence: "The Medtronic Kappa Generation of Pacing Systems offers greater choice in patient management because no two patients are exactly the same." The writers then outline several key features of this product.

Provide Information Your Audience Needs

Audience is an important consideration in all kinds of writing but especially in technical writing, which is far more *user-centered* than other writing. When you write a poem or an essay, for example, you often express your personal feelings and thoughts on the subject. But as a technical writer, your first concern is to provide information *the audience needs*. This is not to say that technical communication involves no thinking and feeling; rather, technical communicators must "write not as isolated individuals but as members of communities," because they are always simultaneously members of several discourse communities, including those of the group in which they work and the audiences for whom they write (Harris, 1989, p. 12).

According to technical communication expert Robert R. Johnson (1997), you can never know every member of your audience, so you always have to do some guessing about audience needs. However, you should, as much as possible, interact with and seek feedback from actual audience members of the community for which you write.

Define Your Primary and Secondary Purposes

All forms of technical communication are also intended for specific *purposes:* the workplace settings, situations, and reasons for a particular form of communication. If the purpose is to persuade, this will influence the form of communication. If the purpose is to inform, this will affect the language, format, and other features of the communication. Many documents have multiple purposes. For example, the primary purpose of most instruction manuals is to teach an audience how to use the product. But for ethical and legal reasons, companies are also concerned that people use the product safely. An instruction manual for a cordless drill (see Figure 2.2), for example, begins with a page of safety instructions.

Any message can be conveyed in numerous ways, depending on how it is constructed for different audiences. Information about a new cancer treatment may appear in a medical journal for health care professionals, a textbook for nursing or medical students, and a newspaper article for the general public. Although health care professionals and nursing or medical students may all be part of the larger community of medical professionals, and although the general public may not be considered part of that community, it is important to understand the language differences within these communities. Because the community of medical professionals can be divided into smaller groups of nursing or medical students, the writer would need to consider the different audience and purpose features of each of these communities.

IMPORTANT SAFETY INSTRUCTIONS

WARNING: When using Electric Tools, [always follow] basic safety precautions to reduce risk of fire, electric shock, and personal injury, including the following:

READ ALL INSTRUCTIONS

1. **KEEP WORK AREA CLEAN.** Cluttered areas and benches invite injuries.
2. **CONSIDER WORK AREA ENVIRONMENT.** Don't expose power tools to rain. Don't use power tools in damp or wet locations. Keep work area well lit.
3. **GUARD AGAINST ELECTRIC SHOCK.** Prevent body contact with grounded surfaces. For example: pipes, radiators, ranges, refrigerator enclosures.
4. **KEEP CHILDREN AWAY.** All visitors should be kept away from work area. Do not let visitors contact tool or extension cord.
5. **STORE IDLE TOOLS.** When not in use, tools should be stored in a dry, and high or locked-up place - out of reach of children.
6. **DON'T FORCE TOOL.** It will do the job better and safer at the rate for which it was intended.
7. **USE RIGHT TOOL.** Don't force small tool or attachment to do the job of a heavy-duty tool. Don't use tool for purpose not intended. For example, don't use a circular saw for cutting tree limbs or logs.
8. **DRESS PROPERLY.** Do not wear loose clothing or jewelry. They can be caught in moving parts. Rubber gloves and non-skid footwear are recommended when working outdoors. Wear protective hair covering to contain long hair.
9. **USE SAFETY GLASSES.** Also use face or dustmask if operation is dusty.
10. **DON'T ABUSE CORD.** Never carry tool by cord or yank it to disconnect from receptacle. Keep cord from heat, oil, and sharp edges.
11. **SECURE WORK.** Use clamps or a vise to hold work. It's safer than using your hand and it frees both hands to operate tool.
12. **DON'T OVERREACH.** Keep proper footing and balance at all times.
13. **MAINTAIN TOOLS WITH CARE.** Keep tools sharp and clean for better and safe performance. Follow instructions for lubricating and changing accessories. Inspect tool cords periodically and if damaged have repaired by authorized service facility. Inspect extension cords periodically and replace if damaged. Keep handles dry, clean, and free from oil and grease.
14. **DISCONNECT TOOLS.** When not in use, before servicing, and when changing accessories, such as blades, bits, cutters.
15. **REMOVE ADJUSTING KEYS AND WRENCHES.** Form habit of checking to see that keys and adjusting wrenches are removed from tool before turning it on.
16. **AVOID UNINTENTIONAL STARTING.** Don't carry plugged-in tool with finger on switch. Be sure switch is off when plugging in.
17. **OUTDOOR USE EXTENSION CORDS.** When tool is used outdoors, use only extension cords intended for use outdoors and so marked. (See page 4 for more information about extension cords.)
18. **STAY ALERT.** Watch what you are doing. Use common sense. Do not operate tool when you are tired.
19. **CHECK DAMAGED PARTS.** Before further use of the tool, a guard or other part that is damaged should be carefully checked to determine that it will operate properly and perform its intended function. Check for alignment of moving parts, binding of moving parts, breakage of parts, mounting, and any other conditions that may affect its operation. A guard or other part that is defective should be properly repaired or replaced by an authorized service center unless otherwise indicated elsewhere in this instruction manual. Have defective switches replaced by authorized service center. Do not use tool if switch does not turn it on and off.
20. **DO NOT OPERATE** portable electric tools near flammable liquids or in gaseous or explosive atmospheres. Motors in these tools normally spark, and the sparks might ignite fumes.

CAUTION: When drilling into walls, floors, or wherever "live" electrical wires may be encountered, DO NOT TOUCH THE CHUCK! Hold the drill only by the plastic handle to prevent electric shock if you drill into a "live" wire.

We understand that safety rules make some pretty dry reading, but they really are important. If you just skimmed them, please go back and thoroughly read them. Thank you.

SAVE THESE INSTRUCTIONS

Figure 2.2 Safety Instructions for Operating a Cordless Drill. This cordless drill manual begins with a page of safety instructions.
Source: Black & Decker Instruction Manual, © 1993. Black & Decker (U.S.) Inc. Reprinted by permission.

Further, an audience of medical professionals understands technical terms, but the general public does not. In terms of purpose, medical students are reading so that they can apply the information, whereas general audiences who read about the same topic in a newspaper are often reading for nonspecific learning. Thus articles for each of these audiences will differ in language, content, organization, illustrations, and overall design. The more you understand about the community membership of your audience and the purpose of your documentation, the more your communication will meet user needs.

Figures 2.3 and 2.4 show two pieces of information, both about the over-the-counter heartburn medication Nexium. The Web site is designed for a general audience of patients who have questions or want more information about this medicine. The page from the *Physicians' Desk Reference* (PDR) is also designed to answer questions and provide information, but it is intended for an audience of physicians and health care professionals, not patients. Both items address the same topic, but they are designed and written for very different audiences. Notice the different uses of language and graphics for these two audiences.

Analyzing Your Audience

In preparing a technical communication product, you generally begin by analyzing your audience through a series of questions like these:

2.2

Sample
audience
analysis
templates

- Who will be reading, listening to, or using this material?
- What special characteristics do they have?
- Which discourse community or communities do they belong to?
- What are their background and attitude toward the subject?

Most people already know more than they think they do about analyzing an audience. Imagine that you are asked to give a presentation on global warming to a group of schoolchildren. Later, you are asked to speak on the same subject to a group of manufacturing executives. In preparing to speak to the children, you would probably think of ways to make the topic understandable—for instance, using simple language and comparing your ideas to things familiar to children. In preparing to speak to the manufacturing executives, you would change your approach, using more technical terms and referring to topics they care about, such as the effects of global warming on their industries.

In short, you would have performed a *basic audience analysis* by assessing the characteristics and interests of the two different audiences and then reshaping the information to fit what you know about each group. Yet it is best to be more systematic about analyzing an audience, because a communicator's assumptions are sometimes wrong. For example, you might assume that the manufacturing executives know quite a bit about global warming and therefore use technical terms or refer to complex concepts. But what if your assumption is wrong? What if these executives actually know very little about the subject? Instead of relying on your assumption, learn as much as possible about the language and social dynamics of the community of manufacturing executives before the presentation. Then you can make informed judgments about the information that needs to be communicated to this group in the presentation.

Most communication situations have an immediate audience. This is your *primary audience.* For instance, a set of instructions for installing new email

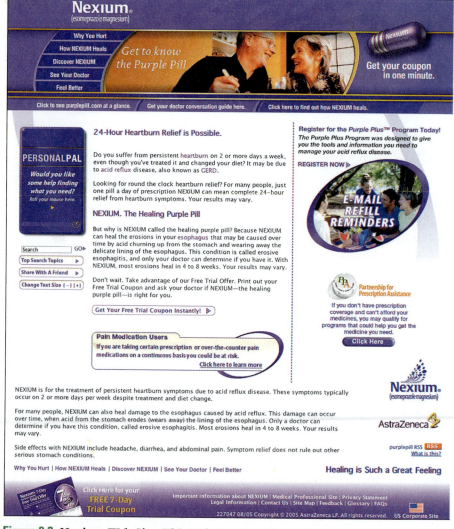

Figure 2.3 Nexium Web Site. This Web site of medical information is designed for a more general audience.

Source: Nexium Web site (http://www.purplepill.com).

NEXIUM®   ℞
(esomeprazole magnesium)
DELAYED-RELEASE CAPSULES
Rx only

DESCRIPTION
The active ingredient in NEXIUM® (esomeprazole magnesium) Delayed-Release Capsules is bis(5-methoxy-2-[(S)-[4-methoxy-3,5-dimethyl-2- pyridinyl)methyl]sulfinyl]-1H-benzimidazole-1-yl) magnesium trihydrate, a compound that inhibits gastric acid secretion. Esomeprazole is the S-isomer of omeprazole, which is a mixture of the S- and R-isomers. Its empirical formula is $(C_{17}H_{18}N_3O_3S)_2Mg \times 3H_2O$ with molecular weight of 767.2 as a trihydrate and 713.1 on an anhydrous basis. The structural formula is:

The magnesium salt is a white to slightly colored crystalline powder. It contains 3 moles of water of solvation and is slightly soluble in water.

The stability of esomeprazole magnesium is a function of pH; it rapidly degrades in acidic media, but it has acceptable stability under alkaline conditions. At pH 6.8 (buffer), the half-life of the magnesium salt is about 19 hours at 25°C and about 8 hours at 37°C.

NEXIUM is supplied as Delayed-Release Capsules for oral administration. Each delayed-release capsule contains 20 mg or 40 mg of esomeprazole (present as 22.3 mg or 44.5 mg esomeprazole magnesium trihydrate) in the form of enteric-coated pellets with the following inactive ingredients: glyceryl monostearate 40-50, hydroxypropyl cellulose, hypromellose, magnesium stearate, methacrylic acid copolymer type C, polysorbate 80, sugar spheres, talc, and triethyl citrate. The capsule shells have the following inactive ingredients: gelatin, FD&C Blue #1, FD&C Red #40, D&C Red #28, titanium dioxide, shellac, ethyl alcohol, isopropyl alcohol, n-butyl alcohol, propylene glycol, sodium hydroxide, polyvinyl pyrrolidone, and D&C Yellow #10.

CLINICAL PHARMACOLOGY
Pharmacokinetics
Absorption
NEXIUM Delayed-Release Capsules contain an enteric-coated pellet formulation of esomeprazole magnesium. After oral administration peak plasma levels (C_{max}) occur at approximately 1.5 hours (T_{max}). The C_{max} increases proportionally when the dose is increased, and there is a three-fold increase in the area under the plasma concentration-time curve (AUC) from 20 to 40 mg. At repeated once-daily dosing with 40 mg, the systemic bioavailability is approximately 90% compared to 64% after a single dose of 40 mg. The mean exposure (AUC) to esomeprazole increases from 4.32 µmol*hr/L on day 1 to 11.2 µmol*hr/L on day 5 after 40 mg once daily dosing. The AUC after administration of a single 40 mg dose of esomeprazole is decreased by 43-53% after food intake compared to fasting conditions. Esomeprazole should be taken at least one hour before meals.

The pharmacokinetic profile of esomeprazole was determined in 36 patients with symptomatic gastroesophageal reflux disease following repeated once daily administration of 20 mg and 40 mg capsules of NEXIUM over a period of five days. The results are shown in the following table:

Pharmacokinetic Parameters of NEXIUM Following Oral Dosing for 5 days

Parameter	NEXIUM 40 mg	NEXIUM 20 mg
AUC (µmol*h/L)	12.6	4.2
Coefficient of variation	42%	59%
C_{max} (µmol/L)	4.7	2.1
T_{max} (h)	1.6	1.6
$t_{1/2}$ (h)	1.5	1.2

Values represent the geometric mean, except the T_{max}, which is the arithmetic mean.

Distribution
Esomeprazole is 97% bound to plasma proteins. Plasmaprotein binding is constant over the concentration range of 2-20 µmol/L. The apparent volume of distribution at steady state in healthy volunteers is approximately 16 L.

Metabolism
Esomeprazole is extensively metabolized in the liver by the cytochrome P450 (CYP) enzyme system. The metabolites of esomeprazole lack antisecretory activity. The major part of esomeprazole's metabolism is dependent upon the CYP2C19 isoenzyme, which forms the hydroxy and desmethyl metabolites. The remaining amount is dependent on CYP3A4 which forms the sulphone metabolite. CYP2C19 isoenzyme exhibits polymorphism in the metabolism of esomeprazole, since some 3% of Caucasians and 15-20% of Asians lack CYP2C19 and are termed Poor metabolizers. At steady state, the ratio of AUC in Poor metabolizerrs to AUC in the rest of the population (Extensive metabolizers) is approximately 2. Following administration of equimolar doses, the S- and R-isomers are metabolized differently by the liver, resulting in higher plasma levels of the S- than of the R-isomer.

Excretion
The plasma elimination half-life of esomeprazole is approximately 1-1.5 hours. Less than 1% of parent drug is excreted in the urine. Approximately 80% of an oral dose of esomeprazole is excreted as inactive metabolites in the feces.

Special Populations
Geriatric
The AUC and C_{max} values were slightly higher (25% and 18%, respectively) in the elderly as compared to younger subjects at steady state. Dosage adjustments based on age is not necessary.

Pediatric
The pharmacokinetics of esomeprazole have not been studied in patients <18 years of age.

Gender
The AUC and C_{max} values were slightly higher (13%) in females than in males at steady state. Dosage adjustment based on gender is not necessary.

Hepatic Insufficiency
The steady state pharmacokinetics of esomeprazole obtained after administration of 40 mg once daily to 4 patients each with mild (Child Pugh A), moderate (Child Pugh Class B), and severe (Child Pugh Class C) liver insufficiency were compared to those obtained in 36 male and female GERD patients with normal liver function. In patients with mild and moderate hepatic insufficiency, the AUCs were within the range that could be expected in

Continued on next page

Consult 2006 PDR® supplements and future editions for revisions

Figure 2.4 **Nexium Information from the *Physicians' Desk References* (PDR).** This information is designed for a specialized audience of medical professionals.
Source: Physicians' Desk Reference (2006), pp. 644–645.

software for the office might be directed primarily at computer support staff. But most documents also have *secondary audiences,* people outside the circle of those who need the information urgently. A secondary audience for software instructions might be managers, who will check the instructions for company policy, or lawyers, who will make sure the instructions meet various legal standards.

Analyzing the Communication Purpose

As you analyze your audience, you also need to consider the purpose of your message by asking questions like these:

- Why is this communication important?
- Why is it needed?
- What will users do with this information?
- Do the users share common membership in a specific discourse community?

People use technical information for various purposes: to perform a task, learn more about a subject, or make a decision. If the communicator has one purpose in mind when preparing the information but the audience has a different purpose, the message will be useless.

For example, you may have encountered Web sites in which the purpose of the page seems at odds with your purpose for visiting the site. Let's say you hear about a new Web site that sells books about bird-watching in South America. As an avid bird-watcher planning a trip to Brazil, you decide to check out this site. When you first connect, you are impressed with the bright colors and cute bird sounds. And as you click on each book selection, you enjoy an array of birds that come flying across your screen. Yet you cannot locate any descriptive information explaining how one book differs from another, and you are not sure whether the prices displayed include shipping. Also, you can't find an order form. It appears that your purpose, to locate and perhaps buy a book, conflicts with the purpose of the page, which appears to be more of a fancy digital advertisement than a place where customers can find information and make a purchase.

Just as there are primary and secondary audiences, there is also more than one level of purpose. The primary purpose of a set of instructions for a new bicycle rack might be to help users assemble the rack, but a secondary purpose might be to meet the company's legal obligation to list all parts and inform users about potential hazards. Therefore, the instructions not only cater to the needs of the community of users but also fulfill the needs of the community of legal professionals working for the company.

Analyzing the Communication Context

Along with audience and purpose, it is also important to understand the context in which the document will be used. Context is related to purpose, but it suggests a slightly different set of questions, such as these:

- What are the organizational settings in which the document will be used? For example, will the document be used in training sessions? As part of overall policy documents? As a Web-based customer support site?
- Are there legal issues to consider? For example, are you using material from another source, and if so, do you need to request permission? Are you discussing company projects that may be confidential?
- How much time do people at this company or with this job title have available to perform a task? For example, a service technician out in the field may have very little time to locate an answer, but a researcher working on a long-term experiment may have more time to mull over the theoretical aspects of a topic.
- Are the readers of this document associated with a larger community of professionals (nurses, scientists, teachers), and if so, what professional values might they bring to the situation? For example, medical professionals value the health and life of the patient above all else.
- Are audience members from one culture only, or is this information directed at a cross-cultural audience? Remember that even the United States contains many diverse cultures: Not everyone in the United States speaks English as their first language, for example.

These and other issues affect every choice you make when writing and designing technical communication.

The following chart summarizes important questions about audience, purpose, and context and provides a template worksheet for your own analysis. Modify this chart to suit your specific situations.

AUDIENCE ANALYSIS WORKSHEET

Communication Aspect	Specific Features
Audience	
Demographic information	Age, gender ratio, education level, ethnicity?
Primary audience	Names, job titles?
Secondary audiences	Names, job titles?
Attitudes toward information	Level of interest and receptivity?
Technical understanding of or experience with topic	Extent of background knowledge?

(continued)

Purpose

Primary purpose:

To learn	List what they want to learn
To obtain background information	List why they need this
To make a decision	List the decisions they will make
To perform a task	List tasks: to build, to design, to install, etc.
Secondary purpose or purposes	Legal, marketing, other

Context

Role within the organization	Managers, engineers, etc.
Political or social situation	Power, decision making
Community membership	Specific vocabulary, discourse, social dynamics
Legal issues	Copyright, patents
Cultural considerations	Cross-cultural audiences
Professional values or affiliations	Engineers, teachers, nurses
Other contextual issues	Due dates, other constraints

Conducting an Audience-Purpose Interview

Some documents have wide audiences: Manuals for household appliances, for example, are sent out to countless users worldwide. You may be able to interview only a few people, but if they represent the average reader or listener, you will have a good sense of how to proceed.

The first step, then, in analyzing your audience is to identify the people available for an interview. Try to interview people from various segments of your audience. Depending on your situation, you may interview people individually or in focus groups (small groups of people brought together for this purpose).

Before the interview, explain what you are doing and ask individuals for an appropriate time to meet or call. Email is a good way to make this initial contact, allowing recipients to respond at their convenience. If you can't set up a face-to-face or phone interview, consider using email to conduct your audience analysis. But don't send out your analysis questions until your respondent has agreed to participate. (See Chapter 4 for more information on conducting interviews.)

During the interview, cover all the items on your audience analysis worksheet. Pay particularly close attention to the following items:

- **Levels of technical understanding.** How much technical knowledge does the reader have? Is the reader part of a discourse community that uses a specific technical vocabulary? Will technical terms be familiar or confusing? How much background will be needed to help explain concepts?
- **International issues.** Are audience members from one culture or country or from several countries and cultures? How can the document be written and designed so it is accessible to everyone?
- **Workplace culture or hierarchy.** In what workplace setting will the document be used? Is there a certain style or tone appropriate to this company? Will all levels of employees be using this material, or is it designed for just one or two groups? Does the company have its own style manual?
- **Gender.** How can the document be written and designed so it is fair to both men and women? For example, if a document needs to refer to a job title, use gender-neutral language (*mail carrier* rather than *mailman*).
- **Mixed audiences.** In preparing a set of procedures, you write one way for experienced users (people who've performed this or similar procedures before) and a different way for inexperienced users. But if your audience consists of both groups, you need to include different levels of information within the same document: some background and explanation of technical terms for the inexperienced users and some technical terms and concepts for those with experience. You can also use an approach called "context-sensitive communication," discussed in Chapter 3.

More Tools for Understanding Audience

2.3
Practice analyzing audiences

Enhance your audience analysis by seeking out other information, such as the following:

- **Corporate style guides.** Stylistic conventions are one of the major factors that regulate a discourse community, and companies often publish style guides with their own rules for corporate communication. These guides offer specific information on everything from grammar and punctuation to tone and style. A company style guide often describes the audiences for its products.
- **User preference documents.** Many manufacturing and software organizations create documents that assess user preferences. These documents are often created after detailed interviews with real customers.
- **Marketing surveys and focus groups.** Marketing departments spend a great deal of time with customers and have a wealth of information to share on customer attitudes, preferences, educational levels, and so on.

Using Information from Your Analysis

A thorough audience and purpose analysis will help you make the following decisions as you prepare your document or presentation.

- **Word choice.** Understanding your audience members' technical level and the linguistic and social conventions of the discourse community to which they belong will govern the kind of language you use. A group of software engineers understand technical language about computing ("remote analog loopback"), but a mixed audience of managers and supervisors may require less technical language and clear definitions of any technical terms you do use. Novices may need nontechnical, reassuring language.

- **Examples.** Good examples can make a technical concept clear and easy to visualize. A document describing how a pacemaker works might compare the pacemaker's action to a more familiar concept, such as a ticking clock.

- **Document format.** An audience often expects a document to conform to a familiar format. Most companies have stylistic conventions that regulate the standard format for communicating new product information, such as a special type of company memo, a prepared form, or an email message with an attachment.

- **Length.** Some audiences, such as busy executives, have no time to read an entire report. In these cases, the report is preceded by an abstract that summarizes key information and conclusions. Length is also important in presentations. Some meetings with a busy agenda often limit individual presentations to 10 or 15 minutes.

- **Document genre.** Is your document meant to persuade or inform? Although all documents are implicitly persuasive (in that you want readers to appreciate the quality of your message), some are expected to be explicitly persuasive as well. A sales proposal, for example, explicitly attempts to persuade its audience to purchase the product or service; on the other hand, a research report is usually intended merely to describe the project and interpret the findings. It is important to remember that not only is the purpose of your document influenced by the genre you use, but the genre you use is also influenced by the conventions of the community for which you write.

- **Information you will include.** Make sure the information you include in the document is interesting and useful to your audience. Consider carefully what to put in and what to leave out, based on what you know about audience and purpose. For example, details of what a new security system is designed to do are of marginal interest to the technician who has been brought in to install it.

Recognizing That Audiences Are Not Passive

Audiences are not merely passive recipients of information, and technical communicators are not merely passive designers of information. Rather, the communities to which technical communicators and their audiences belong should overlap and interact. When people read a manual, listen to a presentation, or explore a Web site, they constantly form opinions of the material, learn new information, and consider new points of view. If they find the information difficult to use, not credible, or insulting, they reject it. Therefore, as you analyze your audience and learn about its community, remember that the communication process works both ways. People will react to your ideas in ways that you may not anticipate. Keep an open mind, and be ready to modify your original ideas based on how your audience reacts.

Typical Audiences and Purposes for Technical Communication

The following categories of audiences and purposes are presented to give you an overview of how to think about different groups of people in different communication contexts and different discourse communities. Obviously, these categories are not exclusive. We are all members of multiple, overlapping discourse communities, and we all shift in and out of various audience roles. For example, at work you may be a nurse or an engineer, but when you go home, you may function more as a member of the general public. Also, in creating categories, we run the risk of stereotyping. It's impossible to speak about *all* engineers or *all* musicians. Yet it is helpful to consider audience types, because a specific type of audience generally shares a concern about a specific type of purpose. Take these concerns into consideration as you plan and design your document or presentation.

- **Scientists** search for knowledge to "understand the world as it is" (Petroski, 1996, p. 2). Scientists look for at least 95 percent probability that chance played no role in a particular outcome. They want to know how well a study was designed and conducted and whether the findings can be replicated. Scientists know that their answers are never "final." Their research is open-ended and ongoing: What seems probable today may well be rendered improbable by tomorrow's research.
- **Engineers** rearrange "the materials and forces of nature" to improve the way things work (Petroski, 1996, p. 1). Engineers solve problems: how to erect a suspension bridge that withstands high winds, how to design a lighter airplane or a smaller pacemaker, how to boost rocket thrust on a space shuttle. The engineer's concern is usually with practical applications, with structures and materials that are tested for safety and dependability.

- **Executives** focus on decision making. In a global business climate of overnight developments (world markets, political strife, military conflicts, natural disasters), executives must often react on the spur of the moment. In such cases, they rely on the best information immediately available—even if this information is incomplete or unverified (Seglin, 1998, p. 54).
- **Managers** oversee the day-to-day operations of their organizations, focusing on problems like how to motivate employees, how to increase productivity, how to save money, or how to avoid workplace accidents. They collaborate with colleagues and supervise various projects. To keep things running smoothly, managers rely on memos, reports, and other forms of information sharing.
- **Lawyers** focus on protecting the organization from liability or corporate sabotage by answering questions like these: Do these instructions contain adequate warnings and cautions? Is there anything about this product that could generate a lawsuit? Have any of our trade secrets been revealed? Lawyers carefully review documents before approving their distribution outside the company.
- **The public** focuses on the big picture—on what pertains to them directly: What does this mean to me? How can I use this product safely and effectively? Why should I even read this? They rely on information for some immediate practical purpose: to complete a task (What do I do next?), to learn more about something (What are the facts, and what do they mean?), to make a judgment (Is this good enough?).

Because audiences' basic purposes vary, every audience expects a message tailored to its own specific interests, social conventions, ways of understanding problems, and information needs.

Checklist for Analyzing Audience, Purpose, and Context

Audience

- Have I identified my exact audience?
- Have I identified this audience's specific interests, information needs, and attitude toward this topic?
- Have I identified this audience's background on this topic?
- Have I interviewed audience members beforehand?

Purpose

- Do I know exactly why this information is needed?
- Do I know exactly what will be done with this information?
- Have I considered all secondary uses of this information?

Context
- Have I considered the settings in which this information will be used?
- Have I considered the political, legal, and cross-cultural issues involving this document?
- Should I refer to a specific style guide for composing this document?
- Can I refer to any user preference or marketing surveys for composing this document?

Exercises

1. Select a topic with which you are familiar; choose from hobbies, your job, or your academic major. Assume that you will be writing a brochure on this topic and that your audience is your classmates. Using the Audience Analysis Worksheet presented in this chapter, interview two or three classmates. From your notes, write an audience and purpose statement. It should begin: "The audience for my brochure is [describe it]. The purpose of my brochure is [describe using verbs: to inform, to train, to convince, etc.]." Trade your statement with a classmate and exchange feedback.

2. **FOCUS ON WRITING.** Based on your experience in Exercise 1, modify the Audience Analysis Worksheet to include other questions, categories, or topics that you will need to learn about in order to understand your audience more fully. Write a memo to your instructor about your findings.

3. **FOCUS ON WRITING.** Find a short article related to your major (or part of a long article or a selection from your textbook for an advanced course). Choose a piece written at the highest level of technicality you can understand. Using the Audience Analysis Worksheet, write down the assumptions about the audience made by the author of this piece. What kind of audience did the author have in mind? What audience characteristics did she or he assume? What are the purposes of this document? Now, working with a partner in class, discuss a different audience (laypeople, mixed audience, novices) for this topic. Write about the changes you might make to turn this article into something accessible to a new audience.

4. **FOCUS ON RESEARCH.** Conduct an online search to identify four Web sites focused on weather information and forecasting. Try to find two that appear to be addressed to technical audiences and two addressed to general, nontechnical, "consumer" audiences. Use the sites listed on the following page as starting points.

    How are these sites designed to present information to a specific audience? Are these sites designed primarily for one audience or one purpose?

How are secondary audiences and purposes addressed? Which site would be most useful to you if you were a meteorologist working on a weekend forecast? Which would be most useful to you if you were planning a family picnic? Why?

Make a list of the key features of each site that appeal to a specific audience, and present your findings in a brief report to your class. Be sure to consider visual presentation, site design, writing style, and other features (the presence or absence of advertisements, for example) when you analyze the sites.

- **http://www.nws.noaa.gov**
  The official site of the National Oceanic and Atmospheric Administration's National Weather Service.
- **http://www.accuweather.com**
  A major commercial weather information site including both general and technical information.
- **http://www.bom.gov.au**
  The official site of the Australian government's Bureau of Meteorology.
- **http://cirrus.sprl.umich.edu/wxnet**
  A site sponsored and hosted by the Department of Atmospheric, Oceanic, and Space Sciences at the University of Michigan. UM Weather includes a comprehensive list of nearly 300 Web sites and other online sources of weather science information.

 The Collaboration Window

Form teams of three to six people. If possible, teammates should be of the same or similar majors (electrical engineering, biology, graphic design, etc.). Address the following situation: An increasing number of first-year students are dropping out of the major because of low grades, stress, or inability to keep up with the work. Your task is to prepare an online "survival guide" for incoming students. The Web site should focus on the challenges and pitfalls of the first year in this major. But before you can prepare the guide, you need to do a thorough analysis of its audience and purpose.

Assuming that some of you are in this major, perform an audience analysis using the Audience Analysis Worksheet on page 25 or a modified version of it. One team member should take notes, but all team members should participate, alternately, both as interviewers and interviewees. Take turns interviewing students one at a time. Once you have a reasonable amount of information, draft an audience and purpose statement for your online survival guide (see Exercise 1).

The Global Window

Many Web sites and technical documents today are designed for truly global audiences. Consider the sites for multinational corporations like Canon and Sony, for example. These sites are explicitly designed for multiple audiences around the globe, with screens in different languages specific to each region and country. Explore these and other international sites, and consider how they are designed to present information to global audiences. Create a list of specific features and elements of each site that differ from region to region. Consider language differences, visual presentation and images, navigation, units of measurement, idioms and slang, cultural biases, and marketing strategies for each. Discuss how you would redesign the site to make it even more accessible to an international audience.

- **http://www.canon.com**
  World gateway site for Canon Inc., a producer of cameras and business machines marketed and sold around the world.
- **http://www.sony.net**
  Sony Global, the world headquarters and Internet portal site for Sony Corp., a leading provider of consumer electronic devices, games, music, and movies.

CHAPTER 3

Designing Usable Information

Usability and Technical Information

When you plan, write, and design a piece of communication—a brochure, manual, online help screen, or report—you are creating a communication product. Like any other product, people will use it only if they can find what they need, understand the language, follow the instructions, and read the graphics. In other words, communication products must be *usable*. Usability means that "people who use the product can do so quickly and easily to accomplish their own tasks" (Dumas & Redish, 1994, p. 4).

To create a usable communication product, begin with a careful audience and purpose analysis (see Chapter 2). This analysis will provide you with much of the basic information you need to design your material. But you can take other, more specific steps to ensure that your document is usable during the planning stages, during the writing and design process, and after the release of your document.

Usability During the Planning Stages

Before you begin writing or designing any information product, learn all you can about your audience and the intended use of your document. Then develop a clear plan.

3.1

Analyzing documents for usability

Perform an Audience and Purpose Analysis

A systematic audience analysis is critical to any successful technical communication. To perform an audience analysis, customize the worksheet provided in Chapter 2 to fit your specific situation.

Perform a Task Analysis

Most audiences approach technical communication material with a series of tasks in mind. These tasks are most evident when the document is a set of instructions: Users want to install a new oil filter, assemble a new gas grill, or install a new word-processing program. But other forms of communication, such as reports, memos, and brochures, also involve user tasks. When reading a report, a manager may need to extract information and write a response. When replying to a memo, a technician may need to make an argument as to why the company should purchase new equipment. In this way, most technical communication is task-oriented. People come to the information wanting to *do* something.

As one pair of experts notes, "It is all too easy to forget that the product exists because human beings are trying to accomplish tasks. Task analysis refocuses attention on users and on their tasks and goals" (Dumas & Redish, 1994, p. 44).

Main task: Assemble the grill

Subtasks   1. Locate all parts.

                  2. Get the required tools.

                  3. Lay out parts in order.

                  4. Assemble parts into smaller units.

                  5. Assemble these smaller units into large units.

Main task: Use the grill

Subtasks   1. Attach the gas canister.

                  2. Turn on the main gas valve.

                  3. Turn on the individual burners.

                  4. Press button to ignite.

Main task: Maintain the grill

Subtasks   1. Turn off the main gas valve when not in use.

                  2. Cover to protect from rain.

                  3. Clean the grate regularly.

Figure 3.1 Sample Task Analysis Worksheet for a Gas Grill Instruction Manual.

For your task analysis, you can create a worksheet similar to the one shown in Figure 3.1. Begin by defining the main tasks. For example, for an instruction manual to accompany a gas grill, you might define the primary user task as "assemble the grill." But this task can be divided into several smaller tasks. Note that the tasks are listed using verb forms (assemble, locate, get, and so on):

1. Locate all parts.
2. Get the required tools.
3. Lay out parts in order.
4. Assemble parts into smaller units.
5. Assemble these smaller units into large units.

Even this list can be subdivided: "Assemble parts into smaller units," for example, probably consists of several smaller steps.

You can determine these tasks by interviewing users and watching them perform the actions. Once you understand the tasks to be performed, you can create an information plan (discussed next). Ultimately, your document will be more useful if you know what your audience wants to *do* with it.

Develop an Information Plan

Once you have a clear picture of the audience and purpose for your document, as well as the intended user tasks, you can draft an information plan: an outline of the assumptions, goals, specifications, and budget for your document. Information plans can be as short as a two- to three-page memo or as long as a five- to ten-page report, depending on your project. Begin with a clearly stated goal ("Users will be able to assemble a gas grill within 30 minutes") so that you can measure when a task has been successfully completed (Rubin, 1994, p. 97). Figure 3.2 is a sample information plan created in a short-memo format.

Do the Research

Developing an information plan might require research. For instance, you might need to determine how often gas grill accidents occur because the burner unit was assembled incorrectly or because a faulty connection has been overlooked. Such data will certainly affect your decisions about what information to include and what to leave out. For more information on conducting research, see Chapter 4.

Usability During the Writing and Design Process

Once you have completed these first steps, you can write, design, and test your document. For a gas grill instruction manual, you would write the instructions, design the graphics, and select a medium (print, CD-ROM, Web) for distributing the information. Most instructions are printed on paper and included with the product. You might choose paper but also make the information available on a Web site. Besides choosing a delivery method, you can take other steps at this stage to ensure usability.

Test Early Versions of Your Communication Product

Allow audience members to provide input as early as possible. If time and budget allow, test your first draft of the brochure, Web page, or report on potential users. Ask people what they find useful and what they find confusing in the document. Or watch people use the material, and measure their performance. If someone were trying to assemble a gas grill, for instance, but could not locate a part because of unclear instructions, knowing about this would be valuable as you revise the material.

Qualitative Testing. To identify which parts of the document work or don't work, observe how users react or what they say or do. Qualitative testing employs either focus groups or protocol analysis (Plain English Network, 2001):

GrillChef Corporation

To: Technical writing design team
From: Erin Green and Geoff Brannigan, team leaders
Date: January 21, 2003
Re: Information plan for gas grill manual

As you know, our team recently performed an analysis of user needs as we prepare to design and write the new User Manual for the new GrillChef Model 2000 double-burner grill. This memo summarizes our findings and presents a plan for proceeding.

Part One: Analysis

Audience—The audience for this manual is very broad. It consists of consumers who purchase the grill. This purchase may be their first gas grill, or they may be replacing an old grill. Some users are making a switch from charcoal to gas. Our analysis revealed that the primary users are male and female, ranging in age from 25–50. From a focus group, we determined that most users are afraid to assemble the grill. But all members expressed enthusiasm about using the grill. Also, according to marketing, this grill is only sold in the United States.

Purpose—The manual has several purposes:
1. Instruct the user in assembling and using the grill.
2. Provide adequate safety instructions. These are to protect the user and to make sure we have complied with our legal requirements.
3. Provide a phone number, Web address, and other contact information if users have questions or need replacement parts.

User tasks—Our task analysis revealed three main tasks this manual must address:
1. How to assemble the grill. Users need clear instructions, a list of parts, and diagrams that can assist them. Users wish to be able to assemble the grill within 30 minutes to one hour.
2. How to use the grill. Users need clear instructions for operating the grill safely. Because some users have never used gas for grilling, we need to stress safety.
3. How to maintain the grill. Users need to know how to keep the grill clean, dry, and operational.

Part Two: Design Plans

Based on our analysis, we suggest designing a manual that is simple, easy to use, and contains information users need. We will follow the layout and format of our other manuals.

Rough outline—Cover with drawing of grill, model number, company name.

Inside front cover: safety warnings (our legal department has indicated that these warnings need to go first).

First section: Exploded diagram, list of parts, drawings of parts, numbered list of instructions for assembly.

Second section: Numbered list of steps for using the grill, accompanied by diagrams.

Third section: Bulleted list of tasks users must perform to maintain the grill.

Final page: Company address, phone number, and Web address.

Production guidelines—Our budget for this project will not allow for color printing or any photographs. We suggest black ink on white paper, 8-1/2 x 11 folded in half vertically. We can use line drawings of the Model 1999 and modify these to the specifications of the Model 2000.

Schedule—The manual must be ready for shipping on April 1, 1999. We will follow our usual production and writing schedule, briefly summarized here:

February 21: First draft of manual is complete. Manual is usability tested on sample customers.

March 1: Manual is revised based on results of usability test.

March 3: Copyediting, proofreading, and final changes. Manual goes to the printer.

March 30: Manual is back from printer and sent to the warehouse.

April 1: Product is shipped.

Figure 3.2 Sample Information Plan for the Gas Grill Manual.

- **Focus groups.** Based on a list of targeted questions about the document's content, organization, style, and design, users discuss what information they think is missing or excessive, what they like or dislike, and what they find easy or hard to understand. They may also suggest ways of revising the document's graphics, format, or level of technical information.
- **Protocol analysis.** In a one-on-one interview, a user reads a specific section of a document and then explains what that section means. For long documents, the interviewer also observes how the person actually reads the document: for example, how often she or he flips pages or refers to the index or table of contents to find information. In another version of protocol analysis, users read the material and think out loud about what they find useful or confusing as they perform the task.

Quantitative Testing. Assess a document's overall effectiveness by using a *control group*. For example, you can compare success rates among people using different versions of your document or count the number of people who performed the task accurately (Plain English Network, 2001). You can also measure the time required to complete a task and the types and frequency of user errors (Hughes, 1999, p. 489). Although it yields hard numerical data, quantitative testing is obviously more complicated, time-consuming, and expensive than its qualitative counterpart.

When to Use Which Test. If time, budget, and available users allow, consider doing both qualitative and quantitative testing. Quantitative testing is ordinarily done last, as a final check on usability. Each test has its benefits and limitations: Quantitative testing "will tell you *if* the new document is a success, but it won't tell you *why* it is or isn't a success" (Plain English Network, 2001). In short, to find out if the document succeeds as a whole, use quantitative testing; to find out exactly which parts of the document work or don't work, use qualitative testing.

Revise Your Plan and Your Product

Revise your information plan and your draft documents to conform to audience feedback. If your audience finds a technical term difficult to understand, define it clearly or use a simpler word or concept. If a graphic makes no sense, devise one that does. It is easier to make these changes earlier rather than later, after your information has already been printed, distributed, or posted to the Web.

Create Documentation That Is Context-Sensitive

A useful way to think about providing documentation for your audiences is to consider documentation *context-sensitive*. Context-sensitive documentation is usually embedded within the software itself and addresses the specific tasks that users want to complete. For example, if a user is creating a memo template in Microsoft Word and clicks Help, the context-sensitive help system will give the user advice on how to create the template. Many online help systems today are context-sensitive, providing audiences with more closely focused help that pertains to their immediate user needs.

Context-sensitive help has not always existed alongside paper-based manuals and user guides. In the past, software documentation was often designed as a series of paper-based materials such as a quick reference card, a "getting started" or "quick start" short manual, or a full-blown large manual. Today, although these types of materials still exist, software documentation can almost always be found on the same installation CD as the software itself and is usually context-sensitive. This kind of online software documentation often accompanies and sometimes replaces paper-based documentation.

Whether documentation is electronic or paper-based, however, you still need to know your audience when designing it. Software users range from novices to experts, and therefore one single type of documentation simply won't suffice. Novices would be confused by the shorthand and technical terms that make sense to experts, whereas experts would be frustrated with the level of detail and explanation needed for a novice user. Depending on their level of expertise, different users need different types of information from documentation, and they should be able to use the documentation to find information that matches their needs. For example, user guides are primarily for novices who want to learn about the product. Quick reference guides are for users who know the product but need a quick reminder. Troubleshooting guides are for both experienced and novice users who don't need the full reference material but need a quick source of answers to solve specific problems. Whether the medium is electronic or paper-based, software documentation should address the specific needs of the users and the tasks for which they use the software.

Usability After the Information Is Released

Even after your instruction manual is on its way to the new gas grill owners or your report is being circulated among other engineers and managers, there are still ways to ensure usability in your information.

Provide Mechanisms for User Feedback

You can include ways for users to provide feedback on the documentation: customer comment cards, email addresses, phone numbers, Web sites. If your instructions contain a mistake on page 6, you can be sure customers will let you know, provided you give them a way to reach you.

Plan for the Next Version or Release

Continue collecting information, researching, and gathering user input as you plan the next version or release of your document. If you will need to write a revised manual in several months, begin collecting data as soon as possible. If the gas grill will be redesigned for next season, learn about the new design so you can plan the new manual. Establish an information file for quick access when you begin revising and updating.

Writing and Organizing Information for Usability

You can dramatically increase the usability of any communication by focusing on three aspects of writing. First, use good grammar and style. Readers can't extract what they need from poorly written information. Moreover, bad writing makes you (and your company) look incompetent. Second, create an overview to give your audience a framework for navigating the document. Third, "chunk" your information into units that make sense for the specific audience and purpose. (Chunking is described later in this chapter.)

Guides for usability assessment

Using Appropriate Grammar and Style

Following is a snapshot of important grammar and style issues for technical writing. For more information, see Appendix A for grammar issues and this book's Companion Website.

Use Proper Punctuation. A poorly punctuated sentence can be hard to interpret. One example is the use of the "series comma," which is a comma inserted before a coordinating conjunction in a list of items; for example:

> The Orb weaver, wood, and lynx varieties are examples of biological diversity in spiders.

Inserting a comma before *and* indicates that there are three items (Orbweaver spider, wood spider, lynx spider) in this series. But some writers, particularly in journalism, omit the final comma before the *and:*

> The Orb weaver, wood and lynx varieties are examples of biological diversity in spiders.

This usage seems to imply that "wood and lynx spiders" are only one kind of spider, which is not the case.

Punctuation is easy once you learn some basic rules. Refer to the chart in Appendix A as you work on your own writing.

Use Active Voice Whenever Possible. In general, readers learn more quickly when communications are written in active voice. In active voice sentences, a clear agent performs a clear action on a recipient:

Active voice	*Agent*	*Action*	*Recipient*
	(subject)	(verb)	(object)
	Joe	lost	your report.

Passive voice, by contrast, reverses this pattern, placing the recipient of the action in the subject slot:

Passive voice	*Recipient*	*Action*	*Agent*
	(subject)	(verb)	(prepositional phrase)
	Your report	was lost	by Joe.

Note that passive voice adds a form of the verb *be* (*was*) next to the actual verb.

Some writers mistakenly rely on passive voice because they think it sounds more objective and important. But passive voice decreases usability by making sentences wordier and harder to understand.

Writers often use passive voice to obscure the agent by leaving out the final phrase:

Passive voice	*Recipient*	*Action*
	(subject)	(verb)
	Your report	was lost.

"Your report was lost" leaves out the responsible party. Who lost the report? Passive voice is unethical if it obscures the person or other agent who performed the action when the person or agent responsible should be identified.

Passive voice is appropriate when the agent is not known or when the object is more important than the subject. For example, if a group of scientists performed an experiment and wanted to explain the results, they might write

| The data were analyzed, and the findings were discussed.

Even here, active voice ("We analyzed the data . . .") would be preferable. But if it was clear who analyzed the data or truly not important who did the work, passive voice might be acceptable. Passive voice can also be used to ease the blow that a direct sentence might deliver; for example:

| You have not paid your bill.

The passive form is indirect and thus less offensive:

| Your bill has not been paid.

Consider this technique when you want to avoid a hostile tone. But in general, to create usable, readable technical information, use active voice.

Avoid Nominalizations. A nominalization is a noun that would be easier to understand as a verb. Verbs are generally easier to read because they are usually short and signal action that can be visualized. You can usually spot a nominalization in two ways.

1. Look for words with a *-tion* ending:

> | My recommendation is for a larger budget.

Strike the ending to find the root verb: *recommend*. Then rewrite the sentence in a more direct form:

> | I recommend a larger budget.

Nominalizations may sound more "important" than a simpler verb form. But this kind of abstraction makes for difficult reading. A usable document is a readable document.

2. Beware "the [*noun*] of [*noun*]" formula:

> | The managing of this project is up to me.

This sentence is wordy and cumbersome. Identify the root verb form (*manage*), and create a more accessible sentence, such as

> | I manage this project.

or

> | Managing this project is my job.

Unpack Nouns. Too many nouns in a row can create confusion and reading difficulty. One noun can modify another (as in "software development"). But when two or more nouns modify a noun, the string of words becomes hard to read and ambiguous; for example:

> | Be sure to leave enough time for today's training session participant evaluation.

Is the evaluation of the session or of the participants? With no articles, prepositions, or verbs, readers cannot sort out the relationships among the nouns. Revise these sentences for clarity and readability:

> | Be sure to leave enough time for participants to evaluate today's training session.

or

> | Be sure to leave enough time to evaluate the participants in today's training session.

Avoid Wordy Phrases, but Don't Overedit. Wordy phrases can often be reduced to one word:

at a rapid rate	=	rapidly
due to the fact that	=	because
aware of the fact that	=	know
in close proximity to	=	near

But don't overedit, leaving out so many words that your audience cannot follow your line of thinking. A sentence such as:

⏐ Proposal to employ retirees almost died.

is confusing. What or who "almost died," the proposal or the retirees? A few more carefully chosen words would help:

⏐ The proposal to employ retirees was nearly defeated.

Short sentences are good, but not at the expense of clarity. Clear information is usable information.

Use Parallel Structure. Parallel structure is a fancy way of saying that similar items should be expressed in similar grammatical form. For example, the structure of the following sentence is not parallel:

⏐ She enjoys many outdoor activities, including running, kayaking, and the design of new hiking trails.

This sentence is essentially a list of items. The first two items, *running* and *kayaking*, are expressed as gerunds, with *-ing* endings. The third item, *the design of new hiking trails*, is not a gerund but a nominalization. To make this sentence parallel, you would revise as follows:

⏐ She enjoys many outdoor activities, including running, kayaking, and designing new hiking trails.

Avoid Unnecessary Jargon. Every profession has its own shorthand and accepted phrases and terms. Among specialists, these terms are an economical way to communicate. For example, *stat* (from the Latin *statim*, "immediately") is medical jargon for "drop everything and deal with this emergency." For computer engineers, a *virus* is not the common cold but a program that makes its way onto a computer's hard drive and causes problems.

Jargon can be useful when you are communicating with specialists. But some jargon is useless in any context. For example, a sentence like

| We will bilaterally optimize our efforts on this project.

may contain some popular buzzwords, but it would be much easier to understand if simplified to

| We will cooperate on this project.

Only use jargon that improves your communication, not jargon that bogs down the information and sounds pretentious. Keep in mind that general audiences are unlikely to know the meaning of jargon that experts use. Depending on the situation, you will need to explain such terms or avoid using them altogether.

Avoid Biased Language. Language that is offensive or makes unwarranted assumptions will put off readers and make your document less effective. Women, for example, who receive a letter addressed to "Dear Sir" will probably throw the letter out and never read the information. Avoid sexist usage such as referring to doctors, lawyers, and other professionals as "him" or "he" while referring to nurses, secretaries, and homemakers as "her" or "she." Words such as *mailman* or *fireman* automatically exclude women; terms such as *mail carrier* or *firefighter* are far more inclusive.

Also, usable communication should respect all people regardless of cultural, racial, or national background, sexual and religious orientation, age, or physical condition. References to individuals and groups should be as neutral as possible. Avoid any expression that is condescending or judgmental or that might violate a reader's sense of appropriateness.

Write from the User's Point of View. As one team of technical communicators notes, "Writing from the user's point of view brings the user into the 'story,' so it is easy for the user to imagine doing what you are describing" (Hargis, Hernandez, Hughes, & Ramaker, 1997, p. 14). Techniques include performing an audience and purpose analysis (so you understand where your audience is coming from), writing in active voice, and creating headings in the form of reader questions. Another technique noted by Hargis and colleagues is to use *you* (second person) or *you* understood whenever possible. Sentences such as "Insert the bolt into the large wheel frame" speak directly to the reader, not to some abstraction, such as "The bolt is next inserted . . ."

Don't Rely Solely on Grammar and Spelling Checkers. Some people mistakenly assume that the computer can solve all grammar and spelling problems. This is simply not true. Both *it's* and *its* are spelled correctly, but only one of them means "it is." The same is true for *their* and *there* (*their* is a possessive pronoun, as in "their books," while *there* is an adverb, as in "There is my mother"). Spelling checkers are very important, because they will find words that are spelled incorrectly, but don't count on them to find words that are *used* incorrectly. Grammar checkers are also fine tools to help you locate possible problems, but do not rely on what the software tells you. For example, not every sentence that the grammar checker flags as "long" should be shortened. Use these tools wisely and with common sense. Also, ask someone to proofread your material. Some companies have full-time technical editors who are happy to look over your writing.

Consider International Issues and Writing for Translation. Technical communication is a global process. Documents may originate in English but then be translated into other languages. In this case, writers must be careful to use English that is easy to translate. Idioms, humor, and analogies are often difficult for translators. One famous example is the case of a U.S. car called the Nova. When translated into Spanish, Nova means "Does Not Go"! In addition to terms, certain grammatical elements are also important for translation. The lack of an article (*a, the*) or of the word *that* in certain crucial places can cause a sentence to be translated inaccurately. Consider the following example (Kohl, 1999, p. 151):

> Programs **that are** currently running in the system are indicated by icons in the lower part of the screen.
>
> Programs currently running in the system are indicated by icons in the lower part of the screen.

The first sentence contains the phrase "that are," which might ordinarily be left out by native English writers, as in the second sentence. This second sentence is harder to translate because the phrase "that are" provides the translator with important clues about the relationship of the words *programs, currently,* and *running.*

Use White Space and Effective Page Design. The proper use of white space, typography, and page design plays a big role in a document's usability. Pages that are set in tiny type with text crammed on the page and no graphics are hard to read. Chapter 9 provides more information on graphics and visuals.

Creating an Overview

Information is usable when people can answer several key questions:

- What will I learn from this document?
- Why am I receiving this information?
- What can I anticipate finding in this document?

To help answer these questions, always provide an overview before launching into the details. Think about it this way: If you were taking a long road trip, you would probably study a map first to get the "big picture" of your journey and to know exactly where you will be headed. Overviews provide a sort of road map.

You can provide an overview in many forms and places within a document. Some documents begin with a section called "About This Document," which previews the entire document. Within a document, you can also provide an overview of each chapter. Figure 3.3 shows a book overview from a manual for an IBM laptop computer. This particular overview explains what users will learn, how long this process should take, and what steps they should already have completed.

Overviews are important in oral communication as well. At the beginning of a presentation, preview for your audience the main points you will be covering. For example, you might begin a presentation about electric cars by saying, "Today, I would like to give you more information about electric cars. Specifically, I will cover three main points: the way electric cars operate, certain new designs in electric batteries, and the usefulness of electric cars in cold climates." Your presentation would then cover these points, in that order.

Chunking Information

Chunking is an organizing technique in which you divide the information into small units or modules based on the topics or types of information that will be covered in a given section. When you chunk information into topics, you should "include information in a topic that the user thinks of as a unit" (Horton, 1990, p. 101).

If you were designing a quick reference card for using an ATM, you might discover that the information falls into three general topics, or chunks:

- How to make a withdrawal
- How to make a deposit
- How to check your balance

You would design the card around these three chunks of information. If any one of the chunks became too long and unwieldy, you might subdivide it. "How to make a deposit," for example, might become two chunks: "How to deposit checks" and "How to deposit cash."

If you've ever created an outline to help you write a paper or speech, you've had experience in breaking down information into smaller units. When you chunk information for an audience, you create these units based on the audience's needs and the document's purpose.

Creating Headings

Another way to enhance usability is to create headings in the form of questions your audience might ask. This approach isn't appropriate for all documents, and overuse of questions can become repetitive and annoying. For certain documents, though, such as patient information brochures, questions can help guide readers to the appropriate section of the document. Questions also create an inviting, user-friendly tone: If the question sounds like something readers would actually ask, they will feel as if the document has been written just for them.

About this book

This book contains information that will help you operate the IBM ThinkPad 240 computer. Be sure to read the *ThinkPad 240 Setup Guide* and Chapter 1 of this book before using the computer.

Chapter 1. "Getting Familiar with Your Computer," acquaints you with the basic features of your computer.

Chapter 2. "Extending the Features of Your Computer," provides information on installing options and using your computer's high-technology features.

Chapter 3. "Protecting Your Computer," provides information on using passwords, and using locks.

Chapter 4. "Solving Computer Problems," describes what to do when you have a computer problem. The chapter includes a trouble-shooting guide on how to recover lost or damaged software.

Chapter 5. "Getting Service," describes various options of IBM's support and service.

Appendix A, Features and specifications describes the features and specifications associated with your computer, including information on power cords.

Appendix B, Product warranties and notices contains the warranty statements for your computer and notices for this book.

The **glossary** defines terms appearing in this book. The book concludes with an index.

v

Figure 3.3 **Book Overview from the IBM Thinkpad 240 Manual.** This page is designed to help users understand the purpose and structure of the manual.
Source: Reprinted by permission from *IBM ThinkPad 240 User's Reference,* 1/e. © by Lenovo.

For example, a patient information brochure about a laparoscopy (a medical procedure that uses a small camera to look inside the body) begins as follows:

> **LAPAROSCOPY**
>
> **Activities**
>
> You should rest until you feel up to resuming your normal activities—usually in a day or two. Do not lift objects weighing more than 20 to 30 pounds for one week.
>
> *Source:* University of Minnesota Hospital and Clinics.

This information would be more useful and friendly if it addressed an actual patient question:

> **WHAT ACTIVITIES CAN I PERFORM AFTER MY LAPAROSCOPY?**
>
> You should rest until you feel up to resuming your normal activities—usually in a day or two. Do not lift objects weighing more than 20 to 30 pounds for one week.

Using the Margins for Commentary

You can use the margins to call out or highlight particularly important information, or you can leave them blank for readers to take notes or write comments (see Figure 3.4). Using white space and marginal cueing areas are discussed in more detail in Chapter 8.

Proofreading Your Final Draft

Writers proofread as a final step, to ensure that everything is just right. No matter how engaging and informative the document, basic errors distract the reader and make the writer look bad. Here are some types of easily correctable errors we can spot with careful proofreading (refer to the page numbers in parentheses for advice on repairing these errors):

3.3
Resources for usability testing

- *Sentence errors,* such as fragments, comma splices, or run-ons (p. 300)
- *Punctuation errors,* such as missing apostrophes or unnecessary commas (p. 296)
- *Usage errors,* such as *it's* for *its, lay* for *lie,* or *their* for *there* (p. 303)
- *Mechanical errors,* such as misspelled words, inaccurate dates, or incorrect abbreviations (p. 308)
- *Format errors,* such as missing page numbers, inconsistent spacing, or incorrect source documentation (p. 134)
- *Typographical errors* (typos), such as repeated or missing words or letters, omitted word endings (such as *-s, -ed,* or *ing*), or left-out quotation marks or parentheses.

Handling the ThinkPad Computer

By using common sense and by following these handling tips, you will get the most use and enjoyment out of your computer for a long time to come.

This section provides tips for handling notebook computers in general. Some descriptions may not suit your situation. Check your shipping checklist to confirm the items you get with your computer.

Notebook computers are precision machines that require careful handling. Though your computer is designed and tested to be a durable notebook computer that functions reliably in normal work environments, you need to use some common sense in handling it.

ThinkPad don'ts

- Do not subject your computer to physical punishment, such as dropping or bumping.
- Do not place heavy objects on your computer.
- Do not spill or allow liquids into your computer.
- Do not use your computer in or near water (to avoid the danger of electrical shock).
- Do not pack your computer in a tightly packed suitcase or bag. Your LCD might be damaged.

A scratchlike marking on your LCD might be a stain transferred from the keyboard (including from the TrackPoint stick) when the cover was pressed from the outside. Wipe such a stain gently with a dry soft cloth. If the stain remains, moisten the cloth with LCD cleaner and wipe the stain again. Be sure to dry the LCD before closing it.

- Do not disassemble your computer. Only an authorized IBM ThinkPad repair technician should disassemble and repair your computer.
- Do not scratch, twist, hit, or push the surface of your computer display.
- Do not place any objects between the display and the keyboard or under the keyboard.
- Do not pick up or hold your computer by the display. When picking up your open computer, hold it by the bottom (keyboard) half.

Figure 3.4 **Page from a User's Reference for an IBM ThinkPad A20.** Note how the page is designed with room in the left margin for users to make notes.
Source: Reprinted by permission from *IBM ThinkPad A20 User's Reference,* 1/e. © by Lenovo.

TIPS FOR PROOFREADING

- **Save it for the final draft.** Proofreading earlier drafts might cause writer's block and distract your focus from the content, organization, and style of your document.

- **Take a break beforehand.** After you complete a final draft, give yourself some time before proofreading. Do something else for at least a couple of hours.

- **Work from hard copy.** Research indicates that people read more perceptively (and with less fatigue) from a printed page than from a computer screen. Also, the page is easier to mark up, scribble on, and so on. Some people like to proofread in a comfy chair or even lying down.

- **Keep it slow.** Read each word—don't skim. Force yourself to slow down by placing a ruler under each line or by moving backward throughout the essay, sentence by sentence.

- **Be especially alert for troublesome areas in your writing.** Do you have trouble spelling? Do you get commas confused with semicolons? Do you make a lot of typographical errors? If punctuation is a problem, for example, make one final pass to check each punctuation mark.

- **Proofread more than once.** The more you do it, the more errors you're likely to spot.

- **Don't rely only on computerized aids.** Your spell checker can root out incorrectly spelled words but not incorrectly *used* words (such as *its* for *it's*) or typos that happen to spell a word (say, *cat* versus *rat*). Grammar checkers often give bizarre or inaccurate advice. In the end, nothing substitutes for your own careful reading.

Checklist for Designing Usable Information

Planning for Usable Communication
- Did I perform an audience and purpose analysis?
- Did I develop an information plan?
- Did I do enough research?

Writing and Designing Usable Communication
- Did I test an early version of the communication product?
- Did I make needed revisions to the plan or product based on testing?

(continued)

> **Writing and Organizing Information with Users in Mind**
> - Does my document use the appropriate grammar and style?
> - Is information appropriately chunked?
> - Did I provide ways for users to give me feedback?

Exercises

1. Identify an activity that could require instructions for a novice to complete. Prepare a task analysis for this activity using a worksheet similar to the one in Figure 3.1. Exchange task analyses with another student in your class, and critique each other's analysis. With your class, discuss the challenges of doing a task analysis and identify strategies for performing a task analysis effectively.

2. **FOCUS ON WRITING**. Find a set of instructions or another type of technical document that is easy to use. Identify specific characteristics of the document that make it usable. Is the document well written? Does it have an overview? Can you quickly find the information you need? Then find a technical document that is hard to use. What characteristics make it unusable? In a memo to your instructor, define specific changes that you would make in revising the document. Submit both examples along with your memo.

3. **FOCUS ON WRITING**. As a technical communicator, you will sometimes encounter technical terms that need to be defined or revised for a nonexpert audience. But how do you define a technical term if you don't fully understand it yourself?

   Usable communication must be written in terminology and language consistent with the audience's background and level of understanding. Online dictionaries and usability resources are tools that technical communicators rely on to help revise the language of documents for nontechnical audiences.

   Find an article in a technical or science journal in your field or area of interest, and create a list of terms appearing in it that are unfamiliar to you. Use the following resources to look up definitions of these terms, and then write your own brief definition of each, directed at a nonspecialist audience.

   - **http://dictionary.langenberg.com**
     A portal site that connects to dozens of online dictionaries of various types and specialties.
   - **http://www.webopedia.com**
     An online dictionary and search engine focused on computer and Internet technology definitions.

- **http://www.techweb.com/encyclopedia**
  Definitions for over 20,000 information technology terms and acronyms.
- **http://www.upassoc.org**
  The Web site for the Usability Professionals' Association.

The Collaboration Window

Bring in some children's connecting blocks, such as TinkerToys or Lego blocks. Form several teams of four to six people, and assign two people as technical writers. The technical writers should assemble a few of the pieces into a simple design (don't use more than three or four pieces). Then the technical writers should write up a quick instruction card explaining how to assemble the pieces into the design they've created. For example, the card for Lego blocks might read

1. Select two large red blocks and two small green blocks.
2. Place one red block on its side.
3. Attach one green block to the red block.

and so on. Then present the "parts" and your instructions to the rest of your team. Watch as your team tries to assemble the blocks according to your instructions. Assess the instructions for usability. Were all tasks accounted for? Did any terms or language confuse the users? Go back and perform a task analysis, and discuss what you could do to improve the usability of your instruction card.

The Global Window

Astronomy and planetary science have become truly global sciences, and space exploration is now conducted by multinational teams. Knowledge about astronomy belongs to everyone, regardless of nationality or language. Do the Web sites representing these disciplines succeed in making themselves accessible to and useful for a global audience?

Explore the Web sites listed on the following page, and assess their usability for international audiences. Would non-English speakers be able to access the information on these sites? What efforts are made to reach international readers? Are language and cultural differences accounted for in the design, content, and interface?

Draw up a list of key elements and features of each site that contribute to or detract from usability for international audiences. What changes would you recommend to make each site more accessible and usable for non-English-speaking readers? Summarize your assessment in a brief memo, including printed copies of specific pages from each Web site that you discuss.

- **http://www.planetary.org**
  Planetary Society
- **http://www.nasa.gov/home**
  National Aeronautics and Space Administration
- **http://www.esa.int/esaCP/index.html**
  European Space Agency

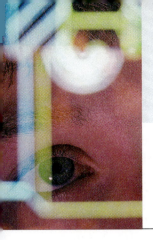

CHAPTER 4

Conducting Research for Technical Communication

Thinking Critically About Research

Primary Research

Internet and Digital Research

Other Electronic Research Tools

Hard Copy Research

Checklist for Research

Exercises

The Collaboration Window

The Global Window

Thinking Critically About Research

Most major decisions in technical communication are based on careful research, often with the findings recorded in a written report, in a long memo, on a Web site, or in some combination of documents. The type of research you will perform as a technical communicator depends largely on your workplace or classroom assignment. For any topic you research, for the classroom or workplace, you can consult numerous information sources. An excellent place to begin is with primary research, where you can get information "from the source" by conducting interviews and surveys and by observing people in action. The Internet is also a great choice, because it's quick and convenient, but you need to verify that the information you find on the Internet is from a credible source. Other electronic sources include CD-ROM databases and online retrieval services. Finally, traditional sources such as encyclopedias, print indexes, and journals can be valuable because their contents are usually subject to close scrutiny before they are published. Many of these traditional sources are also available electronically.

Primary Research

Informative interviews, surveys and questionnaires, inquiry letters, official records, and observations and experiments are considered *primary sources* because they afford an original, firsthand study of a topic.

Informative Interviews

An excellent primary source of information is the interview, conducted in person, by telephone, or by email. Much of what an expert knows may never be published. Also, a respondent might refer you to other experts or sources of information.

Of course, an expert's opinion can be just as mistaken or biased as anyone else's. Like patients who seek second opinions about serious medical conditions, researchers seek a balanced range of expert opinions about a complex problem or controversial issue—not only from a company engineer and environmentalist, for example, but also from independent and presumably more objective third parties such as a professor or journalist who has studied the issue.

Always go into an interview with a clear purpose, and do your homework before the interview so you won't waste time asking questions you could have answered yourself.

INTERVIEW TIPS

- Make each question clear and specific.
- Avoid questions that can be answered yes or no.

- Avoid loaded questions, such as "In what ways do you think the hazards of genetically modified foods have been overstated?" Ask impartial questions instead, such as "In your opinion, have the hazards associated with genetically modified food been accurately stated, overstated, or understated?"
- Save the most difficult, complex, or sensitive questions for last.
- Be polite and professional.
- Let your respondent do most of the talking.
- Ask for clarification if needed, but do not put words in the respondent's mouth. Questions such as "Could you go over that again?" or "What did you mean by [*word*]?" are fine.

Surveys and Questionnaires

Surveys help you form impressions of the concerns, preferences, attitudes, beliefs, or perceptions of a large, identifiable group (a *target population*) by studying representatives of that group (a *sample*).

4.1
Developing
effective
questions

The questionnaire is the tool for conducting surveys. Whereas interviews allow for greater clarity and depth, questionnaires offer an inexpensive way to survey a large group. Respondents can answer privately and anonymously—and often more candidly than in an interview. The following guidelines will help you design effective surveys.

SURVEY AND QUESTIONNAIRE TIPS

- **Define the survey's purpose and target population.** Why is this survey being performed? What, exactly, is it measuring? How much background research do you need? How will the survey findings be used? Who is the exact population being studied (the chronically unemployed, part-time students, computer users)?
- **Identify the sample group.** How will intended respondents be selected? How many respondents will there be? Generally, the larger the sample surveyed, the more dependable the results (assuming a well-chosen and representative sample). Will the sample be randomly chosen? In the statistical sense, *random* does not mean "haphazard": A random sample means that each member of the target population stands an equal chance of being in the sample group.
- **Define the survey method.** What type of data (opinions, ideas, facts, figures) will you collect? Is timing important? How will the survey be administered—in person, by mail, by phone? How will the data be collected, recorded, analyzed, and reported? (Lavin, 1992, p. 277). Phone,
  (continued)

email, and in-person surveys yield fast results and high response rates, but respondents consider phone surveys annoying, and without anonymity, people tend to be less candid. Mail surveys are less expensive than phone surveys over long distances. Electronic surveys, conducted via a Web form or an email message, are the least expensive. But these methods can have pitfalls. Computer connections can fail, and you have less control over how many times the same person completes the survey.

• **Decide on the types of questions.** Questions can take two forms: open-ended and closed-ended. Open-ended questions allow respondents to answer in any way they choose. It is more time-consuming to measure the data gathered, but such questions provide a rich source of information. An open-ended question would be worded like this:

> How much do you know about genetically modified food products?

Closed-ended questions give respondents a limited number of choices, and the data gathered are easier to measure. A closed-ended question would be set up like this:

> Are you concerned about genetically modified food products?
>
> Yes _____   No _____

• **Develop an engaging introduction, and provide appropriate information.** Persuade respondents that the questionnaire relates to their concerns, that their answers matter, and that their anonymity is ensured:

> Your answers will help our company determine the public's views about genetically modified food products. All answers will be kept confidential. Thank you.

• **Make it brief, simple, and inviting.** Respondents don't mind giving up some time to help, but long questionnaires usually don't get many replies. Limit the number and types of questions to the most important topics.

Public Records and Organizational Publications

The Freedom of Information Act and state public-record laws grant public access to an array of government, corporate, and organizational documents. Obtaining these documents (from state or federal agencies) takes time (although more and more such documents are available on the Web), but in them you can find answers to questions like these (Blum, 1997):

- Which universities are being investigated by the Department of Agriculture for mistreating laboratory animals?
- Are auditors for the Internal Revenue Service required to meet quotas?
- How often has a particular nuclear power plant been cited for safety violations?

Organization records (reports, memos, Web pages, and so on) are also good primary sources. Most organizations publish pamphlets, brochures, annual reports, or Web sites for consumers, employees, investors, or voters. Of course, you need to be alert for bias in company literature. In evaluating the safety of a genetically modified food product, you would want the complete picture. Along with the company's literature, you would want to consult studies and reports from government agencies and publications from health and environmental groups.

Personal Observation and Experiments

Observation should be your final step in primary research because you now know what to look for. Know how, where, and when to look, and jot down observations immediately. You might even take photos or make drawings.

Unlike general observations, experiments are controlled forms of observations designed to verify an assumption (e.g., the role of fish oil in preventing heart disease) or to test something untried (e.g., the relationship between background music and productivity). Each field has its own guidelines for experimental design, including the need for all experiments to be reviewed by human subjects review boards to ensure protection of test subjects. Depending on the situation, you may be able to learn about your subject matter by interviewing a scientist who is conducting an experiment or by reading published results.

Finally, workplace research can involve the analysis of samples, such as water, soil, or air for contamination and pollution; foods for nutritional content; or plants for medicinal value. Investigators may analyze material samples to find the cause of airline accidents; engineers may analyze samples of steel, concrete, or other building materials to test for tensile strength or load-bearing capacity; medical specialists may analyze tissue samples for disease. As a researcher, you may be able to access this information through interviews or published reports.

Internet and Digital Research

Almost every form of information—newspapers and magazines, government documents and research reports, corporate-sponsored Web sites, library databases—can be accessed on the Internet. In fact, "Googling" a research topic (searching for the topic using the Google search engine) is fast becoming the method of choice for almost all forms of research. In 2003, for instance, the Pew

4.2

Gathering information on the Internet

Internet and American Life project reported that 80 percent of adult Internet users had researched medical information using the Internet.

The Internet can provide sources ranging from 12-year-olds who have their own blogs to electronic journals and national newspapers. Remember that although the Internet is quick and easy to use, you need to be sure that the source of your information is credible and reliable. (See TIPS for Researching on the Internet). Following is a brief listing and description of various sources of information on the Internet.

Online News Sites and Magazines

Most major news organizations offer online versions of their broadcast outlets and print publications. Examples include online newspapers (http://www.nyt.com) or the Web site for CNN (http://www.cnn.com) or PBS (http://www.pbs.org). Major magazines also offer Web versions. Some news is available *only* electronically—online magazines such as Slate.com and smaller new sites such as NewYorkBusiness.com are examples.

Note: Make sure you understand how the publication obtains and reviews information. Is it a major news site, such as CNN, or is it a smaller site run by a special-interest group? Each type can be useful, but you must evaluate the reliability and objectivity of each source.

Government Research Sites and Other Government Documents

Almost every government organization—local, state, and federal—has a Web site and online access to research and reports. Examples include the National Institutes of Health (http://www.nih.gov), the Census Bureau (http://www.census.gov), and state and local sites that provide information on auto licenses, state tax laws, and local property and land issues. From some of these sites, you can link to specific government-sponsored research projects.

Note: Check the date on the report or data; for instance, if you are using Census Bureau information, make sure the date fits the research question you are trying to answer. Also find out how often the site is updated so that you can determine how current the posted information is.

Community Discussion Groups and Bulletin Boards

For almost any topic under the sun, there is a discussion group or bulletin board on the Web that you can turn to. The good news is that these sites provide you with an abundance of information. But the challenge is to determine how to use this information. Assume that you are studying a health-related issue, such as quitting smoking, and you want to visit a Yahoo group or other discussion site to learn more about the challenges facing smokers who are trying to quit. This information may be very insightful, but it does not represent the full range of input from all smokers.

Note: Look at more than one such site in order to get a broader perspective on the discussion.

Blogs and Wikis

Blogs (Web logs) are Web sites where users post ideas and discussions, and these are displayed in reverse chronological order (see Chapter 5). Blogs can also be used to connect to other similar discussions and to make comments and give feedback. As with discussion groups, you will find more blogs than you can use, so evaluate the information carefully and consider more than one source. Never lose sight of the fact that virtually *everything* posted on a blog reflects personal opinion, not objective evaluation.

Wikis (wikipedias) are community encyclopedias where anyone can add or edit the content of a listing. The original and still most popular wiki is Wikipedia (www.wikipedia.org). The theory of a wiki is that if the information is wrong, someone will eventually correct it. Like many (if not most) Internet sites, wikis do not have a centralized editor or gatekeeper to check the accuracy of the information.

Note: Use blogs and wikis with caution, and check the information against several other peer-reviewed or traditional sources.

Email Lists

Many topics can be researched by subscribing to an email list devoted to that subject. For instance, if you are an engineer studying alternative energy (wind turbines, solar energy), you can probably find an email list for this topic. Unlike the full Internet, email lists are usually very focused on the topic at hand, and subscribers are usually experts in this content area. There are several choices for receiving the information: single email messages or a "digest" format that provides all of the postings in a single email at regular intervals (daily or weekly).

Note: After you join the list, pay attention to the main people who do the postings. If the list is dominated by two or three people, you might want to find another list that has a more diverse set of subscribers.

Library Databases That Are Searchable via the Internet

Almost all libraries now have some form of a Web site where you can search for books and articles, reserve material, and even pay overdue fines. Research libraries, such as the ones located in colleges and universities, also have Web sites that let users search not only the library itself but also the large databases and other digital resources subscribed to by the library: *Applied Science and Technology Abstracts*, which indexes journals in most major scientific areas, is an example.

Note: Before initiating a database search, meet with a librarian. Your local reference librarian can give you a quick tour of the various databases and instructions for searching them most effectively. You can then use the Internet search engine from school or home.

Other Web Sites

There are many other kinds of Web sites that could be useful for research, including corporate information sites, advertising and marketing sites, and sites with specific points of view (e.g., lobbying and special-interest groups). Remember that you must evaluate each Web site carefully. See TIPS for Evaluating and Interpreting Information.

Evaluating Sources from the Web

Regardless of your topic, a Web search typically yields a large number of hits. You need to evaluate every source you intend to use. If you can't clearly identify the author and his or her credentials, you should assume that the source is not credible. Why? Because the Web is a *bottom-up* medium, allowing anyone with the technical resources to create a Web site. Fonts, color, and images can make any site appear credible. Information comes from a multitude of sources, without any form of gatekeeping.

On the other hand, journal articles, newspaper reports, and television or radio stories are considered *top-down* information. These materials are usually subject to editorial or peer review and fact-checking before being printed or delivered on the air. Nevertheless, *all* Web sites require particular critical attention.

For example, imagine you are researching the topic of genetically modified organisms (GMOs); in particular, you are looking into the pros and cons of using genetically modified corn, oats, and other grains for food. You use a search engine and search on the term "GMO." One of your hits is the Web site shown in Figure 4.1.

Too often, people assume that information located via a Web search can be cited without evaluating the source. At first glance, this site appears to have a clear point of view and a clear source: "The Campaign Grassroots Political Action." The left side of the page offers many links to information about GMOs, and the center of the page features the question "Do you know what is in your food? Is it genetically engineered?"

But does this site offer objective information? If you look at the answer to the first question, about what is in your food (look below the bowl of cereal), it states that "[y]ou don't know—because they won't tell you . . .". Clearly, this is a site designed to encourage readers to write to their congressional representatives,

Figure 4.1 A Web Site That Advocates a Particular Viewpoint. One of the Web site hits found during a search on the term "GMO."

Source: The Campaign www.thecampaign.org/. Reprinted by permission.

Federal Register

U.S. Government
Printing Office

U.S. Government
Online Bookstore

Document Links:

Declaration of
Independence

U.S. Constitution

Bill of Rights

Current Bills
in U.S. Congress

Answer: Since genetically engineered soy and corn are used in many processed foods, it is estimated that over 70 percent of the foods in grocery stores in the U.S. and Canada contain genetically engineered ingredients.

Question: Are people all over the world eating genetically engineered foods?

Answer: No, all of the European Union nations, Japan, China, Australia, New Zealand and many other countries require the mandatory labeling of foods that contain genetically engineered ingredients. As a result, food manufacturers in all those countries choose to use non-genetically engineered ingredients.

Question: Are you telling me that people in the United States and Canada are eating a lot more genetically engineered foods than in many other countries in the world?

Answer: Yes, citizens in the United States and Canada are engaged in the largest feeding experiment in human history and most people are not even aware of the fact.

Question: What countries are growing genetically engineered crops?

Answer: There were only five countries that grew about 98 percent of the $44 billion of commercial genetically engineered crops in 2003-2004. Those five countries were: the United States ($27.5 billion), Argentina ($8.9 billion), China ($3.9 billion), Canada ($2.0 billion) and Brazil ($1.6 billion).

Question: What can I do to help properly regulate genetically engineered foods so that I can rest assured that these experimental crops will not harm human health or the environment?

Answer: The single most important step you can take is to mail three letters using the U.S. Postal Service. One letter goes to your Congressional Representative in the U.S. House of Representatives and the other two to your state's two Senators serving in the U.S. Senate. The letters request that they support legislation to label genetically engineered foods. We have form letters on this web site for this purpose. **Click here** for more information.

Copyright © The Campaign.

Figure 4.1 (*Continued*)

corporate officials, the Food and Drug Administration, and others, and lobby for the labeling of any food containing genetically engineered ingredients. The large font asking readers to "Click Here to Take Action" leads to a second page with instructions for writing a letter to Congress. The site offers questions and answers, which provide some useful information but are not intended to be objective or neutral.

Does this mean that the site is an invalid source of information? Not at all. It does mean, however, that this information source advocates a point of view and should therefore be regarded as biased in that direction. Balance your research by also consulting sources such as academic journals, documentary radio or television programs, technical manuals, and reputable media reporting that will reflect a range of other points of view.

Managing Your Information

Walker and Ruszkiewicz (2000) suggest the following options for keeping track of the vast amount of information you are likely to find on the Internet:

- **Cut and paste.** You can copy URLs (World Wide Web addresses) and text from Web sites, newsgroups, or listservs directly into your word-processing or database files. This saves you time because you won't have to retype or rewrite information to integrate it into your own documents.
- **Download or print out files.** If you find information at a site that appears to change frequently or is hard to access, you should either download and save the information or print it out. Make sure you accurately record the URL where you found the information and the date on which you accessed the site. Most Web browsers can be configured to print this information when they print the page—you can usually specify this option in your browser's page setup menu.
- **Use your bookmarks file.** Most browsers provide some kind of bookmarking system that allows you to save and organize links to sites you've found useful. Typically, this feature allows you to create folders for the different kinds of sites that you visit repeatedly or wish to return to. You can also save your bookmark files to floppy disks, which is especially useful if you work in a public computer lab.
- **Use electronic note cards and bibliography programs.** Software programs such as ProCite or Endnote allow you to store complete bibliographic information as well as abstracts and quotations from various kinds of sources. This kind of software provides a useful system for managing all your research, not just Internet research.

4.3
Evaluating online information

TIPS for Researching on the Internet

- Select specific keywords or search phrases that are varied and technical. Some search terms generate more useful hits than others. In addition to "cell phone radiation," for example, try "electromagnetic fields," "cell phones and brain tumors," or "electrical fields." Specialized terms (say, "vertigo" instead of "dizziness") offer the best access to reliable sites.
- Look for Web sites that are discipline-specific. Specialized newsletters and trade publications offer good site listings.
- Expect limited results from any one search engine. No single search engine can index more than a fraction of ever-increasing Web content.

(continued)

- Save or print what you need before it changes or disappears.
- Download only what you need. Unless they are crucial to your research, omit graphics, sound, and video files.
- Before downloading *anything* from the Internet, ask yourself, "Am I violating anyone's privacy (as in forwarding an email or a blog entry)?" or "Am I decreasing the value of this material for its owner in any way?" For information on copyright, see Chapter 6.
- Consider using information retrieval services such as Inquisit or DIALOG. For a monthly fee or per-page fee, users can download full texts of articles. Schools and companies often subscribe to these Internet-accessible databases.

Other Electronic Research Tools

Several other electronic technologies are used for storing and retrieving information. These technologies are accessible at libraries and in many cases via the Web.

Compact Discs

A single CD-ROM can store the equivalent of an entire encyclopedia and serves as a portable database, usually searchable via keyword. One useful CD-ROM for business information is ProQuest. Its ABI/INFORM database indexes countless journals in management, marketing, and business published since 1989; its UMI database indexes major U.S. newspapers. A useful CD-ROM for information about psychology, nursing, education, and social policy is SilverPlatter.

Online Retrieval Services

College libraries and corporations subscribe to online services that can access thousands of databases stored on centralized computers. Compared with CDs, mainframe databases are usually more specialized and more current, often updated daily (as opposed to weekly, monthly, or quarterly). Online retrieval services offer access to three types of databases: bibliographic, full-text, and factual (Lavin, 1992, p. 14):

- *Bibliographic databases* list publications in a particular field and sometimes include abstracts for each entry.
- *Full-text databases* display the entire article or document (usually excluding graphics) directly on the computer screen and will print the article on command.
- *Factual databases* provide facts of all kinds: global and up-to-the-minute stock quotations, weather data, lists of new patents filed, and credit ratings of major companies, to name a few.

Four popular database services are the following:

- **OCLC and RLIN.** You can easily compile a comprehensive list of works on your topic at any library that belongs to an electronic consortium such as the Online Computer Library Center (OCLC) or the Research Libraries Information Network (RLIN). OCLC and RLIN databases are essentially giant electronic card catalogs. Using a networked terminal, you can search the databases by subject, title, or author.
- **DIALOG.** Many libraries subscribe to DIALOG, a network of independent databases covering a wide range of subjects and searched by keywords. This system can provide bibliographies and abstracts of the most recent journal articles on your topic. DIALOG databases include Conference Papers Index, Electronic Yellow Pages (for Retailers, Services, Manufacturers), and ENVIROLINE.
- **BRS.** Bibliographic Retrieval Services, another popular network, provides bibliographies and abstracts from life sciences, physical sciences, business, or social sciences. BRS databases include Dissertation Abstracts International, Harvard Business Review, and Pollution Abstracts.

Comprehensive database networks such as DIALOG and BRS are accessible via the Internet for a fee. Specialized databases, such as MEDLINE and ENVIROLINE, offer free bibliographies and abstracts, and copies of the full text can be ordered for a fee. Ask your librarian for help searching online databases.

Card Catalog

Most library card catalogs aren't made up of cards anymore—rather, they are electronic and can be accessed through the Internet or at terminals in the library. You can search a library's holdings by subject, author, or title in that library's catalog system. Visit the library's Web site, or ask a librarian for help.

Hard Copy Research

Traditional printed research tools are still of great value. Unlike much of what you may find on the Web (especially if you aren't careful about checking the source), most print research tools are carefully reviewed and edited before they are published. True, it may take more time to go to the library and look through a printed book, but often it's a better way to get solid information. In time, many of these sources will become available on the Web (many are now).

Bibliographies

These comprehensive lists of publications about a subject are generally issued yearly or even more frequently. However, they can quickly become dated. To see which bibliographies are published in your field, begin with the *Bibliographic Index,* which is a list (by subject) of bibliographies that contain at least 50 citations.

To look for bibliographies on scientific and technical topics, consult *A Guide to U.S. Government Scientific and Technical Resources,* which is a list of everything published by the government in these broad fields. You might also look for bibliographies focused on a particular subject, such as *Health Hazards of Video Display Terminals: An Annotated Bibliography.*

Encyclopedias

Encyclopedias provide basic information. Examples include the *Encyclopedia of Building and Construction Terms,* the *Encyclopedia of Banking and Finance,* and the *Encyclopedia of Food Technology.* The *Encyclopedia of Associations* lists over 30,000 professional organizations worldwide (American Medical Association, Institute of Electrical and Electronics Engineers, and so on). Most organizations can be accessed via their Web sites.

Dictionaries

Dictionaries may be general, or they may focus on specific disciplines or give biographical information. Examples include the *Dictionary of Engineering and Technology,* the *Dictionary of Telecommunications,* and the *Dictionary of Scientific Biography.*

Handbooks

These research aids gather key facts (formulas, tables, advice, examples) about a field in condensed form. Examples include the *Business Writer's Handbook,* the *Civil Engineering Handbook,* and the *McGraw-Hill Computer Handbook.*

Almanacs

Almanacs contain factual and statistical data. Examples include the *World Almanac and Book of Facts,* the *Almanac for Computers,* and the *Almanac of Business and Industrial Financial Ratios.*

Directories

Directories provide updated information about organizations, companies, people, products, services, or careers, often including addresses and phone numbers. Examples include *The Career Guide: Dun's Employment Opportunities Directory,* the *Directory of American Firms Operating in Foreign Countries,* and *The Internet Directory.*

Guides to Literature

If you simply don't know which books, journals, indexes, and reference works are available for your topic, consult a guide to literature. For a general list of books in various disciplines, see Walford's *Guide to Reference Material* or Sheehy's *Guide to Reference Books.* For scientific and technical literature, consult Malinowsky and Richardson's *Science and Engineering Literature: A Guide to Reference Sources.* Ask your librarian about literature guides for your discipline.

Indexes

Indexes are lists of books, newspaper articles, journal articles, or other works on a particular subject.

Book Indexes. A book index lists works by author, title, or subject. Sample indexes include *Scientific and Technical Books and Serials in Print* (an annual listing of literature in science and technology), *New Technical Books: A Selective List with Descriptive Annotations* (issued ten times yearly), and *Medical Books and Serials in Print* (an annual listing of works from medicine and psychology).

Periodical Indexes. A periodical index provides sources from magazines and journals. First, decide whether you seek general or specialized information. Two general indexes are the *Magazine Index,* a subject index on microfilm, and the *Readers' Guide to Periodical Literature,* which is updated every few weeks.

For specialized information, consult indexes that list journal articles by discipline, such as *Ulrich's International Periodicals Directory,* the *General Science Index,* the *Applied Science and Technology Index,* or the *Business Periodicals Index.* Specific disciplines have their own indexes: Examples include the *Agricultural Index,* the *Index to Legal Periodicals,* and the *International Nursing Index.*

Citation Indexes. Citation indexes allow researchers to trace the development and refinement of a published idea. Using a citation index, you can track down the specific publications in which the original material has been cited, quoted, applied, critiqued, verified, or otherwise amplified (Garfield, 1973, p. 200). In short, you can use them to answer the question "Who else has said what about this idea?"

The *Science Citation Index* cross-references articles on science and technology worldwide. Both the *Science Citation Index* and its counterpart, the *Social Science Citation Index,* are searchable by computer.

Technical Report Indexes. Government and private-sector reports prepared worldwide offer specialized and current information. Examples include *Scientific and Technical Aerospace Reports, Government Reports Announcements and Index,* and the *Monthly Catalog of United States Government Publications.* Proprietary or security restrictions limit public access to certain corporate or government documents.

Patent Indexes. Countless patents are issued yearly to protect rights to new inventions, products, or processes. Information specialists Schenk and Webster

(1984) point out that patents are often overlooked as sources of current information: "Since it is necessary that complete descriptions of the invention be included in patent applications, one can assume that almost everything that is new and original in technology can be found in patents" (p. 121). Examples include the *Index of Patents Issued from the United States Patent and Trademark Office,* the *NASA Patent Abstracts Bibliography,* and the *World Patents Index.*

Patents in various technologies are searchable through databases such as Hi Tech Patents, Data Communications, and World Patents Index.

Abstracts

By indexing and summarizing each article, abstracts can save you from having to track down a journal before deciding whether to read the article or skip it. Abstracts are usually titled by discipline: *Biological Abstracts, Computer Abstracts,* and so on. For some current research, you might consult abstracts of doctoral dissertations in *Dissertation Abstracts International.* Abstracts are increasingly searchable by computer.

Access Tools for U.S. Government Publications

The federal government publishes maps, periodicals, books, pamphlets, manuals, monographs, annual reports, research reports, and other information, often searchable by computer. Examples include *Electromagnetic Fields in Your Environment, Major Oil and Gas Fields of the Free World,* and the *Journal of Research of the National Bureau of Standards.* Your best bet for tapping these complex resources is to request assistance from the librarian in charge of government documents. The basic access tools for documents issued by or published at government expense, as well as for many privately sponsored documents, are the following:

- *Monthly Catalog of the United States Government:* The major pathway to government publications and reports.
- *Government Reports Announcements and Index:* A listing (with summaries) of more than 1 million federally sponsored research reports published and patents issued since 1964.
- *Statistical Abstract of the United States:* Updated yearly, this offers an array of statistics on population, health, employment, and the like. It can be accessed via the Web. CD-ROM versions are available beginning with the 1997 edition.

Many unpublished documents are available under the Freedom of Information Act (FOIA). The FOIA grants public access to all federal agency records except for classified documents, trade secrets, certain law enforcement files, records protected by personal privacy law, and the like. Contact the agency that would hold the records you seek: for workplace accident reports, the Department of Labor; for industrial pollution records, the Environmental Protection Agency; and so on. Government information is increasingly posted to the Internet.

Microforms

Microform technology allows vast quantities of printed information to be stored on microfilm or microfiche. This material is read on machines that magnify the reduced image.

TIPS FOR EVALUATING AND INTERPRETING INFORMATION

Evaluate the Sources

- Check the date of posting or publication. The latest information is not always the best, but keeping up with recent developments is vital.
- Assess the reputation of each printed source. Check the copyright page, for background on the publisher; the bibliography, for the quality and extent of research; and (if available) the author's brief biography, for credentials.
- Identify the study's sponsor. If the study acclaims the crashworthiness of the Hutmobile but is sponsored by the Hutmobile Auto Co., be skeptical.
- Look for corroborating sources. A single study rarely produces dependable findings. Learn what other sources say, why they might agree or disagree, and where most experts stand on the issue.

Evaluate the Evidence

- Decide whether the evidence is sufficient. Evidence should surpass personal experience, anecdote, or news reports. It should be credible enough for reasonable and informed observers to agree on its value and accuracy.
- Look for a reasonable and balanced presentation of evidence. Suspect any claims about "breakthroughs" or "miracle cures" and the like. Expect a discussion of drawbacks as well as benefits.
- Try to verify the evidence. Examine the facts that support the claims. Look for replication of findings.

Interpret Your Findings

- Don't expect certainty. Complex questions mostly are open-ended, and a mere accumulation of facts doesn't prove anything. Even so, the weight of solid evidence usually points toward some reasonable conclusion.
- Identify your personal biases. Don't ignore evidence simply because it contradicts your original assumptions.
- Consider alternative interpretations. What else might this evidence mean?

Check for Weak Spots

- Decide whether the evidence supports the conclusions. Suspect any general claim not limited by a qualifier such as *often, sometimes,* or *rarely.*
- Treat causal claims skeptically. Consider confounding factors (other explanations for the reported outcome).

(continued)

- Look for statistical fallacies. Determine where the numbers come from and how they were collected and analyzed—information that legitimate researchers routinely provide.
- Consider the limits of computer analysis. A computer model is only as accurate as the assumptions and data programmed into it.
- Interpret the reality behind the numbers. Consider the possibility of alternative and possibly more accurate interpretations of the data.
- Consider the study's possible limitations. Small, brief studies are less reliable than large, extended ones; epidemiological studies are less reliable than laboratory studies (which have their own flaws); animal or human exposure studies are often not generalizable to larger human populations; "masked" (or blind) studies are not always as objective as they seem; and measurements are prone to error.
- Look for the whole story. Bad news may be underreported; good news, exaggerated; bad science, camouflaged and sensationalized; or research on promising but unconventional topics (say, alternative energy sources), ignored.

Checklist for Research

Methods

- Are my sources appropriately up-to-date?
- Is each source reputable, trustworthy, relatively unbiased, and borne out by other, similar sources?
- Does the evidence clearly support the conclusions?
- Is a fair balance of viewpoints represented?
- Can all the evidence be verified?

Reasoning

- Can I rule out other possible interpretations or conclusions?
- Have I accounted for all sources of bias, including my own?
- Are my generalizations warranted by the evidence?
- Am I confident that my causal reasoning is accurate?
- Can I rule out confounding factors?
- Can all the numbers, statistics, and interpretations be trusted?
- Can I rule out any possible error or distortion?
- Am I getting the whole story and getting it straight?

Exercises

1. Locate a research article from the past four years (not one that is too recent). Using a citation index, track down the specific publications in which the original material has been cited. If your article is from a scientific or technical field, try the *Science Citation Index.* Based on the number and type of citations of the original article, what is your opinion about the importance of the article's findings?

2. Locate an expert in the field for your major or an upcoming project (such as a long report). Arrange to interview that person. You may wish to make your initial contact via email. Follow the tips on page 56. In groups of three or four, discuss your interview experience and your findings with your classmates.

3. **FOCUS ON WRITING.** Identify two major indexes to locate research articles for your field or topic. One source should be a traditional periodical index, and the other should be an Internet search engine. Find a recent article on a specific topic (for example, privacy laws in your state), and write a short summary.

4. **FOCUS ON RESEARCH.** Researchers often have difficulty determining how to judge the validity of information found on a Web site. Working in small groups of three or four, do some research and develop a set of criteria that can be used when evaluating a Web site for research purposes.

   Begin by visiting one or more of the sites listed here. Compile a working list of criteria based on these sites; then work as a group to expand your list. For example, do you consider good design to be a sign of credibility? What else do you look at when you are assessing the relevance, currency, and validity of information on a particular site? How do you know if a site is commercially or politically biased?

   Test the criteria you have developed by using a search engine to locate Web sites on a current topic (global warming, genetically modified foods, software piracy, or MP3 file downloading, for example). Select one site that interests you, and evaluate its credibility as a source for research information using your own criteria. Revise your list as needed and then format it as a document that can be shared with the rest of your class.

   - **http://www.library.cornell.edu/olinuris/ref/research/webeval.html**
     "Evaluating Web Sites: Criteria and Tools," developed by the library at Cornell University.
   - **http://www.lib.berkeley.edu/TeachingLib/Guides/Internet/Evaluate.html**
     "Evaluating Web Pages: Techniques to Apply and Questions to Ask," from the Library at the University of California, Berkeley.
   - **http://www.library.jhu.edu/researchhelp/general/evaluating/index.html**
     "Evaluating Information Found on the Internet," by Elizabeth E. Kirk, from the Sheridan Libraries at Johns Hopkins University.

The Collaboration Window

Divide into small groups, and prepare a comparative evaluation of literature search media. Each group member will select one of the resources listed here and create an individual bibliography of at least 12 recent and relevant works on a specific topic of interest selected by the group:

- Conventional print media
- Electronic catalogs
- CD-ROM services
- A commercial database service such as DIALOG
- The Internet and the World Wide Web
- An electronic consortium of libraries, if applicable

After carefully recording the findings and keeping track of the time spent in each search, compare the ease of searching and quality of results obtained from each type of search on your group's selected topic. Which medium yielded the most current sources? Which provided abstracts and full texts as well as bibliographic data? Which consumed the most time? Which provided the most dependable sources? The most diverse or varied sources? Which cost the most to use? Finally, which yielded the greatest depth of resources? Prepare a report, and present your findings to the class.

The Global Window

FOCUS ON WRITING

The International Space Station (ISS) is undoubtedly the largest and most complex international scientific project in history. Begun in 1995, the project requires the collaboration, expertise, and technological resources of 16 nations. The ISS has encountered delays and difficulties for a variety of reasons, including funding problems and the grounding of the NASA space shuttle program following the 2003 *Columbia* disaster.

Do some preliminary research on the scope and history of the project by visiting http://www.shuttlepresskit.com/ISS_OVR, and then follow the links from that site to the sites for the European, Japanese, and Canadian space agencies. How do those sites differ from the U.S.-based NASA sites? Do you find any differences in the way the mission of the ISS is described? In the ways the roles of each nation are defined?

Imagine that you have been assigned to produce a campaign to rally and reenergize public support around the world for the ISS project. What information

would you use to persuade citizens of the participating nations that in today's world, it is worth their nation's time and money to support continued development of an international space station? Would you use different strategies to persuade people in different countries? Why?

Develop a one-page proposal that outlines the key features of your campaign, detailing how you would customize the style and argument of your campaign to persuade public audiences in the diverse nations involved in the ISS initiative.

CHAPTER 5

Technical Communication in a Digital World

Communicating in Digital Space

Designing Information for the New Media

Online Documentation and Interface Design

Corresponding over the Wires: Email, Blogs, and Instant Messaging

Telecommuting and Virtual Teams

Presentation Software

Checklist for Digital Communication

Exercises

The Collaboration Window

The Global Window

Communicating in Digital Space

Computer technologies are often touted as the answer to communication problems. Much of what formerly took hours to accomplish by hand takes only seconds on a computer. For example, creating a pie chart or line graph once required careful hand drawing using pen, ink, and colored overlays. Now, clicking on a button in any spreadsheet program to create a chart, graph, or other visual display takes only seconds. Similarly, contacting people by telephone used to be difficult at times, but voice mail and pagers simplify this task.

However, these technologies by themselves do not guarantee quality communication. In fact, the information overload that often results from the use of so many technologies can make communication more, not less, confusing. By understanding the unique features of digital communication, you can use these technologies to create quality technical communication.

Note that all the elements discussed in Chapter 1 (accessibility, usability, and relevance) apply to electronic communication as well. In addition, there are many unique aspects of communication in the digital realm.

Designing Information for the New Media

Web sites, digital television, voice mail systems, and other technologies are often called the "new media" because they blend characteristics of many traditional media types. For example, print newspapers are different from television news. Radio ads are distinct from brochures. Software manuals are distinct from CD-ROMs. Yet the trend today is toward "convergence," meaning that lines between these forms of communication are becoming blurred. Online newspapers blur the distinctions between a newspaper and an interactive Web site, for example. As more and more of this convergence occurs, technical communicators face information design issues unique to the new media.

For instance, if you are a technical writer at a software company, you may be asked not only to research and write the information for a user's guide but also to design this information for a Web site or an online help screen. In many organizations, these tasks are done by different communication specialists. Companies may have employees who focus solely on writing, while others focus on Web design. Even so, each communication specialist must know the principles involved in designing for new media.

Although many types of information can be categorized as new media, this section focuses on Web design. When designing for the Web, you should consider three areas: writing issues, design issues, and technical issues.

Writing Issues

Writing for Web sites, like writing on paper, must conform to the principles of effective technical communication. In addition, writing for Web sites involves several audience considerations.

5.1

Evaluate
sample
Web
Sites

Addressing the needs of impatient readers. Web page readers generally have less patience with on-screen material than with hard copy; one Web expert claims that "when visiting a new site, users often give up on it before its main page has fully downloaded" (Rosenfeld & Morville, 1998, p. 8). Computers are associated with speed, and people are impatient with long blocks of online information. Also, the flickering light patterns of computer screens tire the eyes, causing people to resist reading long passages of text online.

To counter reader impatience, you should write text in a *chunked* format, breaking down the text from one long paragraph into shorter passages that are easy to access and quick to read. Chunking is also used in paper documentation (see Chapter 3), but it is especially important for Web documents.

How you chunk the information depends on the way your audience intends to interact with the site. One pair of experts recommends that chunking of information "be flexible and consistent with common sense, logical organization, and convenience. Let the nature of the content suggest how it should be subdivided and organized" (Lynch & Horton, 2001, p. 39).

Imagine that you are writing text for a Web site intended to explain a medical procedure to patients. After performing an audience analysis, you decide to organize this information by questions users might ask: "How long will the surgery last?" or "When will I be able to return to work?" You would chunk your information into these categories, possibly making each an individual link on the Web site.

Companies increasingly realize that chunked information is cost-effective and strive to create single sources of information that can be reused in various formats. A technical communicator may write the information once, store it in a database, and use the same chunks (or "modules") to create a manual, a brochure, a Web site, and a CD-ROM.

Addressing the needs of nonlinear readers. People do not read Web sites in a linear fashion. A typical Web site displays information in a *hypertext format,* allowing users to jump around, moving from link to link, often out of the originally intended sequence. Each chunk of text on a Web page must make sense, regardless of the order in which it is read.

Addressing the needs of a diverse audience. A Web page's audience may be far broader than originally intended. Unless you are designing an intranet site (available only within a specific company or organization), your Web site can be accessed by almost anyone worldwide. Some Web sites, such as a site for patients seeking specific medical information, begin with a brief description of the intended audience. To accommodate a global audience, take the following steps:

- Provide links to information that might be highly technical or require further explanation.
- Provide a feedback mechanism (email address, Web form) for people who have questions.

- Write short sentences, not only for ease of reading but also for easy translation to Web pages in different languages.

Design Issues

Web pages are designed using *hypertext markup language,* or HTML. This HTML code appears as inserted commands, or "tags," which, when read by a Web browser (such as Microsoft Explorer), cause formatting features to appear on the screen. For example, a line of text tagged as follows:

```
<b><c>Privacy and electronic Commerce</c></b>
```

would appear as bold ($< b >$) and centered ($< c >$) when viewed through a browser:

Privacy and electronic Commerce

The slash tags at the end of the text ($< /b >$ and $< /c >$) tell the browser to turn off the boldface and centering features until these codes are used again.

In the Web's early days, HTML coding was done by experts. Today, it is easy to write a Web page with little or no knowledge of HTML. You can use Web editing software (such as Front Page or Dreamweaver) or even most word-processing programs to create a Web page, much as you would create a word-processing document. The software then translates your document into HTML code.

Even though Web sites are technically easy to produce, effective design is no simple matter. Many sites created by novices are poorly designed and hard to use. Web design is the subject of many books, classes, and workshops. The following are some basic design features to consider.

Organization. One common source of frustration for Web users is the "can't find it" problem (Rosenfeld & Morville, 1998, p. 4). Most of us have visited Web sites that have no links, no overview of the site's content, or no apparent logical organization. A well-designed Web site is clearly organized so that users can follow the information flow (see Figure 5.1). The page should be organized so that the main purpose of the site is represented by the largest item and draws the eye to it. If information is in columns, each column should have a clear purpose, and differently sized fonts as well as visuals should be used to differentiate between the columns of information. White space helps your reader move from section to section.

Typography. Typefaces on a computer screen show up less clearly and with less resolution than on a printed page. Also, predicting exactly how a typeface will appear on a given computer screen is almost impossible, since different browsers present fonts differently. Lynch and Horton (2001) offer these recommendations for type design on the Web:

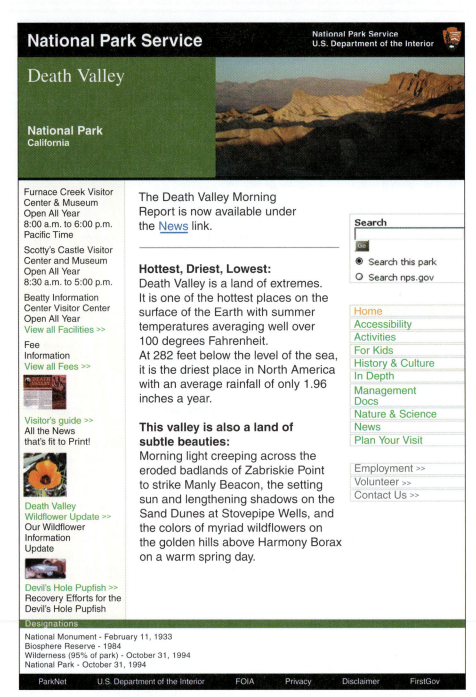

National Park Service

National Park Service
U.S. Department of the Interior

Death Valley

National Park
California

Furnace Creek Visitor
Center & Museum
Open All Year
8:00 a.m. to 6:00 p.m.
Pacific Time

Scotty's Castle Visitor
Center and Museum
Open All Year
8:30 a.m. to 5:00 p.m.

Beatty Information
Center Visitor Center
Open All Year
View all Facilities >>

Fee
Information
View all Fees >>

Visitor's guide >>
All the News
that's fit to Print!

Death Valley
Wildflower Update >>
Our Wildflower
Information
Update

Devil's Hole Pupfish >>
Recovery Efforts for the
Devil's Hole Pupfish

The Death Valley Morning
Report is now available under
the News link.

Hottest, Driest, Lowest:
Death Valley is a land of extremes.
It is one of the hottest places on the
surface of the Earth with summer
temperatures averaging well over
100 degrees Fahrenheit.
At 282 feet below the level of the sea,
it is the driest place in North America
with an average rainfall of only 1.96
inches a year.

**This valley is also a land of
subtle beauties:**
Morning light creeping across the
eroded badlands of Zabriskie Point
to strike Manly Beacon, the setting
sun and lengthening shadows on the
Sand Dunes at Stovepipe Wells, and
the colors of myriad wildflowers on
the golden hills above Harmony Borax
on a warm spring day.

Search

Go
⦿ Search this park
◯ Search nps.gov

Home
Accessibility
Activities
For Kids
History & Culture
In Depth
Management
Docs
Nature & Science
News
Plan Your Visit

Employment >>
Volunteer >>
Contact Us >>

Designations

National Monument - February 11, 1933
Biosphere Reserve - 1984
Wilderness (95% of park) - October 31, 1994
National Park - October 31, 1994

ParkNet   U.S. Department of the Interior   FOIA   Privacy   Disclaimer   FirstGov

Figure 5.1 A Well-Organized Web Page. This home page is pleasing in appearance and well organized. The photograph and text box at the top span the entire width of the page, providing cohesion and unity to the site and directing the eye to this information first. Three columns then provide information and links. Each column uses a different font size to differentiate. The page uses white space effectively and, while it offers a good deal of links and information, it is not overcrowded or cluttered. Small images in the left column provide good balance to the text.

- Present a clear size contrast between one font and another.
- Give attention to the use of capital and lowercase letters. Don't use all caps, which are hard to read.
- Use a serif font for the body text and sans serif for display text.
- Use typefaces designed specifically for reading on computer screens, such as Georgia or Verdana (see Chapter 8 on typography).

Notice how most of these recommendations are embodied in Figure 5.2.

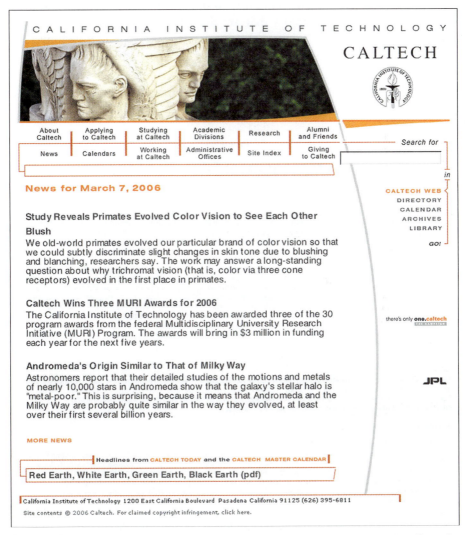

Figure 5.2 **A Typographically Effective Web Page.** This Web site uses typography effectively for the screen. The stretched sans-serif font is clear and readable; the design and color scheme are pleasing to the eye and draw the reader's attention to the Caltech logo.

Source: California Institute of Technology, http://www.caltech.edu.

Line length. Computer screens curve at the edges, making long lines of text hard to follow. Never simply "dump" a page from print text onto a Web site. Instead, chunk the text, as described earlier, into smaller units. Make lines of text at least 1/2 inch narrower than the full screen width (see Figures 5.3a and 5.3b) Also, text set ragged right is easier to read than text set justified right or justified left and right.

5.2
Web design tools and resources

Appearance. A well-designed, visually attractive Web site combines the information power of both printed text and visual information (such as a photograph, illustration, or live video). Color can increase visual appeal, but don't mix too many colors. Select a few colors that complement each other well, and keep your choices simple. Use colors that are appropriate for your audience: The school colors, for example, might make an attractive background for a university Web site.

·O·U·T·R·E·A·C·H·

[Index]

Pesticide Management Education Program

Origin
Pesticides are one of the most important tools in production agriculture, enabling growers to control pests such as insects, weeds, and diseases. Their use has made it possible for agriculture to thrive in producing food and fiber. Pesticides also play an important role in public health for control of nuisance pests and disease vectors such as mosquitoes. Homeowners routinely use pesticides for pest control in and around the home. Pesticides have contributed immensely to the quality of life, as well as helping to provide food and fiber to the world.

The safe use of pesticides has been a major focus of Cornell Cooperative Extension (CCE) programs since 1960. Concerns about pesticide use and effects on the environment prompted Extension to formalize its educational programs on pesticides. Based on this need and the concern for the health of those who use pesticides, including growers, homeowners, and commercial applicators, the Pesticide Applicator Training (PAT) program was begun in the mid–1970s. Since that time PAT has expanded into diverse audiences and topics ranging from rural to urban settings. Topics such as homeowner use, proper storage and disposal, ground and surface water concerns, endangered species, worker protection, food safety, integrated pest management, and risk/use reduction are now covered. To better reflect this progress, the PAT program has undergone a name change as well to reflect the scope of education that takes place. The new title of this program is now Health, Environmental and Pesticide Safety Education.

Mission
The overall mission of the Pesticide Management Education Program (PMEP) is to promote the safe use of pesticides for the user, the consumer, and the environment. PMEP serves as an information center on pesticides for college and field extension staff, as well as growers, commercial applicators, pesticide distributors and formulators, environmental and conservation groups, and private citizens.

Activities

- Health, Environmental and Pesticide Safety Education (HELPS)
  The program is responsible for coordinating the pesticide education programs for New York State. Specifically, this program compiles and provides up–to–date pesticide information on proper application, storage, disposal, decontamination, transportation, and effects on human health and the environment. The program is also responsible for providing information on federal and state regulations and restrictions to producers, homeowners, consumers, pesticide applicators, agribusiness, CCE personnel, and College of Agriculture and Life Sciences staff.

Figure 5.3a Lines That Are Too Long for a Computer Screen. Although the entire text is visible, lines that take up the whole screen are hard to read. Compare with Figure 5.3b.
Source: Pesticide Management Education Program, Cornell University, Ithaca, New York.

Technical Issues

Web sites must be *accessible*. For example, a Web site that contains photographs and illustrations may be visually attractive but hard to access for users whose computers do not have sufficient memory or just aren't fast enough. To make your site as accessible as possible, learn all you can about the computer use of the majority of your audience. Work with your company's technical support staff to use *standard file formats* and design a site that is suited for the browser and computers used by the audience. Web sites for a global audience should be compatible with the current industry-standard browsers (Netscape or Microsoft Explorer, for example). Make

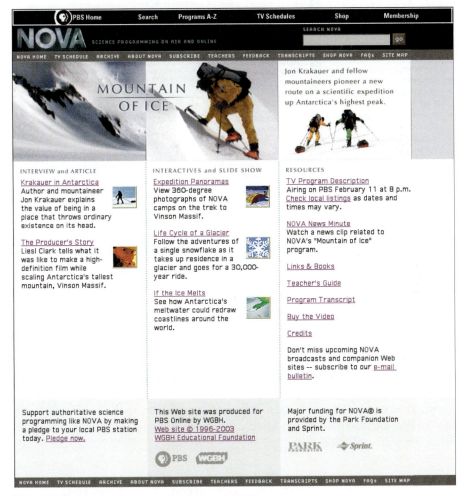

Figure 5.3b Shorter Line Lengths, Easier on the Eye.

Source: Nova, http://www.pbs.org/wgbh/nova/vinson. Copyright © 2003 WGBH/Boston.

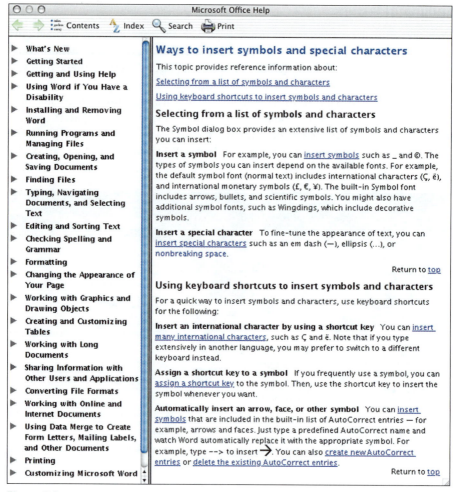

Figure 5.4 Online help from Microsoft Word.
Source: Reprinted by permission from Microsoft Corporation.

sure all links work correctly, and avoid the "gratuitous use of bells and whistles" (Rosenfeld & Morville, 1998, p. 5). Finally, test the site to be sure it is *functional* and *usable.* Most organizations have staff who work specifically on the technical aspects of Web sites and can help you make sure the technical design of your site is appropriate for your audience.

Online Documentation and Interface Design

Online documentation is either delivered to the user via a CD-ROM or built into the software itself. If you have ever used the "help" command in your word-processing software and read the help information on your screen, you have accessed online documentation.

Online Documentation

Online documentation (see Figure 5.4) is very popular with software, because it saves the time and money that would be spent on printing paper documentation and manuals. Also, some online documentation is *context-sensitive:* If a spreadsheet user makes a mistake, for example, the software will recognize the mistake and direct the user to the appropriate help screen. This process is much easier for the user than sifting through pages and pages of a paper manual.

Like Web pages, online information should be written in well-organized chunks and should never be paper documentation dumped into an electronic format. To create effective online documentation, one expert suggests listing all the tasks people perform with the paper document and then deciding whether each task is possible in the online version. If people rely on an index to look up information in a specific manual or report, an index might also be needed in the equivalent online document (Horton, 1990).

You can use special software, such as RoboHelp or Doc-to-Help, to convert textual material into online help files.

Interface Design

The interface is the part of a software application you see on the screen. When you use Microsoft Word, for example, you see a menu bar, buttons to click on, and a background screen. While the heart of the program, computer code, runs silently in the background, the interface, the clickable icons and menus, lets users interact with the machine.

Software interfaces must be well designed: Menu commands must be consistent, visual images must appear in logical places, and features must perform in ways that make sense to the user. Items must be spelled correctly, and screens must appear in the proper order.

Interface design is such a complex subject that many schools offer degrees in this area. Technical communicators often work on the layout, functionality, and wording of software interfaces, and some go on to become interface designers.

Corresponding over the Wires: Email, Blogs, and Instant Messaging

The bulk of today's electronically mediated correspondence occurs via email, blogs, and instant messaging.

Email

A number of features make email attractive for workplace communication.

- **Asynchronicity.** Asynchronous communication does not take place in real time. Unlike a face-to-face conversation, in which two or more people must be physically present, email allows you to communicate with someone at any time, day or night. You can send a message at 2:00 A.M. if that suits your schedule, and the recipient can read it when he or she arrives at the office at 9:00 A.M.
- **Electronic "paper trail."** Unlike phone calls or face-to-face conversations, email messages can be stored and saved for future reference. It is also possible to cut and paste material from an email message into another document.
- **Easy forwarding.** Email messages can be forwarded to others with a single keystroke, thus simplifying the distribution of a message to multiple recipients.
- **Attachments.** Most email programs enable you to send attachments (see Figure 5.5) of entire documents with their original formatting. Word-processing

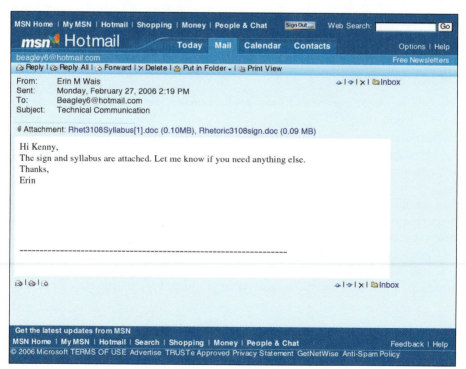

Figure 5.5 An Email Message with Attachment, Using MSN Hotmail. The paper clip icon indicates the attachment.

Source: Reprinted by permission from Microsoft Corporation.

files—of your résumé, a formatted report, or any other document—as well as spreadsheet, sound, or graphics files, can easily be attached to most email messages and read by the recipient. Most popular email programs make attachments between PCs and Macintosh computers interchangeable.

Technical communicators commonly share drafts of material via email or co-author entire reports or other documents by collaborating through email.

The heavy use of email has resulted in new conventions for spelling, phrasing, and expectations of how quickly people will respond. Although many people have tried to outline "netiquette" rules, these continue to evolve. When communicating via email, consider the following issues.

- **Oral or written.** At first glance, email resembles a written document. The standard email format resembles that of a paper memo, with "To," "From," "Date," and "Re:" fields. Yet email tends to be informal and conversational. Even writers who are extremely careful with traditional written correspondence sometimes ignore spelling or grammar, instead writing an email message much as they might speak it. Proofread your email messages, spell-check them whenever possible, and avoid using all capital letters (ALL CAPS in email is considered shouting).

- **Speed and reach.** As with Web sites, people have a short attention span when it comes to reading email. Email is considered a *speedy* medium, because people read messages quickly. Don't send extremely long messages or huge attachments unless you have warned the receiver in advance. Also, remember that accuracy is essential in technical communication. Email seems to inspire writers to send information quickly, without reviewing the content. Be sure to check the content of your message carefully.

  Reach refers to the idea that email messages can be seen by vast audiences across great distances. You never know who will read your message. A message intended only for your manager may accidentally get sent to the entire department. Or your manager may forward a message, intact, to others in the organization—and that message may be the only impression others have of you. In most organizations, email messages belong to the company, not you. Never post an email message that you would not want to be seen by people other than your intended audience.

- **Flaming.** Some people use email to express anger and to personally attack others. Researchers speculate that this behavior, called *flaming*, has various causes, including the speed at which people post messages and the fact that email writers can hide behind the screen, thus avoiding the repercussions of face-to-face rudeness. If your email exchange becomes difficult, confusing, or angry, consider calling a meeting or making some phone calls to resolve the situation.

- **Hierarchy.** Email often lets you bypass "pecking orders" and send messages directly to someone you might never reach by phone. Because email tends to inspire informality, writers often forget that they are not writing to an old college roommate but to a manager, a respected scientist, or an important author. Even with email, politeness is always important; for example, if you don't know the recipient of your message, begin with a salutation—"Dear Dr. Jones"—not with an informal "Hi!" or with no salutation at all.

• **Gender in cyberspace.** Research suggests that females may participate less or be overwhelmed by male opinions on the Internet. While there is no conclusive evidence that this is always the case, researchers know that young girls often get less time at the computer, at home and in school, and that in workplace situations, men often dominate the conversations during meetings. Make sure that everyone involved in an electronic discussion (a series of email messages about a project, for example) has an equal say. If you find that someone (of either gender) is not speaking up, you may wish to encourage that person to contribute. Or if someone on the list is dominating the discussion, privately email that person, asking to allow for other voices.

TIPS FOR USING ELECTRONIC MAIL

Observe Rules of "Netiquette"

• Check and answer your email daily. Unanswered email is annoying. If you're really busy, at least acknowledge receipt and respond later.
• Check your distribution list before each mailing. Verify that your message will reach all intended recipients and no unintended ones.
• Don't use email when a more personal medium is preferable. Sometimes an issue is best resolved with a phone call or even voice mail.
• Don't use email for most formal correspondence. Don't use email to apply for a job, request a raise, resign from a job, or respond to clients or customers unless recipients specifically request this method.
• Allow everyone in an email discussion to participate equally, regardless of gender.

Consider the Ethical, Legal, and Interpersonal Implications

• Assume that your email is permanent and could be read by anyone at any time. Don't write anything you wouldn't say to someone's face.
• Think twice before making wisecracks. What seems amusing to you may be offensive to others, including recipients from different cultures. Any email judged to be harassing or discriminatory brings immediate dismissal and can result in legal action against the company as well as the guilty employee.
• Don't use email for confidential information. Avoid complaining, criticizing, or evaluating people, and handle anything that should be kept private (say, an employee reprimand) in some other way.

- Don't use the company email network for personal correspondence or for anything not work-related. Employers increasingly monitor email networks.
- Before you forward an incoming message, obtain permission from the sender. Assume that anything you receive is the private property of the sender. (Email copyright issues are covered in Chapter 7.)

Make the Message Usable

- Use a clear subject line. Instead of "Test Data" or "Data Request," announce your purpose clearly: "Request for Beta Test Data for Project 16." Recipients scan subject lines when deciding which new mail to read immediately.
- Refer clearly to the message to which you are responding: "Here are the Project 16 Beta Test Data You Requested."
- Keep sentences and paragraphs short.
- Use a block format. Don't indent paragraphs.
- Don't write in FULL CAPS—unless you want to SCREAM!
- Where appropriate in formal emails, use graphic highlighting. Headings, bullets, numbered lists, boldface, and italics improve readability.
- Where appropriate, use formal salutations and closings. When addressing someone you don't know or someone in a position of authority, begin with a formal salutation ("Dear Doctor Gomez") and end with a formal closing ("Sincerely"). For a familiar recipient, you can be less formal ("Hello," "Regards").
- Use smiley faces and abbreviations sparingly. Smiley faces, made from a colon, dash, and right-hand parenthesis :-) are used to signify humor. Use these and other emoticons infrequently and only in informal messages to people you know well. Also, common email abbreviations (for example, FYI, BTW, and HAND—which stand for "for your information," "by the way," and "have a nice day," respectively) may annoy some recipients.
- Close with a signature section. Include the name of your company or department, your telephone and fax number, and other relevant contact information.
- Proofread. A mechanically and grammatically correct message is always more credible than a sloppy one.

Blogs

Blogs, the popular online forums for sharing information and opinions, are increasingly used in the workplace. Easily created with templates and authoring tools downloaded from a site such as Blogger.com, blogs enable colleagues to converse online on day-to-day matters ranging from solving a critical hardware problem at a nuclear power plant to brainstorming for new ideas in game software. Blogs can support collaborative production of documents such as proposals, annual reports, and promotional literature, not to mention usability surveys among customers of various products and services.

One vital benefit of blogs is the gathering of real-time information from custom feeds and e-newsletters on preselected topics—often in a preselected language—from sources, say, in health, science, technology, or business. Newsisfree.com, for example, searches and updates the news from over 20,000 sources every 15 minutes. (Clicking on this site's "Careers" link on April 19, 2005, for example, yielded the article "Common Career Derailers," published in *ComputerWorld* that very day, among countless other up-to-the-minute items.) Knowledge Centers offer the latest research reports on virtually any topic imaginable, ranging from data security to operating systems. Because blogs are inexpensive, efficient, and user-friendly, mainstream applications, in academia as well as the workplace, offer unlimited possibilities.

Several colleges and universities have begun hosting blogs as a way to support classroom teaching, provide space for student discussion, allow faculty to collaborate on research projects, and so on. One excellent example is the University of Minnesota's UThink Project at http://blog.lib.umn.edu. (See page 91 for precautions in relying on blogs as a sole source of information.)

Instant Messaging

A faster medium than email, instant messaging (IM) allows for text-based conversation in real time: The user types a message in a pop-up box, and the recipient can respond instantly. IM groupware enables multiple users to converse and collaborate from various locations. According to *Fortune* magazine, "Instant messaging is rising fast in corporate America, rapidly displacing email for routine communication" (Varchaver, 2003, p. 102).

Although instant messaging has been popular among teens and college students, its more recent advent as a business tool means that few rules govern its use. Also, most current IM software does not automatically save these messages electronically. But as IM becomes more pervasive in the workplace, companies will likely monitor its use by employees and save all messages as a permanent record.

Telecommuting and Virtual Teams

Increasing numbers of employees work from home via a computer and a secure high-speed connection to the Internet. This telecommuting requires great attention to detail. Information can be misconstrued, lost, or difficult to download when sent via computer. Sometimes the network server can go down, email speed can fall behind, or voice mail can be deleted, and when these are your primary connections to the company, you need to have a fallback plan in place. Remember that for any projects conducted via telecommuting technology, you should always back up your data or make a hard copy, just to be safe.

Most organizations offer ways for employees to collaborate from remote locations. You may be on a team with members from various time zones in the United States as well as countries across the globe (China, India, Germany, Australia). Being part of a virtual team is almost a given in today's global business climate. Virtual teams work in two ways: in real time, using instant messaging (IM), videoconferencing, and conference calls, and in ways that don't require real-time presence, such as email lists, blogs or discussion boards, and special tools known as computer-supported cooperative work software. See Chapter 1 for more on virtual teams.

Another example of virtual teamwork is online education. Employees often take distance education courses via the Web. Technical professionals take such courses to enhance their skills or pursue advanced degrees. Technical communicators are often part of the teams that design and deliver these courses.

Presentation Software

Presentation software (such as PowerPoint, discussed in Chapter 9) allows you to enter text, images, and animation and turn this information into presentation slides, which can be displayed via the computer or printed out as overhead transparencies and handouts. Although this software can spice up an oral presentation, offering backgrounds, color, and transitions, it is no substitute for a well-organized and well-prepared presentation. Again, the lure of the technology should never eclipse the principles of effective technical communication.

Checklist for Digital Communication

Content
- Is the information chunked for easy access and quick reading?
- Is each chunk understandable regardless of order or context?
- Are all key terms defined?
- Are all necessary links provided?
- Are feedback and question mechanisms provided?
- Are all sentences short enough to facilitate reading and translation?

(continued)

Design
- Is the document organized top-down?
- Are links structured according to a hierarchy of importance?
- Is the typography appropriate and effective?
- Are the fonts designed to be read on a computer screen?
- Is the information chunked into small units?
- Are text lines left-justified and short?
- Does the document's appearance reflect cultural and organizational preferences?
- Is color used appropriately?

Technical Features and Usability
- Have the technical capabilities of the audience's computers been considered?
- Are standard file formats used?
- Is the Web site compatible with industry-standard browsers?
- Are all links correct?
- Have gratuitous bells and whistles been avoided?
- Has the site been tested to ensure that it is functional and usable?

Email Conventions
- Have rules of netiquette been observed?
- Have all legal, ethical, and interpersonal implications been considered?
- Is the message designed for maximum usability?
- Has the message been proofread for correctness?

Exercises

5.3

Online exercises in Web site analysis

1. **FOCUS ON WRITING.** With a classmate, locate one or two Web sites you might use as research sources for a project. Using the guidelines in this chapter, assess these Web sites for the quality of their writing, design, and technical features. How much does the visual attractiveness or choice of fonts affect your initial view of a Web site? Write up your findings in an email message to your instructor. Include the Web addresses for each of the sites you used.

2. Technical communicators are frequently asked to prepare multiple versions of a document, adapting similar content for presentation on a Web site, in a printed manual, or for a corporate digital archive, for example. Each version may have different purposes and audiences.

   The word-processing software installed on your computer, for example, probably offers both online help and a paper user's manual. (Most companies post PDF versions of their printed user documentation on their Web sites, if you do not have the hard copy available.) Compare the online or on-screen help information to the information in the paper (or PDF) manual. Notice in particular the use of chunking. Is the online information organized differently from the paper? Which is easier to use? Which allows you to find a topic more quickly and accurately?

Write a short report comparing the two types of information. Include both online and hard copy examples.

3. **FOCUS ON RESEARCH.** What are the elements of good Web design? Colorful graphics? Catchy writing? Effective navigation? As the Web has matured and expanded as a medium, principles for effective design have been developed, debated, and agreed on. Do some research to develop your own "top ten" list of effective Web design principles.

Begin by exploring the two Web sites listed here. Then use a search engine to find other resources on Web style and Web design. Based on what you find, put together your list of the ten key elements of effective Web design. Using your list as a guide, find three Web sites that to you best exemplify the principles of effective Web design and style. Prepare a short presentation on your exemplary sites, and explain why you selected them as examples of good design.

- **http://www.webstyleguide.com**
  Web Style Guide, by Lynch and Horton, widely regarded as a "bible" of Web design.
- **http://www.sun.com/980713/webwriting**
  Writing for the Web, by Jakob Nielsen, a leading Web usability expert.

 # The Collaboration Window

Technical professionals often collaborate on projects, and many of them use technology to enhance their collaborations. In class, form teams of three or four people. Assume that you are all located in different parts of the world and must collaborate on a report on a topic that you choose. After determining an audience, purpose, and scope for your report, create a first draft, using the computer to share information. You may wish to set up a Web site where group members can post their sections of the paper or use email attachments to pass the report back and forth.

As you work on this project, ask each team member to keep a log of any technical issues that arise. For example, if you use the Web to post information, can all team members access the Web site? If you use email attachments, are all members able to open the same file types? Combine your log into one list, and based on this list, draft a set of guidelines for collaborating via the Internet. Share these in a brief oral presentation to your class.

The Global Window

Find Web sites that are in different languages or based in different countries. Besides differences in language, note any other differences between non-U.S. Web sites and those that originate in the United States. Here are some features you might look for:

- **Use of color.** Different cultures often associate unique meanings with certain colors. For example, the color red may be used in India to mean procreation or life, while red in the United States is often associated with danger or warnings (Hoft, 1995, p. 267).
- **Issues of privacy.** U.S. sites often give out *cookies* (files sent to your computer that give Web site providers information about you), but other countries, such as Germany, take a different approach, allowing no personal information to be used without an individual's permission. Note if any of the sites mention their privacy policy in this regard.
- **Date formats.** The typical U.S. format for dates is month, date, year (MDY), as in December 6, 2006 or 12/6/06, whereas the European format is date, month, year (DMY), as in 6 December 2006 or 6.12.06 (Hoft, 1995, p. 232).

Keep track of what you find, and present your findings in class. If you can, create a class Web site that describes your findings and links to interesting sites on intercultural communication.

CHAPTER 6

Ethical Issues in Technical Communication

Ethics, Technology, and Communication

Technical communication does not occur in a void. It happens in the world of human beings, politics, and social conditions, a world in which we regularly face ethical dilemmas that pit our sense of what is right against a decision that may be more efficient, profitable, or better for the company.

Ethical questions often revolve around topics related to technology. For example, a new computer chip that secretly collects personal information about a person's Web-surfing habits presents a privacy dilemma. Should users be allowed to choose whether to give out this information? Some people would say yes, but in the United States, few laws address personal privacy at this level. So the decision becomes less a legal one than an ethical one. The communication about this product (a press release announcing it or a user's manual that accompanies the computer) plays a central role in this ethical dilemma. Should the technical writer include this information, exclude it altogether, or deemphasize it by using a small font?

These are not simple questions. Taking an ethical stance requires a personal decision on your part as to how to balance your ethical and moral beliefs with the realities of the job. It requires you to consider the effects of your decisions on the users of your product, on your company, on society at large, and on your job. Sometimes standing your ground on an ethical issue may mean losing your job or suffering retaliation from coworkers.

Examples of Ethical Issues in Technical Communication

6.1
Additional
ethics
cases

The disaster at the Three Mile Island nuclear power plant (Miles, 1989), the explosion of the space shuttle *Challenger* (Gouran, Hirokawa, & Martz, 1986; Gross & Walzer, 1994; Pace, 1988; Winsor, 1988), and the decision to market the Pentium III chip help illustrate the relationship between ethics and technical communication (Electronic Privacy Information Center, 2000; ZDNET, 2000).

Three Mile Island

The case. On March 28, 1979, the Three Mile Island nuclear power plant near Harrisburg, Pennsylvania, accidentally leaked radioactive gases through the plant's venting system. Many experts feared that this leak might lead to a runaway fission reaction and total meltdown, which would have been an environmental and social disaster, not only for the immediate area, but also for the entire region and possibly the nation. At the time, U.S. citizens were questioning the safety of nuclear power, and the Three Mile Island disaster only reinforced their concerns.

The communication situation. In the months that followed, a presidential commission's study of the accident revealed a breakdown in communication among engineers at Babcock & Wilcox, the private company that ran the Three Mile Island plant. One particular memo was directly implicated in the accident.

- **The memo.** Roughly 18 months before the Three Mile Island accident, a similar problem had occurred at another nuclear power plant, also operated by Babcock & Wilcox. As a result, a managing engineer wrote to several other managers, addressing serious concerns within the system. Specifically, the memo suggested that "core uncovery" (meltdown) might occur if this problem was not corrected. Yet the writer placed this vital information in the middle of the memo, where readers often skipped over it. In part because this memo was not emphatic enough, the problem was overlooked until the Three Mile Island plant's near-miss with nuclear disaster.

The Space Shuttle *Challenger*

The case. On January 28, 1986, the space shuttle *Challenger* exploded 43 seconds after launch, killing all seven crew members. The immediate cause was that two rubber O-ring seals in a booster rocket permitted hot exhaust gases to escape, igniting the adjacent fuel tank. However, the O-ring hazard had been recognized since 1977 and documented by engineers but largely ignored by management. (Managers had claimed that the O-ring system was safe because it was "redundant": Each primary O-ring was backed up by a secondary O-ring.)

Moreover, in the final hours, engineers argued against launching because that day's low temperature would drastically increase the danger of both primary and secondary O-ring failure. But under the pressure of deadlines, managers chose to relay only a downplayed version of these warnings to the NASA decision makers who ultimately were to decide on the *Challenger*'s fatal launch.

The communication situation. Various aspects of technical communication were involved in this situation.

- **Organizational role.** Engineers were concerned with safety features, whereas managers were concerned with making the launch on the date and at the time for which it was planned. During meetings, these different points of view often clashed. One engineer was even told to "take off your engineering hat and put on your management hat" (Presidential Commission, 1986, p. 93).
- **Written communication.** Many memos and technical reports circulated during the discussion of whether or not to launch. Writers of these memos had to make choices: Should they emphasize the danger of the situation at the possible expense of losing face with their managers? Should the wording be strong or cautious? One engineer decided to word his memo in the strongest possible terms, but the memo never reached the top-level decision makers at NASA.

The Pentium III Chip

The case. In early 1999, the makers of the personal computer chip called the Pentium announced a new chip, the Pentium III. While the manufacturer and computer makers heralded the chip, privacy advocates were concerned. The chip contained a unique serial number that would automatically activate when the computer was in use. Intel, the chip's manufacturer, argued that this serial number would be useful for e-commerce, because it would give Web sites a unique method to identify a user each time that person connected to the Web site. But privacy groups were concerned that the chip would invade personal privacy—users would be giving up information about their Web activity without consent, and it might be possible for an unauthorized user to access the Pentium serial number and make credit card purchases on the real user's account.

The communication situation. As users became increasingly concerned about the privacy implications of the Pentium III chip, a communication situation developed around the following issues:

- **Email and Internet communication.** The Internet became the main discussion forum for the Pentium III debate. On the one hand, corporate communication from Intel and other computer companies claimed that the chip would pose no privacy problems and that in fact, similar identifying information was already being collected when users logged on to Web sites. Advocates also suggested that the chip, with its unique ID number, could help track down a stolen computer. On the other side, privacy and civil liberties organizations were alarmed that users had no way of turning off the chip and felt that the chip was part of a broader problem of technologies that collect personal information. These discussions took place on Web sites, via discussion lists, and through email that was passed back and forth across the Internet. Some of the information was true; some was inaccurate. Anyone interested in the debate had to sort through this vast amount of information from different perspectives: Intel's information, while technically accurate, was biased toward the company's point of view, privacy advocates were writing from their perspective, and individuals were often mixing factual information with exaggeration.
- **Media reports.** Press releases, newspaper articles, and television and radio reports were equally confusing. Some indicated that the Pentium III chip was a privacy invasion; other sources were more supportive. This information often made its way back to the Internet discussions, causing even more confusion. In the end, the uproar over the chip resulted in Intel's creation of a mechanism that allows consumers to turn the identifying feature on or off. (Privacy advocates were still not convinced that this was a good solution.)

The Pentium III case may not be as clear-cut as the other two in that there is no "smoking gun" (such as the memos in those cases). But this case illustrates how controversial technologies raise ethical issues that are not always easy to sort out. A communicator employed at Intel who disagreed with the Pentium III's approach to collecting private information would have to weigh that ethical stance against the interests of the company. And citizens who wanted to learn more about the chip found mixed information at best.

Virtually all areas of science and technology are involved in issues of communication and ethics:

- *Medical technologies,* such as genetic testing, raise questions about personal privacy and medical insurance.
- *Banking and retail operations,* which increasingly collect personal information on consumers, raise concerns about how this information is used and who has access to it.
- *Environmental pollutants,* such as pesticides or smokestack output, raise serious questions about the long-term health of the planet.

In your own communication, you will often face ethical decisions—about how much information to include, how much to leave out, how to word an issue, or how to shape the information for users and consumers. In the end, communication is never neutral. It always comes with some type of consequence.

Types of Ethical Choices

Throughout time, people have tried to define universal principles of ethics to provide a basis for ethical decision making. The following are three of these theories.

- **Kant's categorical imperative.** Immanuel Kant (1724–1804) argued that certain ethical situations dictate certain actions. Kant suggested that "codes of conduct and morality must be arrived at through reason and be universally applicable to all societal environments at all times." Kant emphasized the individual's responsibility and the intention of the act, not its consequence (Fink, 1988, p. 7).
- **Utilitarianism.** Associated with John Stuart Mill (1806–1873), the ethical principle known as utilitarianism asserts that "ethical conduct should aim at general well-being, creating the greatest happiness for the greatest number of people." Unlike Kant, Mill argued that the outcome, not just the intention of an act, determined how people judge the ethics of that behavior (Fink, 1988, p. 7).
- **Ethical relativism.** Taken to its extreme, ethical relativism suggests that any act may be ethical, depending on the particular ethical, religious, and cultural stance of the individual or group. A more moderate approach to rela-

tivism would suggest that acts need to be considered not against some fixed set of standards, as in Kant's notion, but in the context of the culture and individual circumstance. More recently, some would argue, U.S. culture in particular has gravitated toward a relativistic position regarding ethical behavior.

Such broad ethical principles, however, rarely provide sufficient guidance for the countless ethical decisions technical communicators face today. Kant's codes of ethics or Mills's utilitarianism might have been useful in their given periods of history, but today, most philosophers and ethicists agree that in a complex world, it is more effective to consider the particular situation and to develop standards appropriate for that situation.

For technical communication, you might consider an approach based on *reasonable criteria* (standards that most people consider acceptable), which take the form of obligations, ideals, and consequences (Christians, Tackler, Rotzoll, Brittain-McKee, & Woods, 2005; Ruggiero, 1998, pp. 33–34). *Obligations* are the responsibilities you have to everyone involved:

- Obligation to yourself to act in your own best interest and according to good conscience
- Obligation to stand by the clients and customers to whom you are bound by contract—and who pay the bills
- Obligation to your company to advance its goals, respect its policies, protect confidential information, and expose misconduct that would harm the organization
- Obligation to coworkers to promote their safety and well-being
- Obligation to the community to preserve the local economy, welfare, and quality of life
- Obligation to society to consider the national and global impact of your actions

When the interests of these parties conflict—as they often do—you have to decide where your primary obligations lie.

Ideals are the values that you believe in or stand for: loyalty, friendship, compassion, dignity, fairness, and whatever qualities make you who you are. *Consequences* are the beneficial or harmful results of actions. Consequences may be immediate or delayed, intentional or unintentional, obvious or subtle. Some consequences are easy to predict, some are difficult, and some are impossible. Figure 6.1 depicts the relations among these three criteria.

Legal Versus Ethical

Based on the criteria just given, you can see that just because certain actions are legal does not necessarily mean that they are ethical. Copyright, plagiarism, and privacy examples illustrate this point.

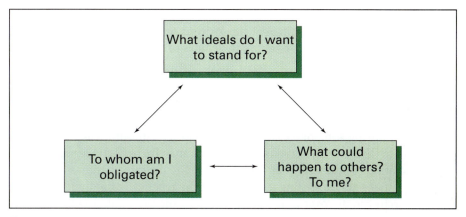

Figure 6.1 Reasonable Criteria for Ethical Judgment.

Copyright

Chapter 7 describes certain circumstances under which you may use copyrighted material without the copyright holder's permission. Under the fair use doctrine, for example, you are allowed to use certain materials for educational purposes. But even though your use of the material may be legal, in some circumstances you should question the ethical implications of that use. Consider the following scenario:

> For a class called "The Language of Cyberspace," you are assigned to do a presentation on the ways in which people form communities on the Web. You locate a Web site for people who are struggling with a certain medical condition, and you notice how the users of this site seem to have formed a community among themselves, discussing specific personal aspects of their condition and seeking advice from each other. You make overhead transparencies of some of these Web discussions, telling yourself that you don't need permission because you are using only a portion of the material and you are using it for educational purposes. You use these transparencies in a class presentation.

Even though this use is legal, is it ethical? Your obligation to your coworkers (fellow students) and to the community should remind you to consider that the people who logged on to this Web site never expected their names and personal information to be put up on an overhead in front of a class. What if one of the users turns out to be the friend of a classmate, and that classmate never knew about the friend's medical condition?

In this case, you should have considered not only the legal aspects of your decision but also the ethical ones. Your obligation to yourself to act in good conscience might lead you to ask how to avoid causing possible embarrassment to the users of this site, either by selecting a different site for your presentation (one that does not use names) or by changing or omitting the names of the users before placing your material on a transparency.

Plagiarism

Plagiarism is using someone else's words and ideas without giving that person proper credit. Even when your use of a source may be perfectly legal, you may still be violating ethical standards if you do not cite the information source.

Assume that you are writing a class report on genetically modified plants. In your research, you discover a very good paper on the Web. You decide that parts of this paper would complement your report quite nicely. Under copyright and fair use guidelines, you can reproduce portions of this paper without permission. And with the Web, it is very easy to cut and paste them into your paper. But does this legal standard and the technical ease with which you can do it mean that you can use someone else's material freely, without giving that person credit? Even though it might be legal under fair use guidelines to reprint the material without notifying the copyright holder, using someone else's material or ideas without giving that person credit is plagiarism.

Plagiarism is a serious infraction in most settings. Students can be suspended or expelled from school. Researchers can lose their jobs and their standing in the academic community. Most important, plagiarism is serious because it violates several of the reasonable criteria for ethical decision making discussed earlier in this chapter. Plagiarism violates your obligation to yourself to be truthful, and it violates your obligation to society to provide fair and accurate information. It also violates your obligation to coworkers—in this case, other students and researchers. Especially in the age of the Internet, when it's easy to use material from Web sites, you need to consider the ethics of the situation.

Privacy

Chapter 7 describes privacy issues in technical communication, especially in light of the capability of Web users to collect personal information over the Internet and the conflicts between U.S. and European approaches to personal privacy. Because one of your ethical obligations should be to society (to consider the national and global impact of your actions), privacy is high on the list of ethical issues to consider.

If you are designing a Web site, for example, should you create a page that asks users for name, address, and other personal information? If this were a business question, you might automatically say yes. Because it is an ethical question, you would need to ask about your obligations to society. A privacy statement such as the one in Figure 7.4 might be one way to address both the business and ethical sides of the question. Another solution is to make sure users have a way to remove their names from your database at any time.

Additional Ways in Which Actions Can Be Unethical

Besides plagiarism or violations of copyright and privacy, your actions can be unethical in other ways. As you read this section of the chapter, consider these situations in relation to the reasonable criteria listed in Figure 6.1. Note that most of these situations relate to workplace issues; Figure 6.2 illustrates how workplace pressures can influence ethical values.

6.2
Real-world issues in ethical communication

Yielding to Social Pressure

Sometimes you may have to choose between doing what you know is right and doing what your employer or organization expects. Suppose that just as your company is about to unveil its new pickup truck, your safety engineering team

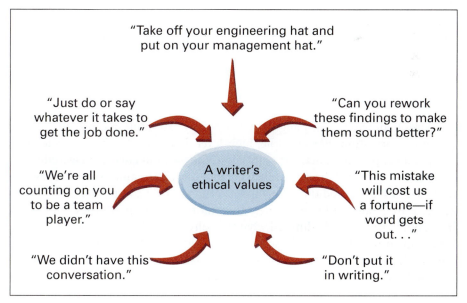

"Take off your engineering hat and put on your management hat."

"Just do or say whatever it takes to get the job done."

"Can you rework these findings to make them sound better?"

A writer's ethical values

"We're all counting on you to be a team player."

"This mistake will cost us a fortune—if word gets out. . ."

"We didn't have this conversation."

"Don't put it in writing."

Figure 6.2 How Workplace Pressures Can Influence Ethical Values.

discovers that the reserve gas tanks (installed beneath the truck but outside the frame) may, in rare circumstances, explode on impact from a side collision. You know that this information should be included in the owner's manual or, at a minimum, in a letter to the car dealers, but the company has spent a fortune building this truck and does not want to hear about this problem.

Companies often face contradictory goals of production (producing a product and making a profit on it) and safety (producing a product but spending money to avoid accidents). When production receives first priority, safety concerns may suffer (Wickens, 1992). In these circumstances, you need to rely on your own ethical standards. In the case of the reserve gas tanks, you may determine that your obligation to society overrides your obligation to yourself or your company. If you make this choice, be prepared to be fired for taking on the company.

Mistaking Groupthink for Teamwork

Some organizations rely on teamwork and collaboration to get a job done; technical communicators frequently operate as part of a larger team of other writers, editors, designers, engineers, and production specialists. Teamwork is important in these situations, but teamwork should not be confused with *groupthink,* which occurs when group pressure prevents individuals from questioning, criticizing, or "making waves" (Janis, 1972). Group members may feel a need to be accepted by the team, often at the expense of making the right decision. To some extent, the *Challenger* case, discussed earlier in this chapter, illustrates groupthink in action. Although several individual engineers had serious concerns about the O-rings in cold temperatures, their concerns were overridden by the sentiments of the group.

Suppressing Knowledge the Public Needs

Pressures to downplay the dangers of technology can result in censorship of important information. For example, high-level employees at the major tobacco companies apparently knew for years about the harmful effects of cigarettes and other nicotine-related products (chewing tobacco, cigars, and so on). Yet lawsuits in the late 1990s proved that many managers and other company decision makers went to great lengths to suppress this information. Should these employees have come forward and admitted what they already knew—that cigarettes cause cancer and other diseases and that nicotine is very addictive? The answer is yes so long as they were prepared to suffer the consequences. You will need to ask if your obligation to the company takes priority over your greater obligation to your fellow citizens. What about your obligation to yourself to be truthful and to act in good conscience? Again, being aware of your own ethical stance is critical in these situations.

Exaggerating Claims About Technology

Organizations that have a stake in a particular technology may be especially tempted to exaggerate its benefits, potential, or safety. Assume that you are a technical writer working on the manual and brochure for an uninterrupted power supply, a device that allows computers and other electronic devices to have power even if the main power goes out. Your company manufactures several models of these power supplies. The low-end model will maintain power for 5 minutes after the main power goes out; the high-end model, for 40 minutes. To emphasize the potential of the product, your manager asks you to use only the 40-minute figure, thereby exaggerating what the other models can do. How would you approach this ethical dilemma? Would you simply do what you were told, or would you find a way to raise the issue with your team and your manager? Your choice will most certainly be affected by your ethical values.

Exploiting Cultural Differences

Cross-cultural communication carries potential for ethical abuses. Based on its level of business experience or its particular social values, a given culture might be especially vulnerable to manipulation or deception. Some countries, for example, place greater reliance on interpersonal trust than on lawyers or legal wording, and a handshake can be worth more than the fine print of a legal contract. If you know something about a culture's habits or business practices and you use this information unfairly to get a sale or make a profit, you are ignoring your obligations to yourself and your community.

Types of Technical Communication Affected by Ethical Issues

Certain forms of communication have specific features worth considering in an ethical context.

Graphics

As noted in Chapter 9, graphics are powerful tools for technical communication, and this power can be used in many ways. Graphs, charts, icons, and other images can provide quick, efficient displays of complex information, but they can also be manipulated to distort information. A line graph that does not have clearly labeled axes, for example, might make a financial trend look better than it really is. Other design features, such as the size or shape of graphical images, can also be misleading. For example, Figure 6.3 misrepresents the data that it is trying to convey. If you compare the first bar in each series with the last, you will

6.3
Assess the ethics of sample graphics

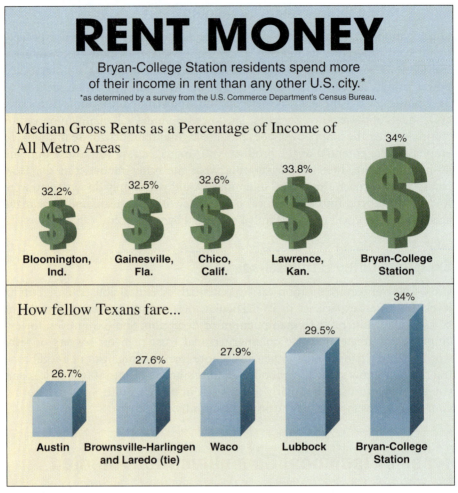

RENT MONEY

Bryan-College Station residents spend more
of their income in rent than any other U.S. city.*

*as determined by a survey from the U.S. Commerce Department's Census Bureau.

**Median Gross Rents as a Percentage of Income of
All Metro Areas**

34%

33.8%

32.6%

32.5%

32.2%

| Bloomington, Ind. | Gainesville, Fla. | Chico, Calif. | Lawrence, Kan. | Bryan-College Station |

How fellow Texans fare...

34%

29.5%

27.9%

27.6%

26.7%

| Austin | Brownsville-Harlingen and Laredo (tie) | Waco | Lubbock | Bryan-College Station |

Figure 6.3 Distorted Pictograph and Bar Graph.
Source: David Howell, "B-CS Renters Dish Out the Dough." *The Eagle.* 12 Nov. 1994, A-1.

think that the rent in Bryan-College Station is almost twice that of Bloomington, IN and Austin, TX. However, if you take the time to read the actual percentages, you learn that the difference is less than 2% (Bloomington comparison) and less than 8% (Austin comparison). These differences are far smaller than the graphics imply.

One study found that technical communicators most frequently based their decisions about such matters on a goal-based philosophy, determining that "the greater the likelihood of deception and the greater the injury to the reader as a consequence of that deception, the more unethical is the design of the document" (Dragga, 1996, pp. 262–263).

Web Pages and the Internet

The power of a Web page to convey information is obvious, and this topic has been discussed elsewhere in this book. Ethically, you need to consider the speed of the Internet, its global reach, and a Web page's ability to combine sound, color, images, text, and interactivity. These features create the potential for manipulation and distortion. Imagine a Web site for a herbal remedy that some people feel is helpful for anxiety. This herbal remedy may not have FDA approval, and it may have harmful side effects. But a Web site promoting this product could easily, and at very little cost, be set up to look extremely scientific and factual. Fancy logos from quasi-scientific organizations might give the page a sense of professional credibility. Statistics, charts, and links to other Web sites might all give this the appearance of a valid medical site. Yet as a communicator, you need to question the possible outcome for users and the overall risks to society of setting up such a site.

Memos

As noted earlier, both the Three Mile Island and *Challenger* cases involved information conveyed in the form of memos. Memos may seem innocuous enough, but the messages they convey can present serious ethical choices. While the problems at Three Mile Island cannot be placed solely on the shoulders of the memo writer, communicators should be aware that the information in a memo often has serious ethical implications.

Instructions

Instructions entail a variety of ethical considerations. For example, many instructions contain safety information. Should this information be placed on the first page, or will this deter some consumers from using the product? Again, the answer to this question rests on an ethical decision balancing the safety needs of society against the company's need for profit. Also, if a set of instructions is not tested for usability, technical communicators have no way of knowing if their material is helpful or not. Is it ethical to send out complicated instructions that have never been tested? Why make a user struggle when a test might have revealed errors in the instructions?

Instructions can also easily mislead users in terms of the time required to complete a task. If the average person needs two hours to assemble a product but the instructions say, "Ready to use in 30 minutes," this information would be unethical.

Reports

Reports must often be kept short to fit a certain page format and to be efficient for readers. For conciseness and focus, reports often leave out unimportant information. But who decides what is unimportant, and on what basis? In preparing

a report about the environmental impact of your company's pulp and paper manufacturing process, for example, you might be tempted to leave out damaging
information, such as the effect of this process on nearby rivers and streams. Or
even if you want to include this information, your team or your manager might
disagree. So you face an ethical decision: Should you include everything? What
will happen if you do or don't? On what basis should information be left out or
included? If you do decide to defy the company, be prepared for anything from a
reprimand to the loss of your job.

Proposals

Proposals present specific plans to get something done. A sales proposal, for example, might present your company's plan to design a Web site for a local community
organization. Because you are probably bidding against other companies, you want
to project the best image and offer the best service for the best price. So you may be
tempted to stretch the truth about the time required to complete the job. Is this
ethical? On the one hand, such projects almost always exceed the deadline, and if
you tell the truth while your competitor lies, you might lose the job. On the other
hand, dishonesty is likely to damage your company's reputation (and your own).
Other ethical questions raised by proposals include costs and materials to be used.

Oral Presentations

In giving an oral presentation, you have the complete attention of your audience.
People are listening to you as an expert on the subject, and this face-to-face situation
elicits trust between presenter and audience members. Whereas a printed document
leaves the writer "invisible," oral presentations create an intimate atmosphere
between speaker and listener. In a position of relative power, the speaker can
convey accurate information in a fair and balanced manner or can use this trust
to manipulate the audience by stirring up emotions without warrant. If your
purpose, for example, is to present technical background on a proposed waste
incinerator in your community, you should offer the facts as best you can rather
than play to the audience's confusion or naiveté.

Responding to Ethical Situations

To ensure that your communication is ethical, consider the reasonable criteria
discussed earlier and shown in Figure 6.1. In addition, many professional organizations have created their own codes of ethics for the particular situations that
people in those professions face. For example, electrical engineers can follow the
Institute of Electrical and Electronics Engineers (IEEE) code, while nurses can
follow the American Nursing Association (ANA) code. Figure 6.4 presents the
ethics code of the Society for Technical Communication.

SOCIETY FOR TECHNICAL COMMUNICATION   3/13/2003

Sexual
Harrassment
(PDF file - 9KB)

Conflict of Interest

Restricting
Services

Tech Comm Policy

General Information

Ethical Principles for Technical Communicators

As technical communicators, we observe the following ethical principles in our professional activities.

Legality
We observe the laws and regulations governing our profession. We meet the terms of contracts we undertake. We ensure that all terms are consistent with laws and regulations locally and globally, as applicable, and with STC ethical principles.

Honesty
We seek to promote the public good in our activities. To the best of our ability, we provide truthful and accurate communications. We also dedicate ourselves to conciseness, clarity, coherence, and creativity, striving to meet the needs of those who use our products and services. We alert our clients and employers when we believe that material is ambiguous. Before using another person's work, we obtain permission. We attribute authorship of material and ideas only to those who make an original and substantive contribution. We do not perform work outside our job scope during hours compensated by clients or employers, except with their permission; nor do we use their facilities, equipment, or supplies without their approval. When we advertise our services, we do so truthfully.

Confidentiality
We respect the confidentiality of our clients, employers, and professional organizations. We disclose business–sensitive information only with their consent or when legally required to do so. We obtain releases from clients and employers before including any business–sensitive materials in our portfolios or commercial demonstrations or before using such materials for another client or employer.

Quality
We endeavor to produce excellence in our communication products. We negotiate realistic agreements with clients and employers on schedules, budgets, and deliverables during project planning. Then we strive to fulfill our obligations in a timely, responsible manner.

Fairness
We respect cultural variety and other aspects of diversity in our clients, employers, development teams, and audiences. We serve the business interests of our clients and employers as long as they are consistent with the public good. Whenever possible, we avoid conflicts of interest in fulfilling our professional responsibilities and activities. If we discern a conflict of interest, we disclose it to those concerned and obtain their approval before proceeding.

Professionalism
We evaluate communication products and services constructively and tactfully, and seek definitive assessments of our own professional performance. We advance technical communication through our integrity and excellence in performing each task we undertake. Additionally, we assist other persons in our profession through mentoring, networking, and instruction. We also pursue professional self–improvement, especially through courses and conferences.

Figure 6.4 Ethical Guidelines for Technical Communication.

Source: Reprinted with permission from the Society for Technical Communication, Arlington, Virginia.

Checklist for Ethical Communication

Use this checklist for any document you prepare or for which you are responsible.

Accuracy

- Have I explored all sides of the issue and all possible alternatives?
- Do I provide enough information and interpretation for recipients to understand the facts as I know them?
- Do I avoid exaggeration, understatement, sugarcoating, or any distortion or omission that leaves recipients at a disadvantage?
- Do I state the case clearly, instead of hiding behind jargon and generalities?

Honesty

- Do I make a clear distinction between what is certain and what is probable?
- Are my information sources valid, reliable, and relatively unbiased?
- Do I actually believe what I'm saying, instead of being a mouthpiece for groupthink or advancing some hidden agenda?
- Would I still advocate this position if I were held publicly accountable for it?
- Do I inform people of the consequences or risks (as I am able to predict) of what I am advocating?
- Do I give candid feedback or criticism, if it is warranted?

Fairness

- Am I reasonably sure this document will not harm innocent persons or damage their reputations?
- Am I respecting all legitimate rights to privacy and confidentiality?
- Am I distributing copies of this document to every person who has the right to know about it?
- Do I credit all contributors and sources of ideas and information?

Sources: Brownell and Fitzgerald (1992), p. 18; Bryan (1992), p. 87; Johannesen (1983), pp. 21–22; Larson (1995), p. 39; Unger (1982), pp. 39–46; Yoos (1979), pp. 50–55.

Exercises

1. Find the professional code of ethics for your major or career. Divide into groups of three or four students, each of whom has a different major. Compare your professional codes, noting similarities and differences. Discuss why each code seems appropriate for that profession.

2. **FOCUS on WRITING.** One of your company's vice presidents has asked you to help the company develop an updated code of ethics. Developing the official

code of ethics will require months of research and collaboration with attorneys, consultants, editors, managers, and other stakeholders. In the meantime, the VP has asked you to develop a brief but practical guide for ethical communication.

Your brief guide to ethical communication will serve as a practical reference for all employees until the final code of ethics has been approved. It will also lay out the key components that will be included in the official code.

Using the material in this chapter and the Web resources listed here, prepare a two-page memo to outline your brief guide to ethical communication. Your purpose is to explain clearly how to avoid major ethical pitfalls in corporate communication.

- **http://www.onlineethics.org**
  The Online Ethics Center for Engineering and Science at Case Western Reserve University. Includes extensive background on ethical issues, case studies, and sample codes of ethics from a number of disciplines.
- **http://ethics. tamu.edu/ethicscasestudies.htm**
  Case studies in engineering ethics, compiled by researchers at Texas A&M University.
- **http://www.iit.edu/departments/csep/codes/codes_index.html**
  A substantial collection of professional codes of ethics, organized by profession and discipline, compiled by the Center for the Study of Ethics in the Professions at the Illinois Institute of Technology.

3. In groups of two or three, locate a piece of technical communication (or use one provided by your instructor), and evaluate its ethical stance. Is the information presented in such a way that ideas or facts are exaggerated or suppressed? Are any cultural issues exploited? Share your thoughts in class, and explain how your team would redo the information.

 # The Collaboration Window

In groups of two or three, locate another piece of technical communication, but this time, actively search for one that seems to take an ethical stance in how it presents its information. If you can, contact the author or one of the writers of this piece and ask how this person made his or her decisions. If you cannot contact the author, speculate on the organizational dynamics, legal issues, and personal choices this person made. How would members of your team go about making the same decisions?

The Global Window

FOCUS ON RESEARCH

Counterfeiting, sometimes known as "intellectual property piracy," has become a major point of tension between the United States and many developing nations. Counterfeit products ranging from computer chips and pharmaceuticals to cigarettes and cell phones now flood markets in Asia and South America, and many may even be found on the streets of New York and other U.S. cities.

Beginning with the Web resources listed here, do some research to learn more about the problems of counterfeit products. What are the advantages and disadvantages, both economically and politically, of trying to crack down on unauthorized copycat products? Why do some countries do little to police such piracy while others, including the United States, view it as a major priority?

Write a brief report to analyze the ethical, economic, and political issues that influence the global debate on counterfeiting, and present your findings in a brief oral presentation to your class.

- **http://www.businessweek.com/magazine/content/05_06/ b3919001_mz001.htm**
  Link to a *Business Week* cover feature on the global counterfeit business.
- **http://www.uschamber.com/issues/index/counterfeiting/default**
  The U.S. Chamber of Commerce issues center page on counterfeiting and piracy.
- **http://www.aacp.org.uk/Fake-Nation.pdf**
  An online report on piracy and intellectual property theft in the United Kingdom, focused on consumer behavior and attitudes.

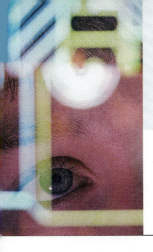

CHAPTER 7

Copyright and Privacy

Why Technical Communicators Need to Understand Copyright and Privacy

Technical communicators rarely create every word, image, or sound from scratch. Often just the right diagram, image, sound, or wording will be found in some other material. You have probably had this experience when preparing a project for a class or work. You begin researching on the Web and find the perfect piece of clip art. Or you are looking through a trade magazine or newspaper, and there it is: exactly the right chart for the "implications" section of your report. Or maybe you need a diagram for an upcoming presentation, and you find one in a magazine. Can you use these materials without permission? What if you scan the image into your computer and modify it first? What if the project is strictly for school: Didn't you hear somewhere that use of material for educational purposes requires no permission? But what if the project is for your company?

Along with copyright concerns, privacy is an issue for technical communicators. If you are working on a project that involves a Web site, you may face the decision of whether to collect personal information from site visitors. Can you collect this information and legally use it without the user's permission? If you are writing a manual, are you allowed to use demographic data about the organization's customers?

Many organizations have legal departments to help you answer these questions. However, if you are a student or a freelance communication consultant or are rushing through a project without time to seek advice, you need to know the basics.

It's especially important to understand copyright and privacy in the age of electronic technologies. Although such concerns existed before the Web, they are heightened by the speed and power of these new technologies. Technical communicators are prime users of these technologies and must be aware of not only the technical aspects but also the legal ones.

SECTION ONE: COPYRIGHT

Copyright—an Overview

WWW

7.1

Guidelines and information on copyright

"Copyright law," says one expert, "is essentially a system of property." However, unlike physical property—your car, your home, your land—"the province of copyright is communication" (Strong, 1993, p. 1). In other words, copyright is the legal system that gives owners rights over their communication products. These products can include books, musical recordings, photographs, drawings, letters, and memos. Any time an idea can be fixed in a tangible medium, that communication product can be copyrighted.

Copyright law originated in England in part to protect the printing trade. The United States Congress established copyright because it seemed the best mechanism for encouraging creativity and for providing the public with a rich source of information. Copyright is essentially a system for "promoting and advancing knowledge" (Cavazos & Morin, 1994, p. 48). Authors and other creators have an incentive to create new works, such as a new novel or a piece of music, because they know that for a limited time, they will own the copyright to their work and others will be legally prohibited from copying it. After a set time, when the copyright expires, the work enters the "public domain" (more on this in the next few sections). Public domain material is accessible to everyone. This access to information is important in a democracy.

Remember that you can't copyright ideas, just expressions of ideas. As copyright experts note (Cavazos & Morin, 1994, p. 50):

> An idea or fact cannot be owned, but the unique description of the idea or fact in original terms can be. An author could not claim ownership [of] the idea of three pigs attempting to outsmart a big, bad wolf, but if the author writes her version of the story, [this version] becomes her property, protected by a copyright.

Naturally, the lines can get a bit blurry, and courts often determine the details of a case. But in general, the thing to remember is that you copyright the expression of an idea when the expression becomes fixed in a tangible medium. If you have an idea for a diagram of the brain, for example, and you create an original diagram (by hand or with a drawing program such as Adobe Illustrator), you hold the copyright to this diagram but not to the idea of the structure of the human brain or other diagrams of the brain.

How Copyright Infringement Differs from Plagiarism

Although the two issues are frequently confused, plagiarism and copyright infringement are not the same. You can plagiarize someone else's work without actually infringing on the copyright. Plagiarism (representing the words, ideas, or perspectives of someone else as your own) is primarily an ethical issue, whereas copyright infringement is a legal and economic issue. (For more on plagiarism, see Chapter 6.)

How Copyright Law Differs from Patent or Trademark Law

Copyright law is part of a broader set of laws that deal with *intellectual property*. Intellectual property is the result of creative expressions, inventions, and designs. Copyright is the arm of intellectual property law designed to deal with creative works. Two other types of intellectual property law that are not discussed at length in this book may interest you at some point in your career.

Patent law. Patent law governs mechanical inventions, machines, and processes. In many engineering and science organizations, as well as research universities, patent specialists make sure that a new invention or process is filed with the patent office.

Trademark law. Trademark law governs icons, symbols, and slogans (Strong, 1993, p. 1). Organizations file for trademark to protect their unique logos, such as the Coca-Cola name or symbol or the Nike "swoosh." The label ™ is used to indicate trademark.

How Individuals and Companies Establish Copyright

First, the individual or company must create an original expression of an idea: a brochure, novel, poem, photograph, diagram, or other tangible work. Since 1976, any communication you create is automatically copyrighted the moment the item becomes fixed in a tangible medium. In other words, the moment you type, write on paper, photograph, draw, or record something, you (or your company) automatically own the copyright.

You can help remind people of the copyright by adding this information somewhere on the product itself:

© 2004 Daniel P. Olsen

© 2004 Central Geology Corporation

To gain full legal protection, you can register the material with the Library of Congress. Should you or your company need to sue for copyright infringement, this registration provides extra evidence.

Even if an author does not add the © symbol, the work is automatically copyrighted. In other words, nearly everything you see in print or on the computer is copyrighted.

What Rights a Copyright Holder Can Claim

Only the copyright holder has the right to reproduce the material, create a derivative work, distribute the work, or display or conduct a public performance of the work. The copyright holder can give permission—limited or full—for others to use the work. So, for example, if you are interested in using the drawing of an anticollision light power supply presented in Figure 7.1, you would need to contact the copyright holder, in this case, the Society for Technical Communication (STC). The drawing was reproduced from the front cover of an issue of the STC's journal. You would not, however, need permission in case of fair use (discussed on page 118).

When You Can and Cannot Use Copyrighted Material

All original works, once they are fixed in a tangible medium, are copyrighted. Any time you download, copy, scan, or otherwise reproduce an item, you may be infringing on someone's copyright. Whether or not you knew the item was copyrighted is immaterial.

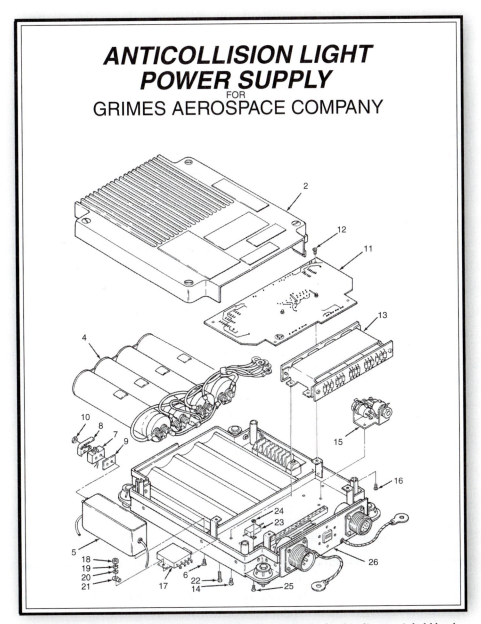

ANTICOLLISION LIGHT POWER SUPPLY
FOR
GRIMES AEROSPACE COMPANY

Figure 7.1 **A Diagram Protected by Copyright.** The copyright for this diagram is held by the Society for Technical Communication.

Source: Reprinted with permission from the Society for Technical Communication, Arlington, Virginia.

You can use a copyrighted work without infringing if you obtain permission from the copyright holder. The holder might grant limited permission, to use the material one time only in one publication only, or might grant unlimited rights.

You can also use material without permission when the materials are in the *public domain*. Copyright holders can place their materials in the public domain; if they do not do so, all materials will eventually become public after the term of protection has expired. It is common on the Web, for example, to find sites labeled "Public Domain Clip Art Files." For works created after 1977, the standard term of protection is the lifetime of the author plus 70 years for individuals and 95 years for corporate authors (Karjala, 1999). (For works created prior to 1977, the law differs, and you can check with your legal department or a legal specialist at your school.)

Note: All government publications and materials are automatically in the public domain (because they are paid for by the public through tax dollars). Ordinarily, source credit is given (to add credibility), but it need not be.

Fair use doctrine. An important but sometimes overlooked legal right to use copyrighted material without seeking permission is the doctrine of *fair use*. Copyright was never intended to be a one-sided policy favoring only copyright holders. Congress established copyright as a balance between the rights of copyright holders and the needs of the public. On the one hand, authors, artists, and other creators need incentives to produce their works. Because they hold the rights to their works for a limited time, they gain financially from their efforts. But if copyright holders were allowed total control of their materials, the public would have very limited sources of information.

So Congress established the doctrine of fair use as a way to balance creators' rights with public access. Fair use states that under certain conditions, it is fair and legal to use copyrighted works without obtaining the copyright holder's permission as long as the source is clearly identified. Courts ask four questions to establish whether a use is fair (see Figure 7.2). They tend to look favorably on cases in which

- Material is being used in an educational setting
- Material has been published
- Only a small part of the material is being used
- Use of the material will not affect the market value of the original

For this reason, classroom use has almost always been considered fair. Instructors and students rarely require permission to use material in a school project (but they must acknowledge the source). However, if you are a consultant or an employee of a for-profit organization, the fair use doctrine may not apply.

Recently, copyright's balancing act has tipped toward the copyright holder. Fair use doctrine is often ignored. For example, if you go to the library or a copy shop to make copies, you may see an ominous warning sign above the machine. These signs rarely mention fair use. Many products, such as software, come with strictly worded statements about what will happen if you make a copy. But these statements never mention that under the fair use doctrine, you have a legal right to make copies under certain conditions.

- **What is the *purpose* of the use?**

  Commercial or educational? If commercial (and thus for profit), courts will view it less favorably than if your use is strictly educational.

- **What is the *publication status* of the material?**

  If the material has been published, it will be viewed more favorably than if it has not been published. For example, your use is more likely to be considered fair if it is from a published magazine than from a series of unpublished letters.

- ***How much* are you using?**

  If you are using only a small part of a text or work, this use will be viewed more favorably than if you are reproducing a large part or the entire work.

- **What will be the *economic impact* of your use on the original work's owner?**

  If your use of the work will not damage the potential market of the original, this use will be viewed more favorably than if it would cause damage.

Figure 7.2 Guidelines for Determining Fair Use of Copyrighted Material.
Source: Adapted from Patry (1985), p. vii.

When Your Company Owns the Material

When you create technical communications as an employee, from manuals to standard operating procedures to Web pages, you are creating copyrightable material. Don't think, however, that *you* own the copyright. Under what is called the *works-for-hire doctrine,* companies in most circumstances automatically own the copyright to all materials created by their full-time employees. If you are not a full-time employee but a consultant, the company may ask you to sign a contract stating that you will automatically give it the rights to products you produce for them. For example, if you are doing freelance writing for a nursing magazine, the publisher will probably ask you to sign your rights for that story over to the corporation that owns the magazine.

Documenting Your Sources

Even if you receive permission to use someone else's ideas or material or if your use qualifies as fair use, you must document the source of this material. You can document your sources by including an in-text reference, a caption, or a statement (if you use the material during an oral presentation). For instance, if you use some copyright-free clip art in a paper for school, you don't need permission, but you should still credit the artist or company by adding a caption that includes the name of the artist or company and the location where you found the material. For more on documenting sources, see Appendix B.

Electronic Technologies and Copyright

Copyright is at a crossroads. On the one hand, the laws governing copyright are clear: All items fixed in a tangible medium are copyrighted. You need to request permission to use these items unless they are in the public domain or meet requirements for fair use. Yet the technology trend encourages just the opposite approach. Copying, scanning, making transparencies, downloading files—all these tasks that have become so common in the workplace and on the Internet are potential violations of someone else's copyright. As a technical communicator, you will be increasingly surrounded by technology that invites you to take files, clip art, images, sounds, and other tangible works and use them in your own material.

Photocopiers and Scanners

Copiers were one of the first technologies to raise serious questions about how to work with copyright in an electronic age. Most copy shops have reacted conservatively, in part due to lawsuits that accused them of violating copyright while making copies of articles and publishing these as student coursepacks. For this reason, you often see harshly worded copyright statements posted above photocopiers.

Copying something without the copyright holder's permission is often an infringement. But remember that the fair use doctrine allows you to make copies for educational purposes. Even in a workplace setting, if you make some copies to distribute at a meeting, you are exercising the educational aspect of fair use. But if you wanted to make a copy of a diagram or illustration for use in your company's annual report, you would need the copyright holder's permission.

The same guidelines apply to scanners. Scanning an image is a violation of copyright unless your use qualifies as fair (see Figure 7.2) or you have permission. However, scanners and image software (such as Adobe Photoshop) allow you to take the scanned image and manipulate it, often to the extent that no one would ever recognize it as the original. Is this a copyright violation? It could be. But what if no one can tell? This becomes a question not just of law but also of your own ethical standards, as discussed in Chapter 6.

The Web as a Marketplace of Ideas and Information

The Web is often billed as an information marketplace, and indeed, you can find endless images, sounds, information, and photographs on almost any topic by searching a few Web sites. The Web is part of the Internet, and the Internet has always been based on the idea of open information. In the early 1980s, when the Internet was still young, researchers and students used the technology to share ideas. The Web continues this tradition. On almost any Web site, you can click on "download source" and obtain the HTML source code for the Web page. You can also obtain the graphics, logos, diagrams, images, and more with a few simple clicks.

This technology thus encourages people to take copyrighted material without ever considering the original work's legal status. In fact, observers have speculated that the Internet might spell the death of copyright law as we know it. Instead, what seems to be happening is that copyright law is being reconsidered—and sometimes strengthened—in light of this technology. So even though the Web might encourage certain behaviors, it is still a good idea to keep copyright law in mind when you use material from the Internet.

Using Material from the Internet

Perhaps you have located a bar chart on the Web that you'd like to use in your report. It is technically very easy to cut and paste or download the bar chart and insert it in your document. But is it legal? You notice that the chart has no copyright symbol (©). But remember: All expressions fixed in a tangible medium are copyrighted. The © symbol is not necessary. Therefore, downloading the chart and using it in your document could be a copyright infringement. You should first consider whether your use is covered by the fair use doctrine (see Figure 7.2). Is your report for commercial or educational purposes? Has the material already been published? (Web pages count as publishing.) How much of the material will you use, and how will your use affect the original? If in doubt, ask permission.

But what if instead of using the bar chart in your printed report, you create a link to it from your company's Web page? Is providing a link to another site equivalent to copying or reproducing that site? This and similar questions related to Internet technologies are hard to answer. If you're worried about a possible lawsuit, check with an attorney who specializes in intellectual property.

Locating Copyright-Free Clip Art

You can safely use copyright-free images, sounds, graphics, or photographs, and many sites on the Internet offer such items. Although these items were copyrighted at one time, the copyright holder decided to place the materials in the public domain. The Internet encourages this kind of sharing, and you can often find exactly what you need on a copyright-free page. Usually, the author or owner will ask that you credit the source, and you should honor this request. For example, if you use an image from a copyright-free page such as the U.S.

7.2

Finding
and using
clip art

Fish & Wildlife Service's online digital media library, you would add the following phrase:

> Copyright-free image from U.S. Fish & Wildlife Service's online digital media library, located at http://images.fws.gov/

or something similar. Often the owner will ask that you use a particular phrase.

Email and Electronic Messages

Remember the recent email message you received from a classmate, your boss, or your mother? That message is copyrighted by the person who created it. So if you forwarded this message to a friend, technically, you infringed on the owner's copyright. The same is true for a posting to a listserv, bulletin board, or other electronic discussion site.

Copyright law will probably bend at some point to accommodate this use of technology. However, if you wish to use an email message or list posting as part of a project, particularly a research or company project that will receive wide publicity, ask the copyright holder's permission (unless your use complies with the fair use doctrine as explained in Figure 7.2).

The posting of email messages beyond where the original author intended also raises privacy concerns, which are addressed in the next section.

CD-ROMs and Multimedia

The more media you work with, the harder the questions about copyright and intellectual property become. If your company plans to produce a CD to accompany a new product, that CD may combine images, music, film clips, and text. Each item will require careful checking to ensure that the proper legal issues have been addressed. Working with multimedia creates a labyrinth of complex legal issues (Helyar & Doudnikoff, 1994, p. 662) that requires close consultation with an intellectual property attorney.

SECTION TWO: PRIVACY

Privacy—an Overview

Like copyright, privacy is a concept people may not consider until it is too late. For example, new technologies make it easier and easier to accumulate data about consumers, and until those data are misused, people rarely stop to think about how much of their personal information resides in numerous databases.

Privacy is a legal concept, and although U.S. citizens frequently talk about their right to privacy, this right is not actually stated in the U.S. Constitution. Instead, privacy law is based on court cases, state law, some federal laws, and constitutional issues such as the Fourth Amendment ban against search and seizure. One pair of experts speculates that the framers of the Constitution did not explicitly write any privacy amendments because in their day, the ways in which privacy could be invaded on today's scale were impossible to imagine (Cavazos & Morin, 1994, p. 13).

Computer Technologies, Privacy, and Technical Communication

What the Constitution's framers could not foresee were the communication technologies that have been developed over the past century. As Cavazos and Morin (1994, p. 13) note:

> Electronic eavesdropping devices, video and sound recording instruments, and large databases of personal information are all now a part of life in this country. Our legal system has had to react constantly to these new developments as they emerge, striving to maintain the proper balance between civil liberties and the needs of society.

Technical communicators are often at the forefront of these issues, because they are involved in designing manuals, software interfaces, Web pages that collect personal data, video training tapes, and other products that require the use of personal data or images.

Privacy in Cyberspace

Web pages can raise important privacy concerns. If you are part of a technical communication team designing a company Web site, you will need to answer certain specific questions related to the privacy of those who visit your site.

www

7.3
Analyze online privacy statements

Shopping Online

In a study by the Pew Internet & American Life project, 31% of those surveyed reported that online shopping decreased the amount of time they spent in stores (http://www.pewinternet.org). Online shopping has become a part of life; AC Nielsen reports that in 2005, 627 million people shopped online. More than a U.S.-based phenomenon, online shopping has audiences around the globe.

Most large stores have both online and physical sites, and many new stores, such as Amazon.com, are completely online. As a technical communicator, you could be involved in projects that require you to work on e-commerce sites, and you will need to make judgments about the usability, privacy, and safety issues associated with these sites. Your end users may have the following questions about your sites.

Is online shopping safe? One question users often have is whether online shopping is safe. There are many technical methods that are used to ensure data privacy,

Figure 7.3 PayPal is one of a number of Web-based services that provide secure ways to exchange funds and shop online.

Source: These materials have been reproduced with the permission of PayPal, Inc. Copyright © 2006 PayPal, Inc. All rights reserved. www.paypal.com.

but to the end user, these methods may not be clear or understandable. Concepts such as "data encryption" do not make sense to the average online shopper. But icons such as the padlock in the locked position (normally in the lower right hand corner of the screen), provide a visual cue for the user. Online financial sites such as PayPal (Figure 7.3) also provide secure methods and do so in ways that are understandable to users.

Is online shopping private? When you help create a Web page, you need to decide if this page will automatically collect information about the users who connect to it. Your team or company may wish to do this, but you should think about having an overall privacy policy for the Web site. Many companies place such privacy statements as links on their Web sites, as in the example in Figure 7.4. Such a statement lets users know how their information will be used and what choices they have,

Figure 7.4 A Privacy Statement from the Amazon.com Web Site.

Source: © 2005 Amazon.com, Inc. All rights reserved. Amazon, Amazon.com and the Amazon.com logo are registered trademarks of Amazon.com, Inc. or its affiliates. Reprinted by permission.

including information on whether the site uses cookies. As a technical communicator, you may be asked to help write such a privacy statement. Privacy statements, outlining the company's approach to consumer privacy, should be readily available on the Web site and should be written in a way that a regular person can understand.

Global Privacy Issues

The Web has made it difficult for U.S. companies to ignore international issues. When you create a Web page and place it on the Internet, almost anyone from anywhere in the world can access the page. Despite countless benefits, this broad reach across international borders also raises concerns about privacy. Different countries and regions have different laws, viewpoints, and practices about issues that a U.S. Web developer might take for granted. Privacy is such an issue.

In the United States, collecting personal data is common practice. When you shop for groceries, the supermarket cashier will scan your special "savings card." This card not only saves you money but also allows the supermarket chain to gather information about the types and brands of items you purchase. Besides being used by the store, this information is often sold to other companies. For example, if you regularly buy a certain brand of cat food, the store may sell your name, and the names of others like you, to marketers who sell pet items.

The same scenario is true for most U.S. direct mailing services. If you make purchases through your favorite catalog, that company is allowed to sell your name and address to other companies. As most of us know, this process can generate lots of junk mail. The same process is now in full swing on the Web. Each time you enter personal information on a Web site when making a purchase, chances are that your name, address, and record of visits to that Web site will be used for marketing purposes and possibly sold to other companies. Cookies and other Web technologies simplify this sort of data collection.

In the United States, your personal information is up for grabs unless you specify that you do not want it sold. You can file your name with a special service that will attempt to take your name off most mailing lists (but the process is never perfect). And under certain laws, especially when your credit history is involved, you have a legal right to correct misinformation. But the burden is on you to take action.

In Europe, however, companies are not allowed to collect information without your permission. They must also provide a clear mechanism for you to change or remove your information. The European Union's Data Privacy Act turned this policy into law. Anyone doing business with a country in the European Union must follow this law.

So when a citizen of the European Union logs on to a U.S.-based Web site and that Web site sends cookies or collects personal information, the company sponsoring the site may be violating the European citizen's legal rights.

In short, going by the laws and habits of U.S. citizens is not always appropriate in designing Web pages with a global reach. To accommodate non-U.S. visitors to your Web site, work with the company's attorney or with colleagues in marketing or international sales. Consider formulating a specific privacy policy for your company Web sites.

Privacy and Documentation

Technical communication and privacy also intersect in documentation. When you prepare documentation (manuals, quick reference cards, brochures, help screens), you may wish to include quotes from customers or examples of how the product is used in other companies. But before you can use such information, you need written permission from the individual customers or companies involved. The same is true if you use any photographs of customers using your product. Although you or your company may hold the copyright to such items, you still need to ask permission so that you are not violating the individual's or company's right to privacy.

Privacy and Videotapes

Technical communicators are often involved in the preparation of training tapes. These tapes are used by company trainers, marketing and sales staff, or customers to help people learn to use a new product or service. For example, if you work for a company that makes gardening equipment, your company may create both a manual and a training tape to accompany a rototiller. Customers could read the manual or watch the tape to learn how to operate and maintain their new machine.

As part of the training tape, you may wish to use video footage taken when your marketing team was out visiting customers. Or you may have other video footage of employees in the company using the equipment. Even though your company may own the copyright to this material, it is still important to obtain permission from the people in the video (employees or customers) to use the footage in a training video.

Checklist for Copyright and Privacy

Using Copyrighted Work

- Does your use of this material explicitly meet all fair use criteria?
- If you do not meet fair use criteria, do you have the owner's written permission to use this material?
- As an employee, are you aware that your company owns any work you produce for your employer?

(continued)

- Have you clearly documented all sources, regardless of whether you have received permission or have met fair use criteria?
- Have you received permission to use any material electronically, including email?
- When in doubt, have you obtained legal counsel?

Respecting Privacy

- Are you aware of the privacy implications of the specific product you're working on?
- Have you obtained permission to use a person's image or personal quotation in any type of document or video?
- For electronic collection of personal data, have you considered the legal issues involved?
- Are you vigilant in protecting your company's trade secrets and other proprietary information?
- When in doubt, have you obtained legal counsel?

 # Exercises

1. Interview a professional in your field to determine how copyright law affects his or her work and company. Consult with the company's legal department if possible. Report your findings in a memo to your instructor.

2. In groups of two or three, discuss two possible situations in which someone else's material might be used for a new purpose—for example, a diagram from a magazine could be scanned in and used for a brochure. Given the details of the situations you describe, decide if the material is being used according to fair use guidelines.

3. **FOCUS on WRITING.** Technical communicators can now find many sources of graphics, sounds, and photographs on the Web. But which ones can be reproduced and which cannot? How do you know when you need permission to use an image or graphic in a brochure or on a Web site? And how do you go about requesting such permission?

   For the first part of this assignment, use a search engine to locate sources of images and graphics on the Web, beginning with the sites listed here. Explore these sites to determine which offer copyright-free images and which do not. Compile a list of your findings and create a handout (or a Web site) to share this list with your class.

   Second, develop a set of guidelines, based on information you find on the sites listed here, on how to assess whether or not a particular image requires permission to be reproduced. Share these guidelines with your class, and discuss how to use images and documents found on the Web while respecting the copyrights and intellectual property of others.

- **http://creative.gettyimages.com/source/home/home.aspx**
  Getty Images, a leading provider of imagery, film, and digital services.
- **http://www.clip-art.com**
  Links to dozens of sources for clip art and animation files.
- **http://www.cpsr.org**
  Home page of Computer Professionals for Social Responsibility.
- **http://www.copyright.gov**
  Home page of the United States Copyright Office.

 ## The Collaboration Window

Form groups according to major, and plan a brochure (or some other form of technical communication) using copyrighted materials. Write up a process by which you would obtain the materials (public domain, request permission). Share your findings with the rest of the class.

 ## The Global Window

Copyright and privacy are subject to the laws of a country or region. The Internet and other technologies complicate matters because data can easily travel around the world without regard for borders. The World Intellectual Property Organization (WIPO) is an international group that considers the global implications of intellectual property issues. You can learn more about WIPO by visiting its Web site at http://www.wipo.org.

If you can, talk to a communication professional who deals with international audiences. Ask about any difficulties the person has encountered with copyright or privacy. Review the WIPO Web site with this professional, and ask how the information on this site might affect the way she or he would write, design, and distribute a document.

CHAPTER 8

Page Layout and Document Design

Creating Visually Effective Documents

Like all decisions related to technical communication, page layout and document design are based on informed choices. You make decisions about fonts, format, headings, page size, and other aspects based on the document's audience and purpose. For example, imagine that you are asked to produce a brochure for a physician's office. The brochure's audience is patients who have a heart condition and may need a specific type of heart surgery. The brochure's purpose is to explain the procedure, answer frequently asked questions, and review the risks while reassuring patients.

Before you would even begin to think about what to write or how to format the document, you would do an audience and purpose analysis (see Chapter 2). If you learned that the brochure also needed to include a list of tasks, such as a checklist of actions patients need to take, you might also conduct a task analysis (explained in Chapter 3). Your analysis would yield important information. For example, you might learn that patients are frightened and that patients are often older and may have difficulty reading small type. These facts would be important not only as you wrote the copy but also as you thought about designing the document. Frightened patients might prefer to read a document that is soothing to look at. You could choose a comforting typeface, pleasant graphics, and a warm color for the paper. Also, because your audience has trouble reading small type, you would make sure the font is large enough to be read easily.

As you can see, document design, like all technical communication, puts audience and purpose first. In designing your document, consider the features discussed in this chapter.

How Page Design Transforms a Document

To appreciate the impact of page design, consider the fact sheets shown in Figures 8.1 and 8.2. The information presented in Figure 8.1 resists interpretation. Without design cues, we have no way of chunking this information into organized units of meaning. Figure 8.2 shows the same information after a design overhaul.

WWW

8.1

Examples of effective page design

How Readers View a Page

When you design information, consider how most readers look at a page. Generally, they view it first as a whole unit, scanning the page quickly to get a sense of the overall layout, look, and structure. Readers try to make sense of the document and determine its "road map." They ask questions such as these:

- What is the main title?
- What are the primary headings?
- Where are the tables and charts?

Mold is a public health problem. Molds are simple organisms that are found virtually everywhere, indoors and outdoors. The potential health effects of indoor mold are a growing concern. Mold can cause or worsen certain illnesses (e.g., some allergic and occupation-related diseases and infections in health care settings). There is not conclusive evidence, however, about whether indoor mold is associated with a multitude of other health problems, such as pulmonary hemorrhage, memory loss, and lack of energy.

The Centers for Disease Control has accomplished much on the problem. The CDC has a mold Web site (http://www.cdc.gov/nceh/airpollution/mold) that provides information on molds and health and links to resources. In conjunction with the Council of State and Territorial Epidemiologists, the CDC has created an inventory of state indoor air quality programs which is available at http://www.cdc.gov/nceh.airpollution/indoor_air.htm. The CDC assists states in responding to mold-related issues, including offering technical assistance with assessment, cleanup efforts, and prevention of further mold growth and unnecessary exposure. The CDC is strengthening state, local and tribal capacity to respond to mold-related issues, including: determining the extent to which state programs establish coordinated responses to indoor mold exposures, working with federal and other organizations to coordinate plans related to indoor air and mold, developing a coordinated public response strategy, and identifying resources for developing and implementing responses. The CDC is also developing an agenda for research, service, and education related to mold. As a first step, the CDC contracted with the Institute of Medicine (IOM) to conduct a study on the relationship between damp or moldy indoor environments and the manifestation of adverse health effects and to provide recommendations for future research. The CDC's mold-related agenda is expected to address subjects such as the following: characterizing environmental conditions that allow mold growth indoors and the association between indoor mold and disease or illness; improving the capacity of state, local, and tribal health departments to prevent, investigate, and control mold exposures; and conducting and supporting research to define the association between damp or moldy indoor environments and harmful health effects.

The next steps the CDC will take include assisting states and others in responding to mold issues and developing an agenda for research, service, and education related to mold as described above. For more information, visit http://www.cdc.gov/nceh/airpollution/mold.

May 2004

Figure 8.1 **Ineffective Page Design.** Notice that the entire page is in the same font and does not provide the reader with any guidance as to how the information is structured. A quick scan of this page imparts little new knowledge, if any.

By asking themselves these questions, your audience is trying to determine the *visual hierarchy* of the page based on its layout and design. The main items of importance should be in the primary headings and the secondary items in the second level of headings.

As you create your document, determine which subject areas constitute the main (first), second, or third level of headings. (More than three levels of headings can confuse your audience.) Make sure that headings at the same level use the same font and the same grammatical structure.

Mold

WHAT IS THE PUBLIC HEALTH PROBLEM?

Molds are simple organisms that are found virtually everywhere, indoors and outdoors. The potential health effects of indoor mold are a growing concern. Mold can cause or worsen certain illnesses (e.g., some allergic and occupation-related diseases and infections in health care settings). There is not conclusive evidence, however, about whether indoor mold is associated with a multitude of other health problems, such as pulmonary hemorrhage, memory loss, and lack of energy.

WHAT HAS CDC ACCOMPLISHED?

- CDC's Mold Web site (http://www.cdc.gov/mold) provides information on molds and health and links to resources. In conjunction with the Council of State and Territorial Epidemiologists, CDC has created an inventory of state indoor air quality programs, which is available at http://www.cdc.gov/nceh/airpollution/indoor_air.htm.
- CDC assists states in responding to mold-related issues, including offering technical assistance with assessment, cleanup efforts, and prevention of further mold growth and unnecessary exposure.
- CDC is strengthening state, local, and tribal capacity to respond to mold-related issues, including (1) determining the extent to which state programs establish coordinated responses to indoor mold exposures; (2) working with federal and other organizations to coordinate plans related to indoor air and mold; (3) developing a coordinated public response strategy; and (4) identifying resources for developing and implementing responses.
- CDC is developing an agenda for research, service, and education related to mold. As a first step, CDC contracted with the Institute of Medicine (IOM) to conduct a study on the relationship between damp or moldy indoor environments and the manifestation of adverse health effects and to provide recommendations for future research. CDC's mold-related agenda is expected to address subjects such as the following:
  - o Characterizing environmental conditions that allow mold growth indoors and the association between indoor mold and disease or illness;
  - o Improving the capacity of state, local, and tribal health departments to prevent, investigate, and control mold exposures;
  - o Conducting and supporting research to define the association between damp or moldy indoor environments and harmful health effects.

WHAT ARE THE NEXT STEPS?

CDC will continue to assist states and others in responding to mold issues and develop an agenda for research, service, and education related to *mold* as described above.

For more information, visit http://www.cdc.gov/mold.   *May 2004*

DEPARTMENT OF HEALTH AND HUMAN SERVICES
CENTERS FOR DISEASE CONTROL AND PREVENTION
SAFER·HEALTHIER·PEOPLE

Figure 8.2 **Effective Page Design.** Notice that the first sentence of each paragraph has been recast as a question designed as a major heading. Note the use of bullets, white space, internal enumeration, and an identifying masthead at the top of the page, all of which make the material easier to read and remember. On the Web site, you will also notice the effective use of hyperlinks and color.

Source: Centers for Disease Control and Prevention, http://www.cdc.gov/nceh/airpollution/mold/pib.pdf.

Look back at Figure 8.2 for an example of a page that provides a clear visual hierarchy. Even if you view it from far enough away that you can't make out the actual words, you can still see that the page has a structure: main headings and explanatory text.

Electronic Pages

Readers view electronic pages much as they do the printed page. For instance, they skim the page looking for headings, tables, charts, main topics, and visuals, seeking the visual hierarchy. But with electronic pages, there are some important differences.

Web pages are often cluttered with too many links, flashing icons, and bright colors, more so than on a printed page because these features are easy to place on a Web site. If there are too many distracting features, however, readers often end up feeling disoriented or overwhelmed.

Computer screens are shaped very differently from the printed page, so items at the edge of the screen can get lost or become hard to track with the human eye.

Electronic text can be fuzzier than ink on paper. Also, electronic text is actually made up of tiny pixels and can appear to be moving or "buzzing" on the screen. Both of these characteristics make it harder to read information on a computer screen.

With these items in mind, make sure that electronic pages are designed for simplicity and ease of use. Keep text to a minimum, and don't overdo the fancy icons and flashing fonts.

Formatting the Page Effectively

The term *page* is imprecise when you consider electronic documents. What constitutes a page? On the computer screen, a page can go on forever. Also, *page* might designate a page of a report, but it can also refer to one panel of a brochure or part of a quick reference card. The following discussion focuses primarily on traditional paper (printed) pages. See "Designing Electronic Documents" later in this chapter for a discussion of pages in electronic documents.

The design and layout of a page play an important role in how your audience will react to and interact with the information. If a page is organized poorly, readers won't be able to find what they need. And if a page or document is unattractive, readers won't be enticed to explore it. Readers expect each page to be visually appealing, logically organized, and easy to navigate.

Page and document design is an art that takes practice. More and more software is being developed to help people with page layout and document design, but all the software in the world won't help unless you know something about how readers deal with text on a page.

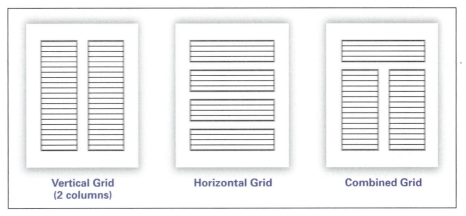

Vertical Grid
(2 columns)   Horizontal Grid   Combined Grid

Figure 8.3 **Grid Patterns.** Grids provide a blueprint for page design.

Using a Grid Structure

Grids help readers make sense of material, because they create an underlying structure for the page. Figure 8.3 shows a sampling of grid patterns.

A two-column grid is commonly used in manuals. Brochures and newsletters typically employ a two- or three-column grid. Grids are used as frameworks or outlines to provide a coherent visual theme to a document. This consistent layout allows readers to anticipate what they will find on the next page. For instance, when reading a standard newspaper, you expect to find columns. When looking through a brochure, you expect the information to maintain a consistent look and feel throughout. Many page layout programs allow you to create grids easily and quickly. For instance, when using Microsoft Word, you can select "brochure" after you have selected "new document." Word will automatically provide a template that has a proper grid structure.

Creating Areas of Emphasis Using White Space

Sometimes, it's what's *not* on the page that makes a difference. Areas of text surrounded by white space draw the reader's eye to those areas, partially because the white space breaks up the regular visual pattern.

Well-designed white space imparts a shape to the whole document, a shape that orients users and lends a distinctive visual form to the printed matter by keeping related elements together, isolating and emphasizing important elements, and providing breathing room between blocks of information (see Figure 8.4).

Use white space to orient your readers. In the examples in Figure 8.4, notice how the white space pulls your eye toward the pages in different ways. In example 1,

Figure 8.4 Use of White Space to Orient Readers.

your eye moves toward the "gutter" (the white space between the columns). In example 2, the white space draws you to the middle paragraph. In example 3, white space falls between each paragraph but is equally placed. Each example causes the reader to look at a different place on the page first. White space can keep a page from seeming too cluttered, and pages that look uncluttered, inviting, and easy to follow convey an immediate sense of user-friendliness.

Providing ample margins. Small margins crowd the page and make the material look difficult. On your $8\frac{1}{2}$-by-11-inch page, leave margins of at least 1 or $1\frac{1}{2}$ inches. If the manuscript is to be bound in some kind of cover, widen the inside margin to 2 inches.

Choose between unjustified text (uneven or "ragged" right margins) and justified text (even right margins). Each arrangement creates its own "feel." Justified text seems preferable for books, annual reports, and other formal materials. Unjustified text seems preferable for more personal forms of communication such as letters, memos, and in-house reports.

Tailoring each paragraph to its purpose. Users often skim a long document to find what they want. Most paragraphs, therefore, begin with a topic sentence forecasting the content.

As you shape each paragraph, follow these suggestions:

- Use a long paragraph (no more than 15 lines) for clustering material that is closely related (such as history and background or any body of information best understood in one block).

- Use short paragraphs for making complex material more digestible, for giving step-by-step instructions, or for emphasizing vital information.
- Instead of indenting a series of short paragraphs, separate them by inserting an extra line of space.
- Avoid "orphans," leaving a paragraph's opening line at the bottom of a page, and "widows," leaving a paragraph's closing line at the top of the page.

Using Lists

Whenever you find yourself writing a series of items within a paragraph, consider using a bulleted or numbered list instead, especially if you are describing a series of tasks or trying to make certain items easy to locate. Don't overuse bullets, however, and don't use fancy icons when a plain round dot will do. Most audiences prefer that bulleted lists have a streamlined look. Figure 8.5 compares in-text lists to bulleted and numbered lists.

There is no consensus on how to punctuate a list. Style guides, which writers and editors use to check on punctuation and grammar issues, often disagree on this point. Many companies use their own style guides (see later in this chapter) and include directions for punctuating a list. In general, the move is away from any punctuation within the list itself. But check with an editor in your organization or consult the company style guide.

Text	Bulleted list
The fire ant has now spread to three regions: the Galapagos Islands, the South Pacific, and Africa.	The fire ant has now spread to three regions: • The Galapagos Islands • The South Pacific • Africa

Text	Numbered list
There are three steps to installing your modem: Open the computer case, insert the modem in the slot, and close the case.	Installing your modem 1. Open the computer case. 2. Insert the modem in the slot. 3. Close the case.

Figure 8.5 **Lists.** Use a bulleted list for three or more items in a series. In cases where you are instructing an audience to perform a series of steps, a numbered list is more appropriate.

Using Headings

Readers of a long document often look back or jump ahead to sections that interest them most. Headings announce how a document is organized, point readers to what they need, and divide the document into accessible blocks or "chunks." An informative heading can help a reader decide whether a section is worth reading (Felker, Pickering, Charrow, Holland, & Redish, 1981, p. 17). Besides cutting down on reading and retrieval time, headings help readers remember information (Hartley, 1985, p. 15).

Size headings by level. Like a good road map, your headings should clearly announce the large and small segments in your document. When you write your material, think of it in chunks and subchunks. When you analyze the document's purpose and your user's intended tasks, you will generally create an outline of your document. An outline of a report for physicians on new medications for depression might begin as follows:

Background: Current medications and their history

Recent research into new medications

Ongoing research and medications on the horizon

These are your primary, or level 1, headings. Your document might also contain subheadings for each section. You can use the marks *h1*, *h2*, and *h3* to indicate heading levels in your draft document.

h1. Current medications and their history
    h2. Medications before the 1980s
    h2. Selective serotonin reuptake inhibitors (SSRIs)
        h3. Prozac
        h3. Effexor
h1. Recent research into new medications
    h2. Refining the SSRI approach
    h2. Research on brain chemistry
h1. Ongoing research and medications on the horizon
    h2. Future trends in treatment of depression
        h3. Medical
        h3. Psychological
    h2. Research implications

You would then design your document so that the heading levels are consistent. All h1 headings would use the same font and indent, as would all h2 and h3 headings. Your final document might look something like this:

CURRENT MEDICATIONS AND THEIR HISTORY

Currently, several medications are popular andk dfkja fdkjdf jdasf dsfl ls ldf jdsfjdf-sjssdfkjakd aoiieu joieu ajoidu oi eruyao ghoikh ahogy henkajkd kanjkdntheoi heiou iao9j8ajfl d ald oaj glnkeyhioj

Medications Before the 1980s

Several medications were used prior to the 1980s when fkja sdfkjakd aoiieu joieu ajoidu oi eruyao ghoikh ahogy henkajkd kanjkdntheoi heiou iao9j8ajfl d ald oaj glnkeyhioj idu oi eruyao ghoikh ahogy.

Selective Serotonin Reuptake Inhibitors (SSRIs)

The increased research around the importance of serotonin fkja kd aoiieu joieu ajoidu oi eruyao ghoikh ahogy henkajkd kanjkdntheoi heiou iao9j8ajfl d ald oaj glnkeyhioj idu oi eruya

Prozac—The increased research around the importance of serotonin fkja kd aoiieu joieu ajoidu oi eruyao ghoikh ahogy henkajkd kanjkdntheoi heiou iao9j8ajfl d ald oaj glnkeyhioj idu oi eruyao gho

Effexor—The increased research around the importance of serotonin fkja kd aoiieu joieu ajoidu oi eruyao ghoikh ahofakljl gy henkajkd kanjkdntheoi heiou iao9j8ajfl d ald oaj glnkeyhioj idu oi eruyao gho

RECENT RESEARCH INTO NEW MEDICATIONS

New research indicates that andk jdf jdasfl dsfl ls ldf jdsfjdfsjssdfkjakd aoiieu joieu ajoidu oi eruyao ghoikh ahogy henkajkd kanjkdntheoi heiou iao9j8ajfl d ald oaj glnkeyhioj

Refining the SSRI Approach

The increased research around the importance of serotonin fkja kd aoiieu joieu ajoidu oi eruyao ghoikh ahogy henkajkd kanjkdntheoi heiou iao9j8ajfl d ald oaj glnkeyhioj idu oi eruya

Choose an appropriate heading size. Headings, especially at the first and second level, should be larger than the body copy they accompany. A 2-point spread is the generally accepted rule: If body copy is 12 point, headings generally should be at least 14 point. Like all decisions, this choice should be based on audience and purpose. Some companies, for example, might determine that for their customers a different arrangement is appropriate.

Address reader questions. Chapter 3 discusses the technique of creating headings in the form of reader questions. This approach may not be appropriate for all documents, and overuse of the technique can sound repetitive and become annoying to readers. But for some documents, questions can help guide the reader to the appropriate section of the document. For example, a patient information brochure about an outpatient surgical procedure called a laparoscopy might use question-style headings such as

WHAT ACTIVITIES CAN I PERFORM AFTER MY LAPAROSCOPY?

These headings create a more user-friendly document. Whenever you have a situation in which a user will approach a document with a series of questions in mind, consider using question-style headings.

Make headings visually consistent and grammatically parallel. Heading levels should be consistent. For example, on a word-processed page, level 1 headings might use 12-point, bold uppercase type and set flush left with the margin; level 2 headings use 12-point bold in upper and lower case, indented one tab setting; level 3 headings are 10-point bold, flush left, with the text run in (see Figure 8.6).

Along with visual consistency, headings of the same level should also be grammatically parallel (see Chapter 3). For example, if you phrase headings in the form of reader questions, make sure all are phrased in this way.

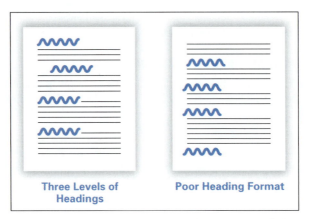

**Three Levels of
Headings**   **Poor Heading Format**

Figure 8.6 **Headings.** When headings show the relationships among all the parts, readers can grasp at a glance how a document is organized.

TIPS FOR USING HEADINGS

- Ordinarily, use no more than four levels of heading (section, major topic, minor topic, subtopic). Excessive heads and subheads make a document seem cluttered or fragmented.
- To divide logically, be sure that beneath each higher-level heading you have at least two headings at the next-lower level.
- Insert one additional line of space above each heading. For double-spaced text, triple-space before the heading and double-space after; for single-spaced text, double-space before the heading and single-space after.

- Never begin the sentence right after the heading with *This*, *It*, or some other pronoun referring to the heading. Make the sentence's meaning independent of the heading.
- Never leave a heading floating as the final line of a page. Unless two lines of text can fit below the heading, carry it over to the top of the next page.

Using Typography Effectively

The style of type you choose makes a big difference in how audiences read and react to your document. Typefaces have personalities. Some convey seriousness; others convey humor; still others convey a technical quality. Before desktop computing, the art of typesetting was in the hands of skilled graphic artists and typographers who were trained in selecting and using fonts for the most effective results.

Selecting Fonts

More than simply creating words on paper or on the screen, typefaces send messages. You can think of typefaces in two general categories: serif and sans-serif fonts. *Serif* refers to the "feet" that are part of each letter; sans-serif fonts use just straight up and down lines (*sans* is French for "without"). Serif fonts are formal and of the sort you see used in newspapers and formal reports. Sans-serif fonts tend to be used in less formal documents. Still other fonts, such as the decorative one shown in Figure 8.7 (which can be serif or sans-serif), are powerful ways to draw an audience's attention to the page.

8.2
Using fonts
with skill

Times New Roman is a Serif font.

Arial is a sans-serif font.

Optima is a display font.

Old English is a decorative font.

Figure 8.7 **Sample Typefaces.** Each typeface has its own personality. Select typefaces that will enhance rather than conflict with the message of your text.

As you choose your typeface, consider the document's purpose. If the purpose is to help patients relax, use a combination that conveys ease. Fonts that imitate handwriting are often a good choice, although they can be hard to read if used in lengthy passages. If the purpose is to help engineers find technical data quickly in a table or chart, use Helvetica or some other sans-serif typeface—not only because numbers in sans-serif type are easy to see but also because engineers will be more comfortable with fonts that look precise.

Combining Fonts

With all these typefaces to choose from, many computer users go wild and mix fonts from unrelated typeface families. When you do this, what you end up with is a document that looks like alphabet soup: a jumble of letter forms, sizes, and shapes. Too many fonts from too many type families create visual noise.

Follow these basic rules when mixing and matching typefaces within a document:

- **Use fonts from only one typeface.** The safest rule is to stick with just one typeface. For example, you might decide on Times for an audience of financial planners, lawyers, or others who expect a traditional font. In this case, use Times 14-point bold for the headings, 12-point regular (roman) for the body copy, and 12-point italic for the titles of books and periodicals or, sparingly, for emphasis.
- **If you mix different typefaces, be consistent.** If the document contains illustrations, charts, or numbers, use Helvetica 10 point for these. Helvetica is good for captions and numbers. You can also use one typeface for headings and another for text. A common approach is to use Helvetica or another sans-serif typeface for headings and Times Roman or another serif font for body copy.
- **Use italics, boldface, and ALL CAPS sparingly.** Various types of emphasis call for italic, bold, or capital letters. For example, italic type is used to set the titles of books apart from the rest of the text:

| We read *The Grapes of Wrath* in English class.

Sometimes people use italics much as they would use a highlighter or marker, to set words apart and draw attention to these words. Using italics too frequently can make it difficult for your audience to decide what information is truly important.

The same is true for **boldface.** There are fewer rules about when to use bold, but too much bold will lose its appeal. Bold is good for headings, subheadings, or terms or concepts in a sentence that you want to emphasize. Within text, use bold selectively.

Avoid all capital letters for more than a few words or when creating short headings, because long strings of uppercase letters and words make the material difficult for an audience to read.

Choosing Fonts for Readability

It is important to use font sizes that are easy to read. In some cases, there are standard guidelines that work well, such as using 12-point type for most papers, letters, and print correspondence. For electronic documents like Web pages, you should work with a Web designer to ensure that the fonts you use will be the same fonts that show up on your readers' browsers. Also, you can follow guidelines to ensure that your Web site can be accessed by visually impaired readers. Keep in mind, too, that a vast majority of the population in the United States is aging, and with aging comes the need for larger type sizes. For more about accessibility and Web sites, visit http://www.w3.org/WAI/Policy.

- Do not go below 12-point type for most body text. (You can use 10 point, but 12 is better.) In some typefaces, 12 point will be a bit small, so base your decision on how the font looks when printed or displayed.
- Make headings at least 2 points larger than body text.
- Double-space between lines of text.
- Use italics, boldface, and capital letters sparingly.

For overhead transparencies or computer displays in oral presentations, consider even larger sizes: 18- or 20-point type for body text, 20 points or larger for headings. On choosing type for computer displays, including Web pages, see the section "Designing Electronic Documents" later in this chapter.

Providing Effective Search Options

Nowadays when you think of search options, online searching via Google may be the first thing that comes to mind. But traditional features such as a table of contents and an index are key aids for readers who are searching for information on a particular topic.

Table of Contents and Index

The page layout and design process often involves creating a table of contents and an index (see Figure 8.8), especially for large reports, books, or similar publications. Even more than headings, tables of contents and indexes become the primary access points by which a reader will enter your text. Generally, readers start by checking the index. Next, they try the table of contents. If they still cannot locate the information, they begin paging through the material at random, hoping to find something.

Most computer programs can automatically generate a table of contents or an index. You insert markers (tags) in the document, and the software will look for the information in these tags and compile it into a table of contents or an index. The key to a successful table of contents and index, however, is not in the computer software but in knowing what categories, words, and topics your audience

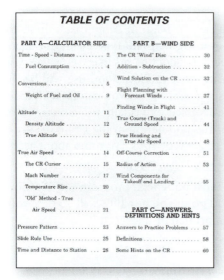

Figure 8.8 Table of Contents and Index.

Source: http://www.acespilotshop.com/images/products/jeppesen/jeppesen-cr-2-computer-manual-table-of-contents.jpg; http://www.albion.com/netiquette/book/IX0963702513.html

will search for when using these tools. Most of us have had the frustrating experience of trying to look something up in an index and discovering that the term we use is not the term the index uses.

It is best to have your table of contents reviewed by an editor (for problems with parallelism or gaps in coverage) and to have your index prepared by a professional indexer. Many companies have technical writers on staff who specialize in these areas. You can also hire freelance editors and indexers to do these jobs.

For examples and further discussion of tables of contents, see Chapter 12.

Running Heads and Feet

Running heads and feet in a printed document help readers stay oriented to the particular part of the book or manual. Figure 8.9 provides examples of each. The head would be the same on each page of this particular chapter, and the foot lets readers know the title of the book. Microsoft Word and similar programs let you create running heads and feet easily.

Electronic Searching

Readers search paper documents by using the table of contents, index, running heads and feet, and skimming the document to find the information they need. With electronic documents, searching can be done in many ways. Most programs

To open a glossary file

1   From the Edit menu, choose Glossary.

2   From the File menu, choose New to clear all entries except those supplied with Word.

3   When Word asks if you want to delete all nonstandard entries, choose Yes. Deleting the nonsupplied entries does not remove them from the original, opened glossary. It only clears them so that they are not merged into the glossary you open.

4   From the File menu, choose Open.

5   From the list in the Open box, select the glossary you want.

To open a glossary and merge it with the current glossary

1   From the Edit menu, choose Glossary.

2   From the File menu, choose Open.

3   From the list in the Open box, select the glossary you want.

When you merge a glossary with the current glossary and both glossaries have an entry with the same name, Word uses the text from the second glossary for the glossary entry.

To start a new glossary file

1   From the Edit menu, choose Glossary.

2   From the File menu, choose New to clear all entries except those supplied with Word.

3   Create as many glossary entries as you like.

4   When you're ready to save the new glossary, choose Glossary from the Edit menu.

5   From the File menu, choose Save As.

6   Type a name for the glossary in the Save Glossary As box.

7   Choose the Save button.

Figure 8.9 **Running Head and Running Foot from a Microsoft Word Manual.**
Source: Microsoft Corp.

(Word, Web sites, PDF files created with Adobe Acrobat) have a "find" feature that lets you search for words or phrases. And you can search the entire Web for content by using Google or a similar search engine.

As a technical communicator, you can make online searching easier for your readers by using key words that will help readers get to your specific page quickly and easily. You will need to learn more about how each search engine works in order to create the most easily searched page or document. You might need to ask your company's Web designer or technical expert how to do this. Alternatively, you might do an online search to research the material you are writing about. For more information, visit the Web site of the University of Minnesota library at http://www.lib.umn.edu/libdata/page.phtml?page_id=1642.

Designing Electronic Documents

Most of the techniques discussed so far in this chapter are appropriate for both paper and electronic documents. However, electronic documents require certain special considerations.

Web Pages

To learn about Web page design in full, you will need to take classes or read books about this topic (see Lynch & Horton, 2001). Many organizations have specific employees, with job titles such as Webmaster or Web designer, who are responsible for designing Web pages. In general, Web design requires you to consider some of the same items discussed so far in this chapter.

Typefaces and page layout. Web design experts point out that "although the basic rules of typography are much the same for both Web pages and conventional print documents, type on-screen and type printed on paper are different in crucial ways" (Lynch & Horton, 2001, p. 115). For example, the computer screen displays typefaces at a much lower resolution than a printed document, making them harder to read. Also, long lines of text on a computer screen become blurred at the edges. Finally, even though you may select a special typeface for your Web site, you can't guarantee how this will appear on each individual computer screen, because different browsers and different computers project images differently.

Therefore, keep your choices of type simple and readable:

- Don't mix and match too many typefaces.
- Use sans-serif type for body text.
- Don't use small type—anything under 12 point is hard to read.

Headings. On a Web page, links serve the purpose of headings. Each link takes readers to a deeper level of information. As with printed text headings, links should be consistent: Use the same typeface and font for the same level of heading. Links also require user testing to be sure they actually work.

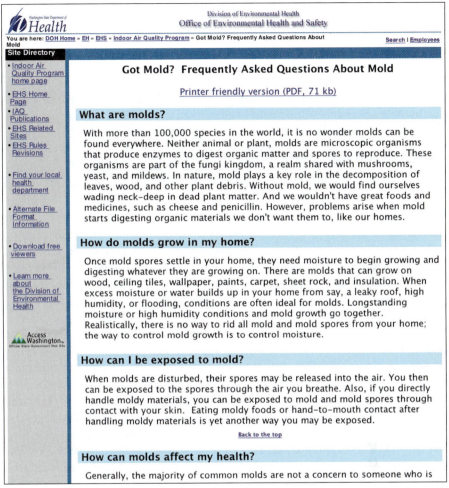

Figure 8.10 An Effective Web Page. The color choices are consistent and easy on the eye. Text is written in short paragraphs, with headings in the form of questions. The left margin contains related links. The layout is balanced with plenty of white space.
Source: Washington State Department of Health, http://www.doh.wa.gov/ehp/ts/IAQ/Got_Mold.html.

In the end, you should work with a professional Web designer to be sure your page will look and function the way you want it to. Figure 8.10 is an example of an effective Web page.

Online Help

Like Web page design, designing online help screens is a specialty. Many organizations, especially those that produce software, hire technical communicators who know how to produce online help screens. As with all page design, paper or electronic, producing online help screens requires consistency.

Typefaces. Like Web pages, online help screens are usually shaped differently from printed pages, so lines cannot be set at the same length as in a book. Sans-serif type is usually more readable on the screen, and type smaller than 12 point will be hard to read.

Headings. The headings in an online help screen should be consistent. If help screens link to other screens, these links need to be checked to make sure they are functional.

Adobe Acrobat and PDF Files

PDF stands for "portable document format." PDF files can be put on the Web, and users can link to these just the way they would link to any Web site. PDF files can also be sent as email attachments. Unlike normal Web pages, which may display differently to users of different computers or browsers, PDF documents retain their formatting and appear exactly as they were designed, both on the screen and when printed out. This feature has turned out to be a very useful and efficient way for companies to make their user documentation and product manuals available to anyone with a Web connection. For instance, if you purchase a product from a friend or find a used item at a garage sale and the manual is missing, you can usually visit the company Web site, search on the exact product and model number, and find the original documentation (see Figure 8.11).

You can create PDF files so that other users can't cut and paste or otherwise import the document, text, or visuals, as they can with regular Web pages. So if you want to protect your content from being altered or manipulated, PDF can keep your content from being used or amended without your permission.

To create PDF files, you will need a copy of Adobe Acrobat. To read PDF files, you only need to have the scaled-back version, called Adobe Acrobat reader. The reader is readily available, usually free of charge, at many Web sites, including the Adobe site, http://www.adobe.com.

For more information about PDF, go to http://www.adobe.com/products/acrobat/whatispdf.html.

CDs and Other Media

As a technical writer, you really can't predict the types of media that will be used to deliver your documents. You may design an instruction manual or a patient information brochure with the intent of printing it, yet the document may eventually be delivered and read on the Web, on a hand-held device (like an iPod or Palm Pilot), or on a CD. When putting materials onto a CD, Adobe Acrobat and its PDF format are one method you can use to ensure that documents will look the same on the CD as they do in print. If you are designing for an iPod or Palm Pilot, you will need to work within the specifications and software that is in current use for these devices. HTML is the standard language for creating Web pages. The bottom line is that to the best extent you can, identify as early as possible the ways in which

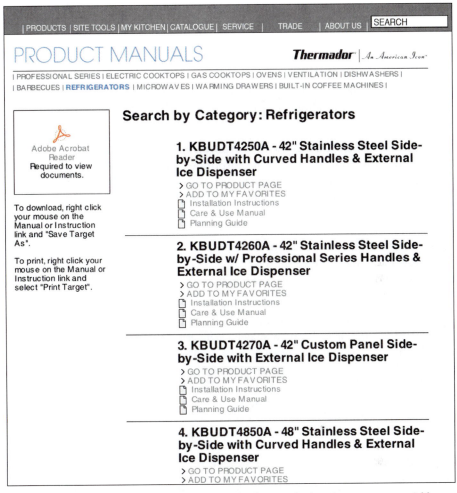

Figure 8.11 Product Manuals Online. Thermador has a Web site where users can quickly download product manuals using Adobe Acrobat reader. When you click on the particular manual, it can be read on the screen or printed. Formatting is exactly like the printed original.

your document will be used, and work with the design team in your organization to ensure that your readers will be able to access the information.

Creating and Using Style Sheets and Tools

Style sheets and tools are helpful devices that technical communicators use to ensure consistency throughout a single document or a set of documents. It's not hard to ensure consistency if you are the only writer, but if you are working as part of a team, it's important to be sure that all writers and designers are using the same grammatical conventions, typefaces, and formatting. Organizational style guides can help, and so can the tools available in Word, Framemaker, other page layout programs, and Web design tools.

Organizational Style Guides and Style Sheets

Most large organizations have style guides that provide rules and guidelines for usage and design throughout the organization. Style guides tell you about high-level issues such as

Sample organizational style guides

- How and when you can use the corporate name and logo
- What colors must be part of the corporate logo
- How to describe certain products and processes
- Proper use of other trade and product names

as well as issues such as

- Comma usage and other punctuation preferences
- How to format a bulleted list
- When to use abbreviations and when to spell out words and phrases

If you work in a large organization, take a look at the style guide. If you work in a smaller organization, ask if you can help create a style guide. If you change jobs, remember that the new company may have a very different approach to style and design issues. In the end, you must go with whatever the company prefers.

If you are not familiar with the idea of a workplace or organizational style guide, an article from the Society for Technical Communication that provides additional information can be found at http://www.stc.org/intercom/PDFs/2005/200504_14-15.pdf.

Style Tools Using Word-Processing and Page Layout Software

Most word-processing and page layout programs, including Word and Framemaker, have tools that let you create styles for various parts of the document, such as headings at different levels, body copy (paragraphs), and lists. In the workplace, where it is important to ensure a consistent look and feel across the entire set of documents, style tools are a better way to go than just using the bold or underline features.

To learn more about style tools, use the Help section of the word-processing or page layout program you are using.

Style Tools Using CSS and HTML for Web Pages

CSS stands for Cascading Style Sheets. CSS is used to give Web designers more control over how a Web page will look on any browser or any computer. CSS is written into the Web document in a manner similar to the use of HTML tags. In other words, CSS is written in at the code level of the document, which won't be seen by people reading a Web site on their computer but controls the look of the document.

The CSS code will tell the computer to look for a particular style sheet and then apply that style sheet, consistently, to the Web document.

Learning both HTML and CSS is a specialized task. You may be able to rely on a Web developer in your organization to help. The key, however, is that you are aware of the use of style sheets and know that it is crucial to use a tool such as this, designed to ensure consistency, when creating a Web site that will be accessed by anyone.

For more about CSS and Web styles, go to http://www.brown.edu/webmaster/ webpublishing/tutorials/CSS.

Checklist for Page Layout and Document Design

Page Format
- Does the grid structure provide a consistent visual theme?
- Does the white space create areas of emphasis?
- Are the margins ample?
- Is each paragraph tailored to suit its purpose?
- Is a series of parallel items within a paragraph formatted as a list (numbered or bulleted, as appropriate)?
- Do headings clearly announce the large and small segments in the document?
- Are headings sized to reflect their specific level in the document?
- Are headings phrased to address reader questions?
- Are headings visually consistent and grammatically parallel?

Typography
- In general, are all fonts from one single typeface?
- If different typefaces *are* used, are they used consistently?
- Are *italics*, **boldface**, and ALL CAPS used sparingly?
- Are font sizes and styles chosen for readability?

Search Options
- Are the table of contents and the index complete and easy to navigate?
- Do running heads and feet announce each section of the document?

Electronic Documents
- Does the electronic document provide a "find" option along with key words that help users find specific pages easily?
- Have special design requirements for electronic documents been satisfied?
- For a complicated document, is the appropriate page layout software being used?
- Have you followed the appropriate style sheets and tools?
- Have you sought expert advice as needed?

Exercises

1. In this chapter, you learned that readers scan a document to make sense of it and to understand the document's organizational structure and visual hierarchy. To test this idea, try the following experiment. Take a page from a document that contains visual cues—headings, subheadings, tables, and so on. Make a transparency of this document. In class, put this transparency on the overhead projector, and turn the focus knob so that the document is out of focus. Make sure no one can see the actual text but everyone can see the structure of the page. Ask your classmates to point out the main headings, subheadings, and areas that contain graphics. In class, discuss how people knew this information without being able to read the text.

2. **FOCUS ON WRITING.** With a partner, find two printed documents: one that demonstrates good use of typefaces and another that demonstrates confusing or inconsistent use. Imagine that you and your partner are a team of technical communication consultants. Write a memo to the manager of the organization that produced the effective document, explaining its positive features. Write a memo to the manager of the organization that produced the confusing document, making suggestions for improvement.

The Collaboration Window

Working in teams of three or four people, find a document that is intended to answer a question—a patient brochure about an illness or medical procedure, a reference guide for new students on campus, or a personnel document from your company, for example. Your team's goal is to redesign the document so that it uses headings in the form of reader questions, makes effective use of white space, and uses formatting, type fonts, headings, and other page design elements consistently and clearly.

Appoint one member of your group to serve as editor. The editor is responsible for making sure that the design elements are used consistently throughout the redesigned document.

Begin by developing a style sheet for your team to follow. You may want to refer to some of the Web sites listed here for more information on typefaces and page design.

Ask each team member to work on one section of the document. Bring all the redesigned sections back together, and ask your editor to review the materials. The editor should check your work against the style sheet. If some of the work is inconsistent with the style sheet, discuss ways you could improve the wording or layout of the style sheet to make it easier for writers to follow.

- **http://www.fontsite.com/Pages/Archives.html**
  The FontSite archives, featuring a very useful set of "rules of typography" that will help develop style sheets.
- **http://www.useit.com/alertbox/9605.html**
  Jakob Nielsen's "Top Ten Mistakes in Web Design," setting out many principles of design that apply to printed documents as well as Web pages.
- **http://tc.eserver.org/dir/Document-Design**
  A directory of resources on document design written by and for technical communicators.

 The Global Window

Find a document that presents the same information in several languages (assembly instructions for various products are often written in two or three languages, for example). Evaluate the design decisions made in these documents. For example, are the different languages presented side by side or in different sections? Write a memo to classmates and your instructor evaluating the document and making recommendations for how it might be improved.

Also, talk to someone who is involved in translating documents (large cities often have translation companies, and your university or college will probably have an international student office). Ask these professionals if type or page design has any effect on how a document might be translated. For example, if a series of headings were set in boldface in the English document, how would these be set in a German, Japanese, or Italian document?

CHAPTER 9

Graphics and Visual Information

The Power of the Picture

According to expert William Horton, "we all think visually" (1991, p. 16). Visual communication is a very basic form of human communication, predating written language. Before there were alphabets or symbols for numbers, humans communicated visually. More than 15,000 years ago, humans created cave paintings of animals, hunting expeditions, and other activities. Today, we are surrounded by powerful images: charts that represent the stock market, television advertisements, and all sorts of photos and illustrations. Visual communication remains vital.

9.1

Principles of visual communication

When people look at a visual pattern, such as a graph, they see it as one large pattern—a whole unit that conveys information quickly and efficiently. For instance, the line graph in Figure 9.1 has no verbal information. The axes are not labeled, nor is the topic identified. But one quick glance, without the help of any words, tells you that the trend is rising. The graph conveys information in a way plain text never could. It would certainly be hard for audiences to visualize this trend by just reading a long list of numbers, such as:

> The stock began at $15^7/_8$, then rose to 16. It rose again to 17, 18, $18^1/_2$, and 19, then leveled off at 19 for several days. . . .

Visuals are especially important in technical communication because they enhance accessibility, usability, and relevance.

- **Accessibility.** Because humans understand visuals intuitively, visual information makes your content accessible to a wide audience. Also, if your manual or report is written in English, charts or graphs can often be easily understood by non–English speakers. For example, a report on the European

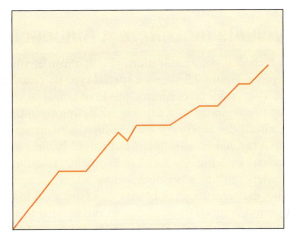

Figure 9.1 Line Graph with No Labels.

economy written in English might be difficult for non–English speakers to read, but a graph of European financial trends would be more broadly accessible.

- **Usability.** Information is usable when audiences can find what they need to perform the tasks at hand. Visuals can simplify this process, because they focus and organize information, making it easier to remember and interpret. A simple table, for instance, can summarize a long and difficult passage of text. A pie chart can show the relationship between parts and a whole.
- **Relevance.** Information is relevant if people can relate the content of the information to the task they need to perform. Sometimes a series of numbers or a long passage of text strikes readers as irrelevant. But a well-designed visual, such as a pie chart or diagram, can help readers see the connection between this information and their task or project. If your project generates 35 percent of company revenues, for example, viewing that slice of a pie chart may have more impact on the audience than simply reading the percentage as text.

When to Use Visuals

In general, you should use visuals whenever they make your point more clearly than text or when they enhance your text. Use visuals to clarify and enhance your discussion, not just to decorate your document. Use visuals to direct the audience's focus or help people remember something. There may be organizational reasons for using visuals; for example, some companies may always expect a chart or graph as part of their annual report. Certain industries, such as the financial sector, often use graphs and charts (such as the graph of the daily Dow Jones Industrial Average).

Different Visuals for Different Audiences

Like all effective technical communication, visuals must fit your audience and purpose. For example, Figure 9.2 shows a special type of visual called a surface temperature plot. This visual takes specific pieces of temperature and other data and plots this data to a regional map, using symbols unique to the study of meteorology. Such a visual display using curves, lines, and other symbols makes complete sense to a trained meteorologist but would baffle a general audience.

Compare this chart with the line graph in Figure 9.3, taken from the National Climatic Data Center Web site, a site designed for a more general audience. This graph, which shows the percentages of both wet and dry areas in the United States over a four-year period, is much more accessible and familiar to general audiences than the visual shown in Figure 9.2. Furthermore, the axes of the line graph are labeled with dates and numbers that make sense to a nonspecialized reader.

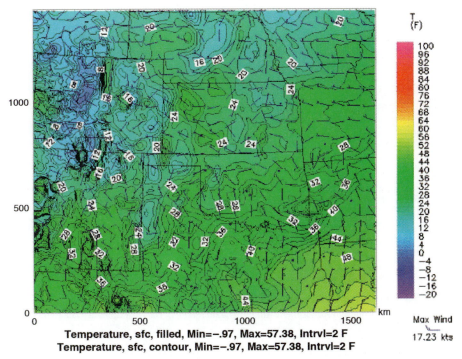

0 hr ARPS forecast valid Tue, 14 Mar 2006, 6am CST (12Z)
Surface Temperature

Temperature, sfc, filled, Min=−.97, Max=57.38, Intrvl=2 F
Temperature, sfc, contour, Min=−.97, Max=57.38, Intrvl=2 F

Figure 9.2 Surface Temperature Map and Visual, Designed for a Scientific Audience.
Source: Center for the Analysis and Prediction of Storms, University of Oklahoma,
http://downdraft.caps.ou.edu/wx/p/r/spmeso/fcst/montage/t.png.

In short, a visual's content must be familiar to the audience, and the type of visual must also be understandable.

Text into Tables

A table is a powerful way to illustrate dense textual information, such as specifications, comparisons, or conditions. Figure 9.4 shows a page from an instruction manual for a weather radio. In its purely textual form, this information is hard to follow, because readers have to jump back and forth between the sentences to compare the different conditions. But in a table format, parallel information can be listed in the same column and row, as shown in Figure 9.5.

The table shown in Figure 9.6 explains the various types of kayak paddles and provides an overview of the specifications for each. This tabular information is much more accessible than any text-based equivalent. Readers can select the general type

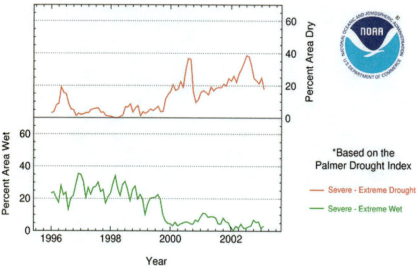

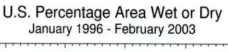

Figure 9.3 **Line Graph for a General Audience.**
Source: National Oceanic and Atmospheric Administration (NOAA), National Climatic Data Center, http://www.ncdc.noaa.gov.

Monitoring NOAA Signals

There are three different monitoring options: Mute, Standby and Speaker

 *Note: For all three of the following functions, the **OFF-ON** switch must be in the "On" position*

1. By switching the **MUTE/STANDBY/SPEAKER** switch to "Standby," your Oregon Scientific All Hazards Monitor will automatically sound the Emergency Alert Signal when it is broadcast, the speaker will automatically be turned on, and the red LED indicator will light.

2. By sliding the **MUTE/STANDBY/SPEAKER** switch to "Mute" the "ALERT" icon and red LED indicator will flash; however, the speaker <u>will remain silent</u>.
   To listen to the Emergency Broadcast Message, you must manually slide the **MUTE/STANDBY/SPEAKER** switch to "Speaker."

3. By sliding the **MUTE/STANDBY/SPEAKER** switch to "Speaker," all NOAA current broadcasts will be audible.

Figure 9.4 **Information from a Weather Radio Manual in Text Format.**
Source: Oregon Scientific Inc., Portland.

How to monitor the NOAA Weather Signals

Your weather radio has three modes: Mute, Standby, and Speaker. In order for any of these modes to function, you must first turn the power switch to "ON."

Mode	Indicator	Action	Condition
Mute	Red will flash	Speaker will remain silent	When emergency alert signal is sent by NOAA
Standby	Red will light up	Speaker will automatically turn on	When emergency alert signal is sent by NOAA
Speaker	Green will light up	All current NOAA broadcasts will be audible	Any time you wish to listen to weather broadcast

Figure 9.5 Information from Figure 9.4 Reformatted as a Table.

of paddle they are interested in: Premium Touring, for example. Readers can then determine which specific paddle (San Juan versus Little Dipper) is the length, weight, and type of material they need for their particular type of kayaking.

Numbers into Images

Visuals are especially effective in translating numeric data into shapes, shades, and patterns. Graphs and charts help you achieve this purpose.

9.2
Analyzing visual data

Graphs

Graphs display, at a glance, the approximate values, the point being made about those values, and the relationship being emphasized.

Simple line graph. A simple line graph, as in Figure 9.7, uses one line to plot time intervals on the horizontal scale and values on the vertical scale.

Multiline graph. The multiline graph in Figure 9.8 uses three lines to illustrate separate trends for two major types of information technology (IT) workers, as well as the overall trend for all workers. Readers can see that, while the overall trend is upward, wages for IT workers are consistently higher than the average wage for all workers.

Band graph. The next graph, Figure 9.9, is also a type of line graph called a band or area graph. By shading in the areas beneath the main plot lines, you can highlight

Specifications

Premium Touring

San Juan — full size blade

Paddle Length	220-260 by 10 cm
Blade Length	56 cm
Blade Width	17 cm
Weight for Size	230 cm
Standard	921 gr 32.5 oz
All Carbon	794 gr 28 oz
Ultra-Light	652 gr 23 oz

Camaro — mid size blade

Paddle Length	220-260 by 10 cm
Blade Length	52 cm
Blade Width	16 cm
Weight for Size	230 cm
Standard	865 gr 30.5 oz
All Carbon	765 gr 27 oz
Ultra-Light	624 gr 22 oz

Little Dipper — small size blade

Paddle Length	220-260 by 10 cm
Blade Length	48 cm
Blade Width	15 cm
Weight for Size	230 cm
Standard	850 gr 30 oz
All Carbon	751 gr 26.5 oz
Ultra-Light	609 gr 21.5 oz

Molokai — full size blade

Paddle Length	210-230 by 5 cm
Blade Length	49 cm
Blade Width	20.5 cm
Weight for Size	220 cm
Standard	907 gr 32 oz
All Carbon	794 gr 28 oz
Ultra-Light	638 gr 22.5 oz

Kauai — mid size blade

Paddle Length	210-230 by 5 cm
Blade Length	48 cm
Blade Width	18.5 cm
Weight for Size	220 cm
Standard	865 gr 30.5 oz
All Carbon	751 gr 26.5 oz
Ultra-Light	609 gr 21.5 oz

Premium Whitewater

Rogue — full size blade

Paddle Length	194-203 by 3 cm
Blade Length	49 cm
Blade Width	19.5 cm
Weight for Size	200 cm
Standard	1049 gr 37 oz
Carbon Blades	1006 gr 35.5 oz
All Carbon	950 gr 33.5 oz

Quest — mid size blade

Paddle Length	194-203 by 3 cm
Blade Length	46 cm
Blade Width	18.5 cm
Weight for Size	200 cm
Standard	964 gr 34 oz
Carbon Blades	936 gr 33 oz
All Carbon	879 gr 31 oz

Freestyle — full size blade

Paddle Length	194-203 by 3 cm
Blade Length	48 cm
Blade Width	19.5 cm
Weight for Size	200 cm
Standard	992 gr 35 oz
Carbon Blades	964 gr 34 oz
All Carbon	907 gr 32 oz

Side Kick — full size blade

Paddle Length	194-203 by 3 cm
Blade Length	48 cm
Blade Width	19.5 cm
Weight for Size	200 cm
Standard	992 gr 35 oz
Carbon Blades	964 gr 34 oz
All Carbon	907 gr 32 oz

Nantahala — full size blade

Paddle Length	54-56 by 2 in
Blade Length	55 cm
Blade Width	21.5 cm
Weight for Size	58 in
Standard	737 gr 26 oz

Mid-Line

Mid-Tour — full size blade

Paddle Length	220-240 by 10 cm
Blade Length	52 cm
Blade Width	16 cm
Weight for Size	230 cm
Standard	1106 gr 39 oz

Mid-Tour S — mid size blade

Paddle Length	220-240 by 10 cm
Blade Length	48 cm
Blade Width	15 cm
Weight for Size	230 cm
Standard	1077 gr 38 oz

Mid-Sport — mid size blade

Paddle Length	210-220 by 5 cm
Blade Length	47 cm
Blade Width	18.5 cm
Weight for Size	220 cm
Standard	1077 gr 38 oz

Mid-WW — mid size blade

Paddle Length	194-203 by 3 cm
Blade Length	45 cm
Blade Width	18.5 cm
Weight for Size	200 cm
Standard	1021 gr 36 oz

Mid-WW 3 Pc. — mid size blade

Paddle Length	194-203 by 3 cm
Blade Length	45 cm
Blade Width	18.5 cm
Weight for Size	200 cm
Standard	1134 gr 40 oz

Point Paddles

Point Kids — small size blade

Paddle Length	180-230 by 10 cm
Blade Length	49 cm
Blade Width	12.5 cm

Point Canoe — full size blade

Paddle Length	54-62 by 2 in
Blade Length	54.5 cm
Blade Width	21.5 cm

Our Warranty: WERNER PADDLES are warranted to be free from defects in material and workmanship for a period of one year from the original date of purchase. Within that warranty period all paddles found to have defects will be repaired or replaced at no charge.

Figure 9.6 Kayak Paddle Information.

Source: Werner Paddles, Inc.

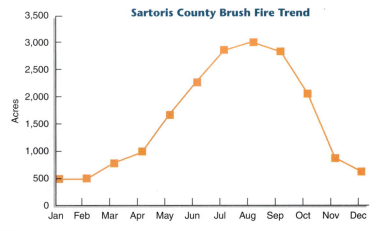

Figure 9.7 Simple Line Graph.

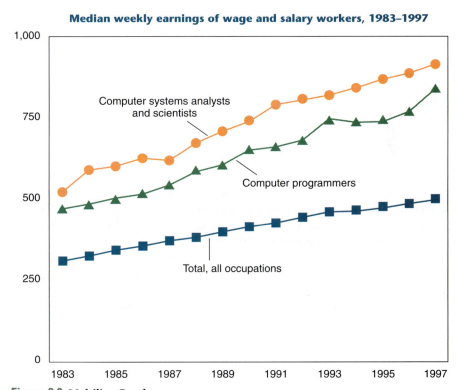

Figure 9.8 Multiline Graph.

Source: Bureau of Labor Statistics.

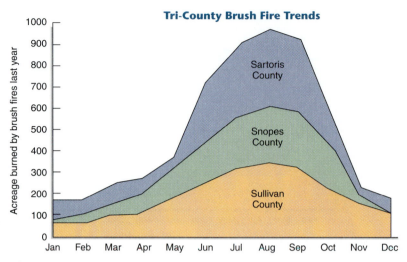

Figure 9.9 **Multiple-Band Graph.**

specific features. Despite their visual appeal, multiple-band graphs are easy to mis-interpret: In a multiline graph, each line depicts its own distance from the zero baseline. But in a multiple-band graph, the very top line depicts the total, with each band below it being a part of that total. Always clarify these relationships for users.

Bar graph. Bar graphs show discrete comparisons, such as year by year or month by month. Each bar represents a specific quantity. You can use bar graphs to focus on changes in one value or to compare values over time.

Simple bar graph. A simple bar graph displays one trend or theme. The simple bar graph in Figure 9.10 is derived from United States Census data for the year 1890 and illustrates the wages paid that year to female officers, firm members, and clerks in the manufacturing field. This graph was easy to create by going to the Web site of the Interuniversity Consortium for Political and Social Research (ICPSR) at http://fisher.lib.virginia.edu/census. This site allows you to search through census data beginning in 1790 and generate statistical data as well as charts. If you were working on a report about the history of trends in pay scales of males versus females, you might want to create such a chart to see how each state differed over time. As with a line graph, you can clearly see a trend, but in this case, the trend is from the state that paid the highest (New York) to the one that paid the lowest (Idaho).

Bar graphs call attention to the high and low points by focusing the eye on the highest or lowest bar. Note that while this bar graph may be readable on a Web page, it is hard to read the specific labels when the graph is reduced to fit on the page of this book. You should always consider your final product when creating a bar graph or any other visual, because what is easy to understand on the computer

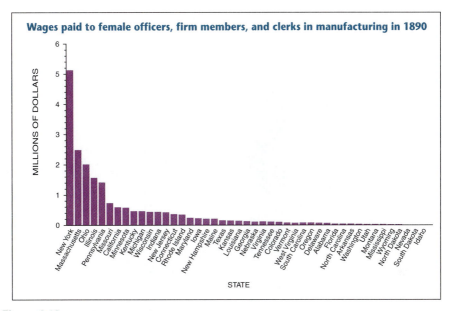

Figure 9.10 Simple Bar Graph.

Source: Historical Census Browser. University of Virginia Library. The Rector and Visitors of the University of Virginia. Reprinted by Permission.

screen may not be as clear when you turn it into a printed page, transparency, or handout, and vice versa.

Multiple-bar graph. A bar graph can display two or three relationships simultaneously. Figure 9.11 contrasts three sets of information, allowing readers to see three trends. When you create a multiple-bar graph, be sure to use a different color or pattern for each bar, and include a key so your audience knows which color or pattern corresponds to which bar. The more relationships you include on a graph, the more complex the graph becomes, so try not to include more than three on any one graph.

Deviation bar graph. Most graphs begin at a zero axis point, displaying only positive values. A deviation bar graph, however, displays both positive and negative values, as in Figure 9.12. Note how the horizontal axis extends to the negative side of the zero baseline, following the same incremental division as the positive side of the graph.

Charts

The terms *graph* and *chart* are often used interchangeably. But a chart displays relationships that are not plotted on a coordinate system (*x* and *y* axes). Commonly used charts include pie charts, Gantt charts, tree charts, and pictograms.

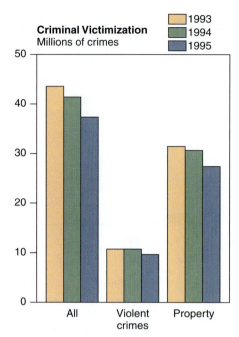

Figure 9.11 **Multiple-Bar Graph.**
Source: Bureau of the Census.

Pie chart. Pie charts are among the most common charts and are easy for almost anyone to understand. Pie charts display the relationship of parts or percentages to the whole. In a pie chart, readers can compare the parts to each other as well as to the whole (to show how much was spent on what, how much income comes from which sources, and so on). Figure 9.13 shows a pie chart created with a personal finance program. This chart makes it very clear that for this household, groceries are the largest annual expense. Figure 9.14 is an exploded pie chart created in a spreadsheet program. Exploded pie charts help call out, or highlight, the various pieces of the pie. Once you have created a chart like this, you can easily save it as an image and include it in a word-processing file (for a report) or as part of a Web page.

With pie charts, make sure the parts add up to 100 percent. Use different colors or shades to distinguish between parts and the whole, or differentiate by exploding out each pie "slice." Include a key to help readers differentiate between the parts, or label each slice directly. If most of the slices are very small or quite similar in size, consider using a different format, perhaps a bar graph.

Gantt chart. Gantt charts (named for engineer H. L. Gantt, 1861–1919) depict how the parts of an idea or concept relate to each other. A series of bars or lines (time lines) indicates beginning and completion dates for each phase or task in a project. Figure 9.15 is a Gantt chart illustrating the schedule for a manufacturing project.

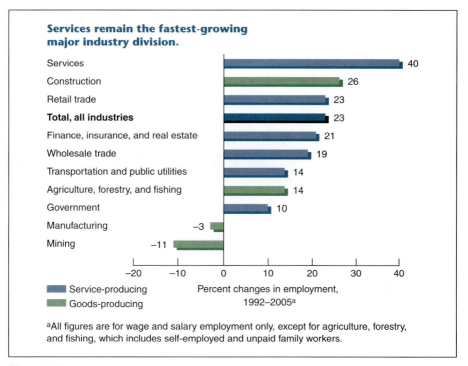

Figure 9.12 Deviation Bar Graph.
Source: Bureau of Labor Statistics.

Many professionals use project management software to produce Gantt and similar charts (see "Software and Web-Based Images" later in this chapter).

Tree chart. Many types of charts can be generally categorized as "tree" charts. These include the following:

- Flowcharts, which use a tree structure to trace a procedure from beginning to end
- Software charts, which use a tree structure to outline the logical steps in a computer program
- Organization charts, which show the hierarchy and relationships between different departments and other units in an organization

Figure 9.16 shows an organizational tree chart.

Pictogram. Pictograms are something of a cross between a bar graph and a chart. Like line graphs, pictograms display numeric data, often by plotting it across x and y axes. But like a chart, pictograms use icons, symbols, and other graphic devices rather than simple lines or bars. Figure 9.17 is a pictogram that uses stick

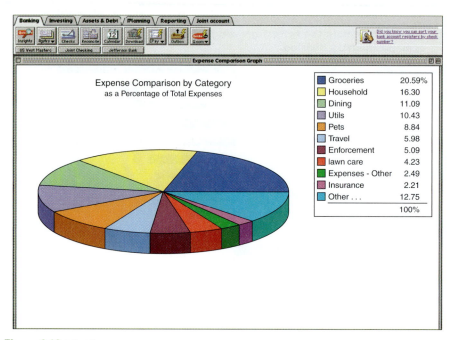

Figure 9.13 Pie Chart.
Source: From Quicken™. Screen shots © Intuit, Inc. All rights reserved. Reprinted by permission.

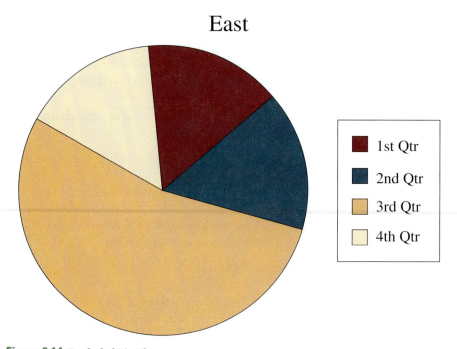

Figure 9.14 Exploded Pie Chart.
Source: Reprinted with permission from Microsoft Corp.

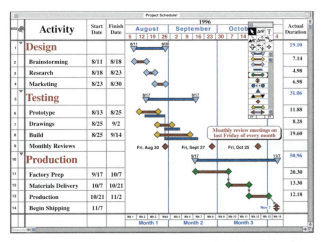

Figure 9.15 Gantt Chart Showing the Schedule for a Manufacturing Project.
Source: Chart created in Fast Track Schedule™.

figure icons to illustrate population at different times. Pictograms are visually appealing and can be especially useful for nontechnical audiences. Graphics software makes it easy to create pictograms.

Illustrations

An illustration is sometimes the best and only way to convey information. Illustrations can be drawings, diagrams, symbols, icons, photographs, maps, or any other visual that relies on pictures rather than on data or words. For example, the

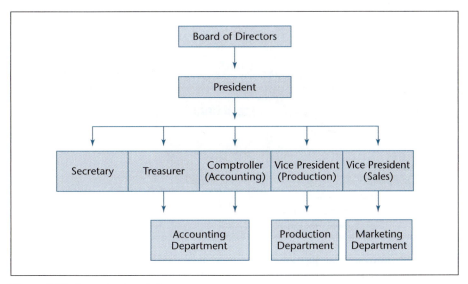

Figure 9.16 Organizational Chart.

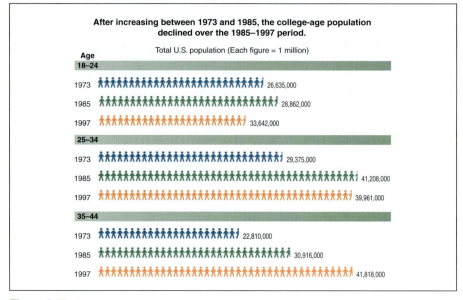

Figure 9.17 Pictogram.
Source: Bureau of the Census.

drawing of the brain in Figure 9.18 accomplishes what plain text cannot: It offers an overview of the brain's shape, the relative sizes of its segments, and its structure. Illustrations are especially valuable when you need to convey spatial relationships or help your audience see what something actually looks like. Drawings can be

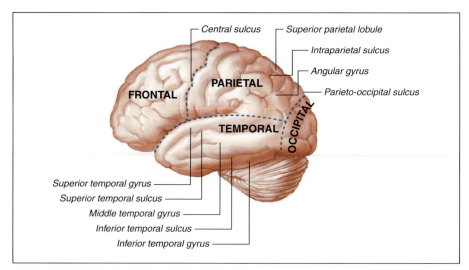

Figure 9.18 Illustration of the Brain.
Source: Davidoff, J. (1991). *Cognition through color.* Cambridge, MA: MIT Press.

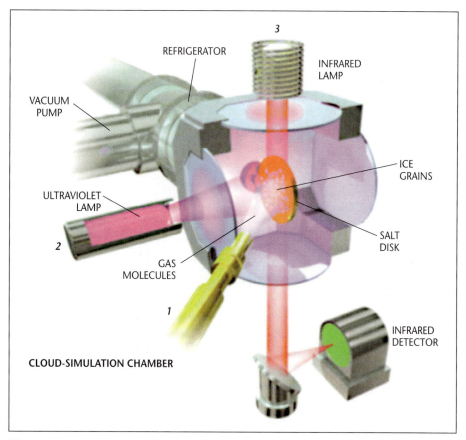

Figure 9.19 **Cloud Simulation Chamber.** Diagrams are useful for illustrating devices.
Source: Bernstein, M. P., et al. (1999, July). Life's far-flung raw materials. *Scientific American,* 42–49. Used by permission of Slim Films.

more effective than photographs, because in a drawing, you can simplify the view, remove any unnecessary features, and focus on what is important.

Diagrams

Diagrams are a useful way to illustrate a device or part of a device. Figure 9.19 is a diagram of a cloud-simulation chamber that provides readers with an understanding of the device as a whole and of the parts that make up the device.

Exploded Diagrams

An exploded diagram can help you explain how a component fits or how a user should assemble a product. The exploded diagram in Figure 9.20 illustrates how to assemble a field mill, which measures fluctuations in the earth's electrical field.

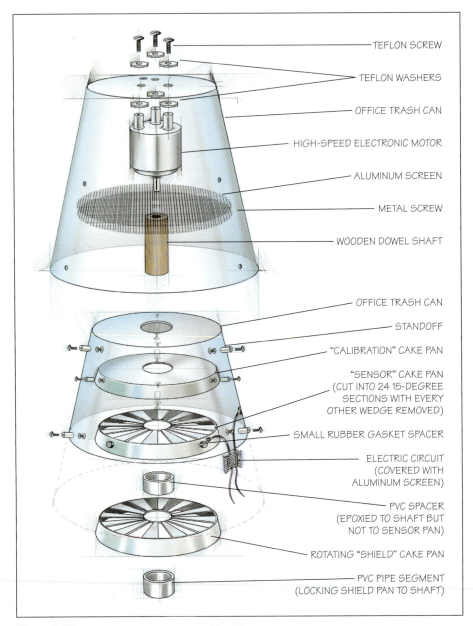

TEFLON SCREW

TEFLON WASHERS

OFFICE TRASH CAN

HIGH-SPEED ELECTRONIC MOTOR

ALUMINUM SCREEN

METAL SCREW

WOODEN DOWEL SHAFT

OFFICE TRASH CAN

STANDOFF

"CALIBRATION" CAKE PAN

"SENSOR" CAKE PAN
(CUT INTO 24 15-DEGREE
SECTIONS WITH EVERY
OTHER WEDGE REMOVED)

SMALL RUBBER GASKET SPACER

ELECTRIC CIRCUIT
(COVERED WITH
ALUMINUM SCREEN)

PVC SPACER
(EPOXIED TO SHAFT BUT
NOT TO SENSOR PAN)

ROTATING "SHIELD" CAKE PAN

PVC PIPE SEGMENT
(LOCKING SHIELD PAN TO SHAFT)

Figure 9.20 **Exploded Diagram of a Field Mill.**
Source: Carlson, S. (1999, July). Detecting earth's electricity. *Scientific American,* 94–95.

Cutaway Diagrams

Cutaway diagrams are extremely useful for showing your audience what is inside of a device or helping explain how a device works. The cutaway diagram in Figure 9.21 illustrates how fireworks operate.

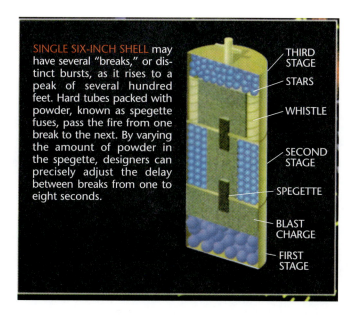

SINGLE SIX-INCH SHELL may have several "breaks," or distinct bursts, as it rises to a peak of several hundred feet. Hard tubes packed with powder, known as spegette fuses, pass the fire from one break to the next. By varying the amount of powder in the spegette, designers can precisely adjust the delay between breaks from one to eight seconds.

THIRD STAGE

STARS

WHISTLE

SECOND STAGE

SPEGETTE

BLAST CHARGE

FIRST STAGE

Figure 9.21 Cutaway Diagram.
Source: Zambelli, G. R., Sr. (1999, July). Aerial fireworks. *Scientific American,* 108.

Symbols and Icons

Symbols and icons are useful ways to make information available to a wide range of audiences. Because such visuals do not rely on text, they are often more easily understood by international audiences, children, and people who may have difficulty reading. Symbols and icons are used in airports, shopping malls, restaurants, and other public places. They are also used in documentation, manuals, or training material, especially when the audience is international. Some of these symbols are developed and approved by the International Standards Organization (ISO). The ISO makes sure the symbols have universal appeal and are standard, whether used in a printed document or on an elevator wall.

The words *symbol* and *icon* are often used interchangeably. Technically, icons tend to resemble the thing they represent: An icon of a file folder on your computer, for example, looks like a real file folder. Symbols can be more abstract; symbols still get the meaning across but may not resemble, precisely, what they represent.

Figure 9.22 shows some international symbols used in airports and other public places. You should have no difficulty guessing what each means.

Note that the first three symbols represent nouns: things or objects. The last symbol (the arrow), however, represents a verb. It indicates that the person looking at it should do something—in this case, turn right. Nouns are easier to represent than verbs, because drawing a thing is easier than drawing an action.

Figure 9.22 **Internationally Recognized Symbols.**
Source: 4YEO.com, http://www.4yeo.com/ICONS/signs/index.htm.

If you are creating a brochure, Web site, manual, or other information product for an international audience, consider using some ISO symbols. Check the ISO Web site at http://www.iso.ch and related sites, which you can locate using a Web search engine.

Wordless Instruction

Many organizations with international audiences rely on wordless instruction: symbols, drawings, and diagrams that convey information completely without words. Flight information cards in the seat pockets of commercial airplanes are an example of wordless instruction, because they use diagrams, photographs, and drawings to explain how passengers can exit an aircraft in the event of an emergency. Figure 9.23 shows how the manufacturer of an automatic coffeemaker uses wordless instruction for its international audience.

Photographs

Photographs are especially useful for showing what something looks like. Unlike a diagram, which often highlights certain parts of an item, photographs show everything. So while a photograph can be extremely useful, it can also provide too much detail or fail to emphasize the parts you want your audience to focus on (see Figure 9.24). To obtain the most effective photograph, use a professional photographer who knows all about angles, lighting, lenses, and special film or digital editing options.

Maps

Besides being visually engaging, maps are especially useful for showing comparisons and helping users visualize position, location, and relationships among various data. The map in Figure 9.25 synthesizes information about various states, regions, and agricultural product values in the United States.

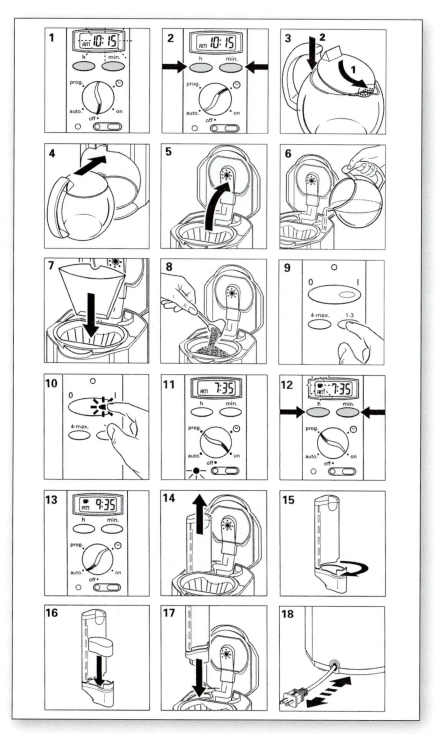

Figure 9.23 Wordless Instructions in a Coffeemaker User's Manual.
Source: Courtesy of Krups, Inc.

Figure 9.24 **Photograph.** Photographs provide a good view of the entire product, such as this electronic car.
Source: Topham © The Image Works. Reprinted by permission.

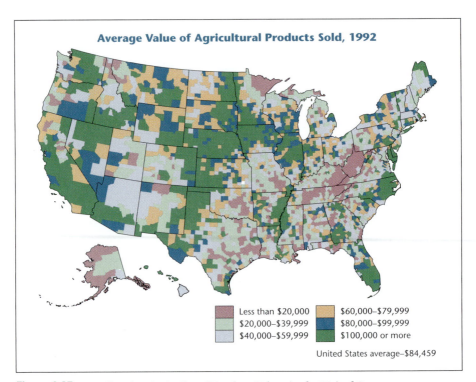

Figure 9.25 **Map Showing Agricultural Product Values in the United States.**
Source: U.S. Department of Commerce.

Visualization and Medical Imaging

Certain techniques from science and medicine can provide powerful and useful visuals for technical communication. Visualization is a process whereby scientists load complex mathematical data into a high-speed computer, and the computer generates an image. The image becomes a tool that can be used to understand the data. For example, images of the surface of Mars are sent back as numbers. Complex software then takes this numeric information and creates an image. The structure of DNA, which is also represented mathematically, can be converted into a visual image that scientists use to envision how DNA works.

Similarly, medical images such as CAT scans, ultrasounds, and photographs of the inside of the body via a laparoscopic camera give us a picture of organs, muscles, and tissue not visible from outside the body. These images, which are often available on the Web, might be appropriate in a medical textbook or in a manual used by physicians to learn about a new imaging product.

Software and Web-Based Images

You can create most of the visuals discussed in this chapter with the wide assortment of computer graphics software, spreadsheets, presentation software, and related products available today. Also, you can find clip art, icons and symbols, medical images, and a vast assortment of other visuals on the Web. (See Chapter 7 for information on copyright and Web-based graphics.)

9.3
Creating graphics for Web use

Consider taking a class in computer graphics. With the continued growth of the Web, the Internet, cable television, personal computing, and other visually based technologies, anyone's career can be enhanced by learning about visuals and computer technology.

Knowing about the following categories of computer software will definitely enhance your abilities as a technical communicator, whether this is your full-time job or just part of your job.

- *Graphics software,* such as Adobe Illustrator or CorelDraw, allows you to draw and illustrate.
- *Photography software,* such as Adobe Photoshop, allows you to work with photographs, scanned images, or other files (such as graphics files taken from the Web). You can manipulate these images to make them fit your document or to make them more appropriate for your audience and purpose. But don't change the items so much that you change the meaning.
- *Presentation software,* such as Microsoft PowerPoint, lets you create slides, computer presentations, and overhead transparency sheets. Other types of presentation software, such as Macromedia Director, are designed to create complex multimedia presentations that include sound and video.

- *Project management software,* such as Microsoft Project, makes it easy to create Gantt charts or organizational tree charts.
- *Spreadsheet software,* such as Microsoft Excel, makes it simple to create pie charts, bar graphs, line graphs, and so on.
- *Word-processing programs,* such as Corel WordPerfect or Microsoft Word, include simple image editors ("draw" feature) and other tools for working with visuals. More sophisticated page layout programs, such as Adobe InDesign, also provide ways for you to work with visuals.

Using Color

Years ago, it was expensive and difficult to use color in anything but the most prestigious documents. Adding color often meant adding cost, because color usually involved cleaning the printing press, using new ink, and then cleaning the press again for a different color job. Smaller color projects, such as overhead transparencies, were often colored by hand. Today, color computer screens and inexpensive color ink-jet printers can make the task, especially for small jobs, far easier and cheaper. Color is an effective tool in a visual, because it helps focus reader attention and makes the document more visually interesting. Color can help you organize your visual. It can also help you orient your reader and emphasize certain areas of your visual or document. Yet too much color, or the wrong color combinations, can be worse than no color at all. Color can greatly enhance how audiences understand technical data, but there is still much we can learn about how people perceive color.

Figure 9.26 illustrates an effective use of color on the Web site for Best Buy, an electronics company. Best Buy uses yellow on its storefront signs, and the Web page continues this theme. The company logo is black type on a bright yellow background. The rest of the Web site integrates various shades of yellow, drawing the reader's eye to key locations. Other text is in blue, which complements the yellow and stands out against the white background. The page does not overuse the yellow.

When using color, remember the following guidelines:

- **Use colors consistently.** A particular color should mean the same thing throughout the visual or the document.
- **Use colors selectively.** Too many colors create "visual noise." Don't mix too many colors, and use colors to help organize the page. Avoid using light colors on a light background: Darker print provides more contrast with a light background.
- **Consider audience and purpose.** Certain audiences and situations may call for certain colors. For example, if your document addresses university students, you might wish to use the school colors. Also, not all audiences will see color as you do. Approximately 9 percent of people have color-deficient vision (Fortner & Meyer, 1997, p. 58), which prevents them from discriminating

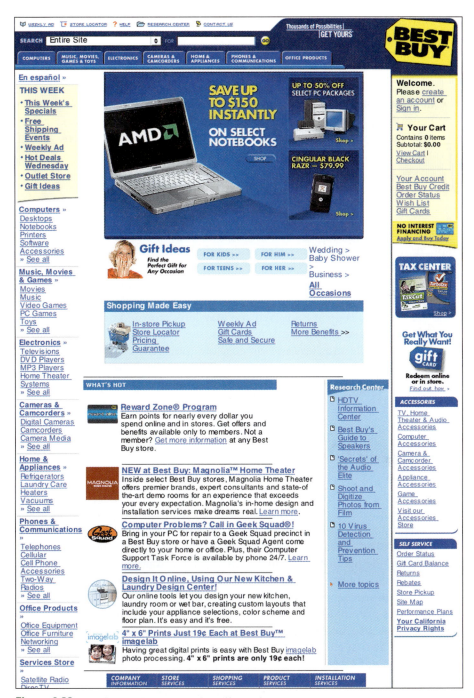

Figure 9.26 A Web Site That Uses Color Effectively.

between certain shades or colors. Whenever possible, test your color choices on audience members.

- **Consider intercultural issues.** Colors have different meanings in different countries. In China, red may mean prosperity, while in the United States, red often indicates danger (Hoft, 1995, p. 267).
- **Consider the medium.** It is cheaper and easier to add color to a Web page or PowerPoint presentation than to use color on a glossy brochure. Consider how your document will be published before making color choices.

Avoiding Visual Noise

Too many visuals, or visuals that are crowded with too much information, create "visual noise." People have an easy time processing visuals, but not if the chart, graph, or other visual is so crowded or disorderly that it cannot be understood. One expert refers to this as "chartjunk" (Tufte, 1990, p. 34): too many bells and whistles at the expense of readable, credible visual information.

Visuals that look fine in one format may appear crowded in another. For instance, what looks great on a Web site may look crowded or out of proportion on a print page. When creating visuals, use a minimalist approach. Keep your designs simple and elegant. Don't use too much clip art, too many colors, or too many images. Test your visuals to be sure they make sense to your audience. If your organization has an in-house graphics designer, ask that person's opinion.

Visuals and Ethics

Although you are perfectly justified in presenting data in their best light, you are ethically responsible for avoiding misrepresentation. Any one set of data can support contradictory conclusions. Even though your numbers may be accurate, your visual display could be misleading. And with currently available computer software, it is easy to create misleading visuals. When bar charts use pictures, not just bars (see "Pictogram" earlier in this chapter), for example, the relative size of the bar and type of picture might convey a particular bias (Kostelnick & Roberts, 1998, p. 292). In another example, a brighter color on one bar and lighter colors on another might prevent a reader from seeing all the data equally.

Graphs can also be confusing or misleading if the axes are not labeled. Readers assume that an axis begins at zero, but this may not always be the case if an image is not labeled. Image labels can also be confusing if they are too small for readers to see or, worse yet, missing. Photographs and other images can easily be manipulated using software. Copyright (see Chapter 7) is also a consideration, because an image you obtain on the Web, for example, may be protected by copyright.

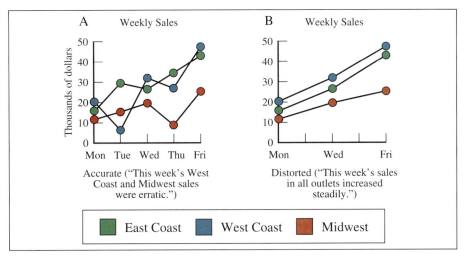

Figure 9.27 An Accurate Line Graph and a Distorted Version. Selective omission of data points in graph (b) causes the lines to flatten, implying a steady increase rather than an erratic pattern of sales, as more accurately shown in graph (a).

Aim for fairness and accuracy. Label the axes of charts and graphs. Indicate the source of your data. Use color appropriately and evenly. If your visual accompanies text, indicate how this visual supports the textual information.

Without getting bogged down in needless detail, an accurate visual includes all essential data. Figure 9.27 shows how distortion occurs when data that would provide a complete picture are selectively omitted. Graph (A) accurately depicts the numeric relationships measured from the value scale. In graph (B), too few points are plotted to give an accurate picture of sales trends.

Decide carefully what to include and what to leave out of your visual display.

Cultural Considerations

Although groups such as the ISO have tried to standardize a wide range of visual information across cultures, you will not always use ISO symbols for your visuals. Visual communication does have global appeal, but charts, graphs, tables, and other visual forms are not universal. As one expert notes, "Visual communication can make cultural assumptions that are inappropriate or offensive" (Hoft, 1995, p. 4). Not all cultures read from left to right, so a chart that is supposed to be read left to right that is read in the opposite direction could be misunderstood. Color is also a cultural consideration. Representations of images that might be used in a computer icon or diagram, for example, may be culturally offensive if they portray sensitive images, such as certain animals (the cow in Hindu culture) or gender roles (women with bare heads in certain Arabic cultures).

Checklist for Visual Communication

- Does the visual serve a legitimate purpose (clarification, not mere ornamentation)?
- Is this the best type of visual for your purpose and audience?
- Is the level of complexity appropriate for the audience?
- Is the visual titled and numbered?
- Are all patterns in the visual identified by label or legend?
- Are all values or units of measurement specified (grams per ounce, millions of dollars)?
- Is color used tastefully and appropriately?
- Do the visual relationships represent the numeric relationships accurately?
- Are all data sources cited?
- Has written permission been obtained for reproducing or adapting a visual from a copyrighted source in any type of work to be published?
- Is the visual introduced, discussed, interpreted, integrated with the text, and referred to by number?
- Is the visual easy to locate?
- Is the visual uncrowded, uncluttered, and free of "visual noise"?
- Is the visual ethically acceptable?
- Does the document respect users' cultural values?

Exercises

1. Find an article in a newspaper, journal, or magazine that does not include visuals necessary to support the communication purpose or meet the audience's needs. Analyze the article, and identify where visuals would be helpful. Make a list of the visuals you would recommend to the article's author or the publication's editor.

2. From the list you drew up in Exercise 1, select two proposed visuals and create them using the graphics component of a word-processing program or graphics software. In a presentation to your class, explain how additional visuals would improve the usability of your article, and show the visuals you created.

3. **FOCUS on WRITING.** Looking at printed materials and sites on the Web, find an example of each of the kinds of visuals discussed in this chapter (diagram, table, pie chart, simple bar chart, deviation bar graph, etc.). Critique each visual: Does it convey the information effectively? Would a different type of visual be more effective? Is visual noise distracting? What would you do to make the visual more effective or more appropriate to audience and purpose? Write up your findings as a short memo to your instructor.

4. Obtain an instruction manual for a piece of technology with which you are familiar. Before looking at the manual, list the visuals you think might be included in the manual and consider the role each of those visuals would play in making the manual usable. Then compare your list with the visuals that are actually in the manual, and analyze the differences between the manual and your list:

   - For visuals that are in the manual and on your list, compare the role in the manual and the role that you defined.
   - For visuals in the manual but not on your list, evaluate the role and effectiveness of the visuals. Do you agree with the decision to include those visuals in the manual? Why or why not?
   - For visuals not in the manual but on your list, evaluate the role that you defined and the effectiveness of that segment of the manual as it exists without the visual. Do you agree with the decision not to include those visuals in the manual? Why or why not?

 ## The Collaboration Window

Return to the teams you worked in for the collaborative exercise at the end of Chapter 2, and examine the audience and purpose statements you created for the survival guide for incoming students. (If you have not done the exercise in Chapter 2, review it now.) List the topics you are likely to include in the guide. Then list the visuals that you believe would effectively support the purpose of each section of the guide. As a team, present your plans to the class, explaining the rationale for each proposed visual.

 ## The Global Window

The International Standards Organization (ISO) is a group devoted to standardizing a range of material, including technical specifications and visual information. If you've ever been in an airport and seen the many international signs directing travelers to the restroom or to the smoking area (or informing them not to smoke), you have seen ISO signs. Go to the ISO Web site at http://www.iso.ch to learn about ISO symbols. Prepare a short report and presentation for class explaining how these symbols are developed. Show some of the symbols, and explain why these work for international communication.

Technical Communication Situations and Applications

Communication Situations

The three chapters in Part Two describe a variety of communication situations and include information about approaches and formats that are in most cases appropriate for these situations. Depending on your particular profession, company, and unique communication situation, these categories may not always be a perfect fit. Ultimately, all situations are unique, and your choices should be driven by a clear and thorough understanding of your audience, purpose, and the company or organization. For example, a situation that might call for a long report in one company might be handled by a memo or short report in another. One organization might produce all of its user documentation in printed books, while another might place all of this information on a Web site. And in some companies, email is the preferred method of communicating, while in others, a combination of email and paper memos is the norm.

Moreover, in actual workplace applications, the categories in these chapters usually overlap. As described here, they are meant to allow you to practice discrete forms of writing and communication: writing a definition or description, writing a memo, writing a set of brief instructions. But on the job, you may need to write a memo that contains some specifications and some description, or you may need to write a short report that contains some documentation and proposes a set of actions for the company to take.

Use these three chapters as opportunities to practice and explore. In class, discuss any experiences you may have had on the job or during an internship that differ from what you read in this book. Consider creating a class Web site that lists the most common communication situations you and your classmates encounter, and then list the types of documents you most frequently work on.

Here are the situations described in the next three chapters:

Everyday situations. Some situations require correspondence that takes place on a regular basis in most organizations (such as email or memos).

Product-oriented situations. Other situations require you to describe, explain, document, or market a technical product or service.

Complex situations. Still other situations require more complex approaches, which may include long reports or proposals.

Each chapter ends with a set of exercises. The Web site for this textbook (http://www.ablongman.com/gurak) contains links to sample documents online as well as exercises related to different document types.

No matter what the circumstance or the document, certain guidelines always apply:

- Perform a thorough audience and purpose analysis.
- Create your product with usability in mind.
- Carefully select a visual format and medium.
- Consider copyright issues.

Everyday Communication Situations

Email

Email has become a major form of business and technical communication, surpassing much of what used to be accomplished with paper letters and memos. Unlike paper, email can be used to quickly and efficiently address an individual, a group within an organization, or a group of interested users from outside the organization. It can reach thousands of readers in a matter of seconds, and these readers can continue forwarding the email message to others. Although paper documents can be photocopied and redistributed, few people take the time to do so. But with email, all it takes is one or two simple keystrokes, and the message has been forwarded.

Email is extremely useful in situations where people are in different time zones or have different working schedules: You can send an email at 2:00 A.M. if you are a night owl, and your early-bird colleague can read it in the morning. Email is useful if you want an electronic paper trail to track the communication—useful for helping you remember details about a project and for legal reasons, too.

Audience and Purpose Analysis

Unlike paper documents, with email you don't have much control over the final audience. You may intend for your note to reach only a small group of people, but because email is so easily forwarded, your audience could turn out to be much larger. People also tend to be more casual and off-the-cuff on email, sometimes more so than they would be in person; therefore, audience consideration becomes crucial. Suppose, for example, that after a long week of work on a particularly tough engineering design project, you send a quick email message to another manager. In your message, you complain about one of the engineers not holding up his end of things. You quickly press "Send" and head out the door. On Monday, at a status meeting, you are surprised to find that your message was forwarded to several other engineers, and they're talking about it! Clearly, your original message was not intended for them, but either by accident or on purpose, someone forwarded it along.

So be sure you understand a cardinal rule about audience, purpose, and email: Always assume that your message will go far beyond its original recipient, and don't send anything via email that isn't appropriate for a wider audience or that would make you uncomfortable if used for a different purpose.

Types of Email

Email messages usually follow the same basic format, with a memo style heading (Subject, Date, From, To), but often use salutations (Dear Laura) and closings (Thanks, Sam) like a letter. Email can be used for a variety of purposes and situations: to exchange information, share ideas, schedule meetings, and collaborate on work projects (see Figure 10.1).

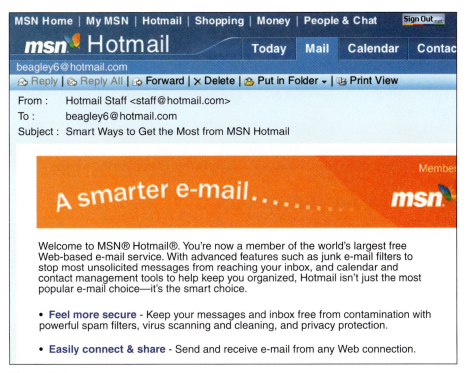

Figure 10.1 An Email Message Using Hotmail.

Typical Components of Email

Most email messages have the following parts.

Header information. This information includes the standard fields from a memo (Subject, Date, From, To). Also, depending on the email program, the header may include more detailed information, such as the following:

- *Host server:* the computer that generated the message
- *Time of receipt:* the exact time the computer received the message
- *Return path:* an email address the computer can use if the message bounces (fails to reach its destination)
- *Message ID number:* a number that the network uses to track the individual message

The header also includes a list of other recipients who received the message as a courtesy copy ("cc").

Message body. The text of the message.

Attachments. Formatted documents, software, photographs, scanned images, and other files can be sent as attachments to an email message.

Usability Considerations

Keep it short. Readers are impatient and don't want to scroll down through long screens full of information. Also, unbroken text is hard to read on the screen. So keep email messages brief and to the point. If you need to, put larger, related files of information on a Web page or use an attachment, where readers can read at their leisure.

Break up the information. Don't write one long block of text with no paragraph breaks. Use numbered lists, headings, and indents to break up the message.

Include links to Web sites. Include links to other relevant Web sites when necessary.

Don't send huge attachments without checking first. Not all email browsers are capable of handling attachments (formatted files, photos, images). Also, if recipients have slow Internet connections or pay by the minute for connect time, they will be annoyed by large attachments that take forever to download. Before sending an attachment, inquire as to what file types the recipient's equipment can handle and if his or her browser can accept attachments.

Pay attention to spelling and formality. Email users lean toward an informal writing style. Even though many email programs contain spell-checkers, people rarely use them. Yet a correctly spelled message will be more credible than a sloppy one. Also, when composing a message for someone you don't know or someone in a position of authority, begin with a formal salutation ("Dear Professor May").

Avoid flaming. *Flaming* refers to email that is unnecessarily angry and makes extreme personal attacks. Because email users are not communicating face-to-face, they sometimes use email to let off steam. Always read over your message, especially in a tense or delicate situation, before sending it. Strive for messages that are informative and useful, not emotionally charged.

Don't use ALL CAPS. Words in all capital letters are hard to read. And in email, they have a special meaning: All caps is the equivalent of shouting. So don't shout unless you mean to.

Use smiley faces sparingly. Smiley faces, made from a colon, dash, and right-hand parenthesis :-), are used to convey humor. Use these and other "emoticons" infrequently, and don't use them in a formal message or in a message to someone you don't know.

Checklist for Email

Netiquette
- Do you check and answer your email daily?
- Have you checked your distribution list before mailing, to verify that the message reaches only intended recipients?
- Do you avoid flaming?
- Have you chosen an alternative medium for any formal correspondence?
- Before sending a long attachment, have you checked with the recipient?

Ethical, Legal, and Interpersonal Implications
- Have you avoided writing anything you couldn't say face-to-face?
- Have humor and wisecracks been avoided?
- Have you avoided using email for confidential information?
- Have you avoided using the workplace network for personal correspondence?
- Before forwarding an incoming message, have you obtained permission from the sender?

Readability
- Is there a clear subject line?
- Do you refer clearly to the message to which you are responding?
- Are sentences and paragraphs short?
- Do you avoid paragraph indentations and FULL CAPS?
- Are formal salutations and closings used, when appropriate?
- Are smiley faces used sparingly?
- Have you included a signature section?
- Have you proofread carefully?

Memos

People in almost every profession use memos to communicate business or technical information within the company, to outside vendors, to clients, or to other relevant parties. Today, the paper memo is rapidly being replaced by email. Even so, paper memos are often called for, especially if the situation is more formal or the discussion is somewhat lengthy. Use a memo when you need to

- Transmit information to a group
- Make a short evaluation or recommendation
- Distribute minutes from a meeting
- Provide follow-up on a discussion

Different organizations have different standards and practices for memos. For example, at some companies, memos are used only to convey formal information and are always written on letterhead. Other, less formal information is sent via email.

Audience and Purpose Analysis

To determine the length, content, tone, and approach of a memo, pay attention to the various audience members who will receive it. Some companies use standard memo distribution lists: a list for all managers, a list for all software developers, and so on. The purpose of your memo should be clear: Is it to inform your audience? To persuade people? To convince them to take action? The organization and writing style of the memo should match this purpose.

Types of Memos

Memos cover every conceivable topic. See Figure 10.2 for one example. Common types are described next.

Memo of transmittal. Like a letter of transmittal, a transmittal memo is used with a package of material, such as a report, a manuscript, or a proposal. The transmittal memo introduces the material, explains what is enclosed, and offers short comments or information not provided in the document itself. Transmittal memos may be as simple as a sentence or a bulleted list describing what is enclosed.

Meeting minutes. Memos are often used to transmit minutes from a meeting. If the minutes go beyond two pages, the memo is probably not the best format, and you might want to opt for a short report instead.

Brief report. The memo format is often used as the basis for very brief reports. Instead of writing a longer report with great detail, the writer will create a short, concise version, using the basic template of a memo structure. You will learn more about short reports later in this chapter.

Typical Components of a Memo

Memos differ across organizations and professions, but most paper memos contain the following parts.

Name of organization. Most paper memos are printed on company letterhead, so you won't need to actually insert the name or address of the organization.

The word *memo* or *memorandum*. This can be centered or set flush with the left margin.

GREENTREE BIONOMICS, INC.

MEMORANDUM

TO:	D. SPRING, PERSONNEL DIRECTOR
FROM:	M. NOLL, BIOLOGY DIVISION
SUBJECT:	NEED TO HIRE MORE PERSONNEL
DATE:	1/16/2007
CC:	E. BRAGIN, CHEMISTRY DIVISION

With 26 active employees, Greentree has been unable to keep up with scheduled contract. As a result, we have a contract backlog of roughly $500,000. To increase our production and ease the workload, I recommend that we hire three general lab assistants.

I have attached a short report outlining the cost benefits of these hires. Could we meet sometime next week to discuss this in detail? I will contact you on Monday.

Figure 10.2 Sample Memo. This memo informs employees about a workplace hiring situation.

To, From, Subject, Date. These four fields are set flush with the left margin and followed by a colon:

To:	Julian Barker
From:	Riley O'Donnell
Subject:	Internal price list
Date:	15 January 2006

Sometimes, the word *Re* is used in place of *Subject*. Also, these fields may occur in a different order, depending on the particular situation. In some companies, the order may be Date, To, From, Subject.

Memo body. The body copy should be set in several short paragraphs. Use lists to display prices, specifications, or other features. Use the direct approach pattern (see Figure 10.6 on page 201) whenever possible, and get to the point quickly.

Typist's initials, distribution and enclosure notations. These items are described under "Letters" and are used in a similar manner with memos.

Usability Considerations

Distribute the memo to all the right people. With email this is easy because you can send it to an electronic list of names. With a paper memo, however, each copy needs to be placed in a mailbox or mailed in an envelope. You may need to ask for assistance with this task; office staff often have preaddressed labels you can use.

Put the important information in an area of emphasis. Don't bury the important information in a large block of text midway through the memo. Preview the key point in the subject line, and follow the top-down approach if possible, presenting the important information clearly in the first paragraph. (See also Figure 10.6.)

Keep it short and to the point. Unless you are writing a short report in memo format (see "Short Reports"), keep your memo as brief as possible, limiting it to one page if you can.

Check spelling, grammar, and style. Run the spelling and grammar checkers, but also proofread or ask a colleague to proofread the memo.

Make sure all appropriate parties receive a copy. No one appreciates being left out of the loop, so be sure to include everyone who should be informed.

Letters

Although many people use email in place of letters, traditional paper letters are still an important part of technical communication. Letters are used to address a single individual, a committee, or an organization. Letters can be short or long, depending on the context. Letters also tend to be more formal than memos, email, spoken communication, or voice mail messages, because letter writers tend to be more careful than they would be with electronic communication. A letter takes time to write, print, and proofread, and in that time, a writer may decide to make a few changes or perhaps to not even send the letter at all, whereas email is quicker to compose and send.

Use a letter when you need to

- Explain something you've enclosed, such as your résumé, a report, or a manuscript
- Inquire about a product, service, or organization
- Complain about or praise a product or service
- Request technical information

Different professions have different standards for letter writing. In most engineering and science professions, letters are generally short and to the point. In certain circumstances, a longer letter may be required to provide the appropriate amount of information.

Audience and Purpose Analysis

To determine the length, content, tone, and approach to a letter, pay attention to audience and purpose. Imagine, for example, that you are a technical writer working on a new Web site, and you order updated font software. After installing the software, you discover that it does not perform as promised. The company from which you purchased the software has a strict no-refund policy on opened software. You are rather angry about the situation, so you decide to write a letter to the software manufacturer.

Who will be the audience for this letter? What is the primary purpose of your correspondence? Too often, people in this situation don't consider that their actual purpose is to obtain a refund, not to express anger. Consider the following opening:

> When I learned that your software does not perform as promised, and when I could not return it to the store, I was furious. How could you sell such a defective product?

Instead of making the recipient defensive, try to establish common ground and show that you are a reasonable person seeking a reasonable solution:

> I have always been a loyal user of your company's products, so I was disappointed that this software did not perform as stated in your marketing material. Because CompCity does not allow software returns, I ask that you refund the price. I will be glad to send the product back to you.

Along with your choice of words and tone, consider the following:

- Address your letter to the correct person or persons.
- Understand how that person will feel about your request. If the person receives hundreds of letters a day, for example, he or she might feel short-tempered and might appreciate a friendly—but determined—tone.
- Make sure other interested parties receive copies of the letter.

Types of Letters

There are many types of letters, including the following.

Letter of transmittal. The transmittal letter accompanies a package of material, such as a report, a manuscript, or a proposal. Usually more formal than a transmittal memo and addressed to a recipient outside your organization, the transmittal letter introduces the material, explains what is enclosed, and provides any additional comments or information not offered in the document itself. Transmittal letters often include a sentence describing what is enclosed, such as

> This package contains a 12-page proposal, a price list, and my business card.

Make sure you address your transmittal letter to the correct person.

10.1

Additional sample cover letter

Cover letter for a job application. One type of transmittal letter is the cover letter that accompanies a résumé and job application (see Figure 10.3). The purpose of a job application cover letter is to explain how your credentials fit this particular job and to convey a sufficiently professional persona for the prospective employer to decide that you warrant an interview. Another purpose is to highlight some specific qualifications or skills. For example, you may have "C++ programming" listed on your résumé under the category "Programming Languages." But for one particular job application, you may wish to accentuate this item. You could do so in your cover letter:

> You will note on my résumé that I am experienced with C++ programming. In fact, I am not only a skilled C++ programmer, but I have also taught evening programming classes at Metro Community College.

Make sure the first paragraph of your cover letter states the position you are applying for, especially if you are applying to the Human Resources Department. For example, you could begin as shown on page 196:

203 Elmwood Avenue
San Jose, CA 95111
April 22, 2006

Sara Costanza
Personnel Director
Liberty International, Inc.
Lansdowne, PA 19050

Dear Ms. Costanza:

Please consider my application for a junior management position at
your Lake Geneva resort. I will graduate from San Jose City College
on May 30 with an Associate of Arts degree in Hotel and Restaurant
Management. Dr. H. V. Garlid, my nutrition professor, described his
experience as a consultant for Liberty International and encouraged
me to apply.

For two years I worked as a part-time desk clerk, and I am now the
desk manager at a 200-unit resort. This experience, combined with
earlier customer relations work in a variety of situations, has given
me a clear and practical understanding of customers' needs and
expectations.

As an amateur chef, I know of the effort, attention, and patience
required to prepare fine food. Moreover, my skiing and sailing
background might be assets to your resort's recreation program.

I have confidence in my hospitality management skills. My experience
and education have prepared me to work well with others and to
respond creatively to changes, crises, and added responsibilities.

Should my background meet your needs, please phone me any
weekday after 4 p.m. at (214) 316-2419.

Sincerely,

James D. Purdy
James D. Purdy

Enclosure

Figure 10.3 **Sample Cover Letter for a Job Application.**

> Please consider my application for the senior software position advertised in this week's *Chronicle*.

Inquiry letter. You may need to inquire about a product, service, set of specifications, or other item. As with most technical communication, keep your inquiry letter short and to the point. Follow the direct approach (see Figure 10.6 on page 201), and state clearly at the outset what you are requesting and why. Make sure you provide multiple ways for the recipient of the material to reach you: email, fax, phone, surface mail.

Word-processing templates. When discussing letters, it's important to note that most word-processing software (such as Microsoft Word) allows you to select from templates or predesigned letter formats. These templates usually provide fields for you to insert your name, your company name, and your message. Some templates provide background artwork or other decorative features. As tempting as it may be to simply choose a template, make sure the one you use is appropriate for your audience and purpose. If not, either use a blank document, or modify the template to suit your needs. Figure 10.4 shows a selection of typical word-processing templates.

Typical Components of a Letter

Most letters have the same basic components. Many organizations have set formats they follow for writing letters, so depending on where you work, these parts may appear in different locations on the page. But in general, a letter contains the elements listed here.

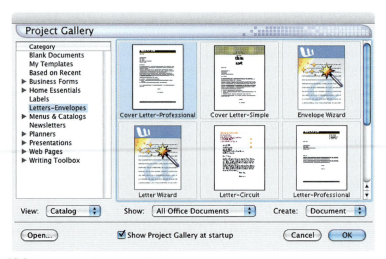

Figure 10.4 **Letter Templates in Microsoft Word.** You can choose from a variety of templates designed for different situations, or even customize one to fulfill your needs.
Source: Reprinted with permission from Microsoft Corp.

Heading and date. If your stationery has a company letterhead, simply include the date two lines below the letterhead at the right or left margin. On blank stationery, include your return address and the date (but not your name):

> 154 Sea Lane
> Harwich, MA 02646
> July 15, 2003

Use the Postal Service's two-letter abbreviations (e.g., MA for Massachusetts, NY for New York, ND for North Dakota) in your heading, in the inside address, and on the envelope.

Inside address. Two line spaces (returns) after the heading and date information, flush against the left margin, is the inside address (the address to which you are sending the letter):

> Dr. Ann Mello, Dean of Students
> Western University
> 30 Mogul Hill Road
> Stowe, VT 05672

When possible, address a specific person and include his or her title.

Salutation. The salutation, two line spaces (returns) below the inside address, begins with "Dear" and ends with a colon ("Dear Ms. Smith:"). If you don't know the person's name, use the position title ("Dear Manager:"). Only address the recipient by first name if that is the way you would address that individual in person. Examples of salutations include

> Dear Ms. Martinez:
> Dear Managing Editor:
> Dear Professor Lee:

Remember not to use sexist language, such as "Dear Sir" or "Dear Madam." Instead, use the position title ("Dear Sales Manager").

Body text. Typically, your letter text begins two line spaces (returns) below the salutation. Workplace letters typically include

- A brief introductory paragraph identifying you and your purpose
- One or more body paragraphs containing the details of your message
- A conclusion paragraph that sums up and encourages action

Keep the paragraphs short whenever possible. If the body section is too long, divide it into shorter paragraphs or place some items in a list (see Figure 10.5).

Complimentary close. The closing, two line spaces (returns) below the last line of text, should parallel the level of formality used in the salutation and should reflect your relationship to the recipient (polite but not overly intimate). The following closings are listed in decreasing order of formality:

> Sincerely, Very truly yours, *or* Sincerely yours,
>
> Respectfully,
>
> Cordially,
>
> Best wishes, *or* Warmest wishes,
>
> Best regards, *or* Regards,

Align the closing flush against the left margin.

Signature. Type your full name and title on the fourth and fifth lines below the closing, aligned flush left. Sign your name in the triple space between the closing and your typed name.

> Sincerely,
>
> *Meredith M. Curtin*
>
> Meredith M. Curtin
>
> Principal Researcher

Specialized Components of a Letter

Some letters also have specialized parts, such as the following.

Attention line. Use an attention line when you write to an organization and do not know your recipient's name but are directing the letter to a specific department or position. Place the attention line flush with the left margin two line spaces (returns) below the inside address.

> Glaxol Industries, Inc.
>
> 232 Rogaline Circle
>
> Missoula, MT 69808
>
> ATTENTION: Director of Research and Development

Subject line. Typically, subject lines are used with memos, but if the recipient is not expecting your letter, a subject line is a good way of catching a busy reader's attention.

LEVERETT LAND & TIMBER COMPANY, INC. | creative land use
quality building materials
architectural construction

January 17, 2006

Mr. Thomas E. Muffin
Clearwater Drive
Amherst, MA 01022

Dear Mr. Muffin:

I have examined the damage to your home caused by the ruptured water pipe
and consider the following repairs to be necessary and of immediate concern:

> Exterior:
>> Remove plywood soffit panels beneath overhangs
>> Replace damaged insulation and plumbing
>> Remove all built-up ice within floor framing
>> Replace plywood panels and finish as required
>
> Northeast Bedroom—Lower Level:
>> Remove and replace all sheetrock, including closet
>> Remove and replace all door casings and baseboards
>> Remove and repair windowsill extensions and moldings
>> Remove and reinstall electric heaters
>> Respray ceilings and repaint all surfaces

This appraisal of damage repair does not include repairs and/or replacements
of carpets, tile work, or vinyl flooring. Also, this appraisal assumes that the
plywood subflooring on the main level has not been severely damaged.

Leverett Land & Timber Company, Inc., proposes to furnish the necessary
materials and labor to perform the described damage repairs for the amount of
six thousand one hundred and eighty dollars ($6,180).

Sincerely,

G.A. Jackson

Gerald A. Jackson, President
GAJ/ob
Enc. Itemized estimate

Phone: 410-555-9879   Fax: 410-555-6874   Email: llt@yonet.com

Figure 10.5 **Sample Business Letter.**

> SUBJECT: *New patent for hybrid wheat crop*

Place the subject line below the inside address or attention line. You can underline the subject to make it more prominent.

Typist's initials, distribution and enclosure notations. These items typically go at the bottom of the page. If someone else types your letter for you (common in the days of typewriters but rare today), your initials and your typist's initials appear as follows:

> GLJ/pl

If you distribute copies of your letter to other recipients, indicate this by inserting the notation "cc." This notation once stood for "carbon copy," but no one uses carbon paper anymore, so now it is said to stand for "courtesy copy."

> cc: J. Hailey, S. Patel

Similarly, if you enclose any items, you can note this at the bottom of the page:

> Enclosures: Certified checks (2), KBX plans (1)

Usability Considerations

Organize for the situation. You can choose from two basic organizing patterns. The first is *direct,* in which you begin with the most important information (your request or the conclusion of your ideas) and then give the details supporting your case. The second is *indirect,* in which you start with the details and build toward a request or conclusion.

Figure 10.6 illustrates each approach. A direct approach is usually better, because readers can get right to the main point. But when you have to convey bad news or make a request that could be received unfavorably, it's often better to build your case first and then make your claim or request toward the end. When complaining about a faulty product, for example, a direct approach would probably be better, because the customer service person, who could easily receive hundreds of letters each day, will get to the point quickly. But for a letter requesting a raise in your consulting fee, an indirect approach is more appropriate.

Address the letter properly. A letter that is addressed to the wrong person will not be very effective. Before sending a letter, spend time researching the name of a person to whom you should send it.

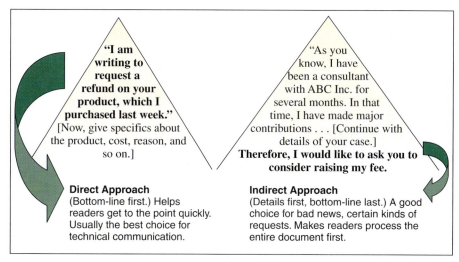

Direct Approach
(Bottom-line first.) Helps readers get to the point quickly. Usually the best choice for technical communication.

Indirect Approach
(Details first, bottom-line last.) A good choice for bad news, certain kinds of requests. Makes readers process the entire document first.

Figure 10.6 **Deciding on Your Writing Approach.** It is appropriate to use a direct approach most of the time, but use an indirect approach when you have negative information to convey. If you do use the indirect approach, keep your information short and to the point, so your reader does not need to read a long narrative to get to the point.

Use language at an appropriate technical level. If your letter is too technical, recipients will not understand it. But if your letter is too simplistic, you may insult or bore your reader. Learn all you can about your audience's level of expertise so you can choose appropriate language.

Include all necessary information. If you are writing to ask for an updated version of your software but you forget to include the current version number, the recipient will not be able to help. If you are lucky, that person will try to reach you and ask for more information. But quite possibly, your letter will be moved to the "get back to this" pile, and you may never receive a reply. Provide all the details your recipient will need.

Check spelling of proper nouns. Make sure you spell the name of the recipient, the company, and the product correctly. If the company is known as "Electronics, Inc.," don't use "Electronic Corp." And it may sound obvious, but be sure you've spelled your own name correctly, too!

Clearly state the main point. Whether you use a direct or indirect organizational pattern, state your main point clearly and directly. If you want a refund on a product, *make sure* you say, "I am writing to request a refund" or something equally direct.

Avoid puffed-up language. Avoid the stuffy, puffed-up, tired phrases some writers think they need to make their letters sound important. Here are a few of the old standards with some clearer, more direct translations:

Avoid	Use instead
As per your request	As you requested
Contingent upon receipt of	As soon as we receive
Please be advised that I	I
In accordance with your request	As you requested
Due to the fact that	Because

In the legal profession (and others), certain phrases such as these are known as "terms of art" and connote a specific concept. In these cases, you may not be able to avoid such phrases. But otherwise, strive for a simple, clear style.

Checklist for Letters

Content
- Is the letter addressed to the correct and specifically named person?
- Have you identified the name and position of your recipient?
- Does the letter contain all of the typical components?
- Does the letter have all needed specialized components?
- Is the letter's main point clearly stated?
- Is all the necessary information included?

Arrangement
- Does the introduction immediately engage the reader and lead naturally to the body section?
- Is the direct or indirect pattern used appropriately?
- Does the conclusion encourage the reader to act?

Style
- Is the language at an appropriate technical level?
- Is the tone conversational (free of puffed-up language)?
- Does the tone reflect your relationship with the recipient?
- Are spelling and grammar correct?

Résumés

The current job market is very competitive; companies may receive hundreds or even thousands of applications for only a few available positions. In order for you to stand out from the competition, you must have a résumé that appears attractive to potential employers. Attractive résumés look good, read easily, and provide information the employer needs to determine if the person should be interviewed. Employers initially spend only 15 to 45 seconds looking at a résumé; during this scan, they are looking for qualifications that fit their needs. Therefore, a good résumé is one that responds to the needs of the potential employer.

Audience and Purpose Analysis

Each résumé you send should be tailored to the wants and needs of the potential employer. If most recent work experience is considered most valuable by an employer, it should be listed first, rather than education or personal information. Since each employer and employment situation is different, your résumé will change as you apply for different jobs or gain new skills and experiences. The purpose of each résumé is to impress your potential employer enough for you to be scheduled for an interview or for your application to be passed along in the employment process.

Typical Components of a Résumé

There are several basic components to a résumé: contact information, career objectives, education, work experience, personal data, personal interests, and references.

10.2
Additional sample résumé

Contact information. Be sure to provide current information where prospective employers can reach you; if you are between addresses, be sure to provide both sets of information and check each regularly. Much business communication is now done via email or phone, so be sure that both your email address and your phone number are accurate.

Career objectives. This is your opportunity to spell out to your employer what kind of job you want. Your objectives project an image of who you are to your potential employer. To give a distinct and positive image, you need to be specific about your goals and avoid vague statements (see Figures 10.7 and 10.8).

Education. When listing your education, begin with your most recent school and work backward. You need to include the name of the school, degree completed, year completed, and your major and minor (if applicable). If your grade point average or class rank is favorable, list them. In addition to degrees, be sure to list any coursework that might be relevant to the position you are applying for.

Work experience. List your most recent job first and then earlier jobs. Include the dates you were employed, the employers' names, and their contact information; also be sure to describe your exact job duties and any promotions and honors received. If it is to your advantage, specifically state why you left each job. In addition, include military experience and relevant volunteer work.

Personal data. By law, you are not required to reveal your sex, religion, race, age, national origin, disability, or marital status; however, if this information is relevant and might be helpful in attaining your goal, you should include it. (See Figures 10.7 and 10.8.)

Personal interests. List any hobbies or interests that are relevant to the position that you are applying for. Also list any work-related skills such as foreign languages, computer skills, and other applicable skills.

References. List three to five people who have agreed to provide strong assessments of your qualifications. It is key that these people be informed about your job search, know you well, and be able to speak concretely on your behalf. Your references should not be family members but rather former employers, professors, and community figures who know you well.

Organization of a Résumé

The organization of your résumé should emphasize your strongest skills and experiences. Your experiences will dictate the organization of your résumé. If you wish to show a pattern of job experience, you should use *reverse chronological organization*. This organization lists your most recent experience first and then moves backward in time toward your earlier experiences. If you have gaps in your job record, you should use *functional organization,* which allows you to focus on skills, abilities, and experiences instead of on employment chronology. *Combined organization* is often used when résumés are to be electronically scanned; this method combines highlighting specific job skills with reverse chronological ordering.

Online Résumé Services

There are a variety of online sources that will help you get your résumé written and placed in a database for potential employers to see. Web services like Monster.com give you a variety of options when it comes to posting your résumé on the Web. You can use a service's own template to create a résumé tailored to its system, upload your own electronic résumé, or copy and paste your résumé into the service's system. With so many employers searching the Web for future employees, an online service is a good way to get your résumé seen by potential employers.

New Types of Résumés

In today's information age, there are various new types of résumés, each addressing a different audience. Besides the standard print résumé, there is the scannable résumé, a résumé made from a template, and an electronic résumé.

Scannable résumés. Many companies feed résumés through an optical scanner that then stores the résumés electronically in a database. Such a system allows an

LISA SAMPLE
1234 Main Street, Minneapolis, Minnesota 55105
home: (612) 555-1234, cell: (612) 555-5678, email: lsample@umn.edu

OBJECTIVE

To obtain a challenging entry-level position as a Clinical Dietitian in a hospital or clinic setting.

EDUCATION

Master of Science in Nutrition, January 2005. University of Minnesota – Twin Cities, GPA: 3.86.

Bachelor of Science in Biology, minor in Chemistry, May 1999. University of Tulsa, GPA: 3.09.

EXPERIENCE

Dietetic Intern, University of Minnesota – Twin Cities, July 2004 – Present. (Registration eligible January 14, 2005)
- Clinical rotations – Reviewed charts and assessed nutritional status of patients; developed a plan of care for each patient. Educated patients regarding diet and nutrition information.
- Community rotations – Established a short basic cooking course for underprivileged teens. Assisted with WIC certifications of families in need. Developed resource information sheet for diabetics in the Indian community.
- Food Service rotations – Developed a four-week menu rotation. Implemented new recipe ideas.

Teaching Assistant, University of Minnesota – Twin Cities, August 2003 – May 2004.
- Assisted Professor in teaching a web-based dietary supplements course.
- Aided students in understanding course materials via email communication.
- Graded course assignments.

Research Assistant, University of Minnesota – Twin Cities, June 2001 – May 2003.
- Established methodology to sterilely place indwelling catheters in the jugular veins of mice.
- Performed infusions of isotopically labeled palmitate and acetate to quantitate fatty acid flux.
- Completed indirect calorimetry to quantitate substrate oxidation in mice.

Clinical Laboratory Scientist III, Memorial Blood Centers, Minneapolis, Minnesota June1999 – June 2001.
- Performed screening on donor and clinical samples for serological markers of infectious diseases.

GRADUATE ACTIVITIES

Publications
- Lisa Sample, Carlus S Dingfelder, Lisa A Smith, Dave A Bernlohr, Chaodong Wu, Alex J Lange, and Elizabeth J Parks. Investigation of in vivo fatty acid metabolism in AFABP/aP^2 mice. *American Journal of Physiology – Endocrinology and Metabolism, In Press.*

Presentations
- Investigation of in vivo fatty acid metabolism in AFABP/aP^2 mice. Presented at Experimental Biology, Washington, DC, April 2004.
- Investigation of in vivo fatty acid metabolism in AFABP/aP^2 mice. Presented at the Minnesota Obesity Center Fall Retreat, Minneapolis, MN, November 2003.

Figure 10.7 Sample Entry-Level Résumé
Source: University of Minnesota, St. Paul Campus Career Center.

Nadine Wolf
2222 Harriet Avenue, Minneapolis, MN 55105
Phone: (651) 444-4444
Email: Nwolf@umn.edu

Objective	To obtain a position as an Environmental Educator/Naturalist working at a Nature Center using my skills in alternative teaching techniques and conservation promotion.

Education   **Bachelor of Science**, Natural Resources and Environmental Studies
University of Minnesota, Twin Cities College of Natural Resources
- Emphasized major in Environmental Education
- Minor in Recreational Resource Management
- Maintaining three jobs while attending school full time

**Related
Experience**

Tour Guide, Bell Museum of Natural History-
University of Minnesota, Minneapolis   September 2004-Present
- Lead several educated guided tours that are one to two hours each day for preschool to sixth graders from diverse twin city's schools and played relative indoor activities games to increase their knowledge
- Teach kids about the natural history of Minnesota & promote conservation
- Care for and handle 13 reptiles and 5 amphibians
- Supervise and engage visitors with knowledge and information by using the objects, materials & resources available in the Touch and See Room

Youth Program Leader, Ann Sullivan School-YMCA-
Minneapolis, Minnesota   September 2004-Present
- Manage 15 third graders in an after school Beckons Program
- Plan, create and implement 45 minutes of curriculum activities each day
- Encourage positive behavior while being an enthusiastic role model
- Supervise the kids during snack and academic time

Environmental Education Intern, Carpenter Nature Center-
Hastings, Minnesota   June 2004-August 2004
- Learned and implemented community environmental educational curriculum
- Taught and observed summer programs held for preschool to seventh graders
- Experienced the world of a naturalist through day to day routines
- Cared for and handled the many different animals every day in the summer
- Learned and gained knowledge about bee keeping while conducted bee keeping once a week with a Naturalist at the nature center
- Designed and constructed an interactive display on geology and dendrology for the interpretative center

**Volunteer
Experience**

Primary Leader, Center for Outdoor Adventure-
University of Minnesota, Minneapolis   May 2004-Present
- Plan, prepare, and lead outdoor adventure trips with college participants on weekends
- Created advertisement online and with flyers to promote trip programs

Outreach primary leader, MN Inner City Outings-
Twin Cities, Minnesota   May 2002-Present
- Lead 8-12 year-old at-risk youth on outdoor activities to increase their understanding of nature
- Plan & create outings ideas for future trips, what to teach and where to go
- Conduct safe wilderness experiences and promote the ideal of conservation to the youth

Program Helper, Ginew/Golden Eagle Program-
Minneapolis, Minnesota   September 2001-2002
- Helped American Indian youth strengthen and develop life skills
- Participated in cultural activities to help youth increase their self-esteem
- Developed activities that promoted knowledge for healthy life choices

Certifications   American Red Cross Adult CPR/AED & First Aid   Expires October 2005
Fifteen Passenger Van Training At the University of Minnesota

---

Figure 10.8   **Sample Résumé with "Experience" Grouped Into Two Sections.**
Source: University of Minnesota, St. Paul Campus Career Center.

employer to search through literally thousands of résumés using keywords. In order to prepare such a résumé, nouns should be used as keywords, and you should list all of your skills, credentials, and job titles. Since the résumé is stored electronically, it can be longer than a print résumé.

Résumés from a template. Programs such as Microsoft Word provide electronic templates that can be filled in with an individual's own personal data. Such programs organize the information put into the template, and the organization can be easily changed as the template is shifted.

Electronic résumés. A résumé can be submitted electronically via email to a potential employer. This type of résumé can be an electronic copy of a print résumé or can take the form of a hyperlinked résumé. A hyperlinked résumé allows pieces of your portfolio, your personal statement, writing samples, and other information about you to be directly accessed on the Web.

Checklist for Résumés

Content
- Is all of your contact information accurate?
- Is your career objective clear?
- Do you put your strongest characteristics forward?
- Do you accurately describe your previous jobs?
- Have you included all necessary contact information for your previous employers?

Form
- Is the type of résumé appropriate for the job you are applying for?
- Does the organization of your résumé put your best characteristics forward?
- If you have a scannable résumé, does it use keywords effectively?
- If your résumé has hyperlinks, are they all functioning?

Overall
- Is everything spelled correctly? Is your résumé free of grammatical errors?
- If you have a print résumé, is it on quality paper?
- Is your résumé uncluttered and tasteful?
- Does your résumé read easily?

Short Reports

Reports present ideas and facts to interested parties, decision makers, and other audiences. Technical professionals rely on short reports as a basis for informed decisions on matters as diverse as the most comfortable office chairs to buy or the best recruit to hire for management training. Unlike long reports, short ones (two to five pages) do not contain a lot of detail. For example, a long report describing the geologic conditions of an area might include an appendix with detailed comparisons of topsoil, groundwater, and other conditions. A short report would summarize this information in a brief table or, depending on the audience's prior knowledge, omit this information altogether.

Short reports are appropriate in a variety of situations. When the purpose of your communication is to inform an audience, offer a solution to a problem, report progress, or make a recommendation, you may wish to use a short report. Short reports often use a memolike structure, starting with a memo-style header and breaking the text up into chunks separated by headings, but they contain more information than the typical memo.

Audience and Purpose Analysis

Do your best to determine who will read this report. For instance, even if the report is addressed to team members, it may be sent on to other managers, the legal department, or sales and marketing. If you can learn about the actual audience members in advance, you can anticipate their needs as you create the report. Also, before you start the report, be clear about its true purpose. For example, you may be under the impression that the report is intended simply to inform your colleagues about the new technical specifications for a component part. But after you interview some audience members and begin researching the content, you learn that what your audience really wants is a report that makes recommendations. Should your company invest in these new parts, or should it continue with the parts it currently uses? Recommending is different from informing. It requires you to weigh the evidence, examine the data, and decide what you think is right.

Types of Short Reports

Short reports come in many types, depending on the situation. Common types include the following.

10.3

Sample recommendation report

Recommendations. Recommendation reports interpret data, draw conclusions, and make recommendations, often in response to a specific request. The recommendation report in Figure 10.9 is addressed to the writer's boss. This is just one example of a short report used to examine a problem and recommend a solution.

Progress reports. Many organizations depend on progress reports (also called status reports) to track activities, issues, and progress on various projects. Some professions require regular progress reports (daily, weekly, monthly), while others may use these documents on an ad hoc basis, as needed to explain a specific

Trans Globe Airlines

MEMORANDUM

To: R. Ames, Vice President, Personnel
From: B. Doakes, Health and Safety
Date: August 15, 20xx
Subject: **Recommendations for Reducing Agents' Discomfort**

In our July 20 staff meeting, we discussed physical discomfort among reservation and booking agents, who spend eight hours daily at automated workstations. Our agents complain of headaches, eyestrain and irritation, blurred or double vision, backaches, and stiff joints. This report outlines the apparent causes and recommends ways of reducing discomfort.

Causes of Agents' Discomfort
For the time being, I have ruled out the computer display screens as a cause of headaches and eye problems for the following reasons:

1. Our new display screens have excellent contrast and no flicker.
2. Research findings about the effects of low-level radiation from computer screens are inconclusive.

The headaches and eye problems seem to be caused by the excessive glare on display screens from background lighting.

Other discomforts, such as backaches and stiffness, apparently result from the agents' sitting in one position for up to two hours between breaks.

Recommended Changes
We can eliminate much discomfort by improving background lighting, workstation conditions, and work routines and habits.

Background Lighting. To reduce the glare on display screens, these are recommended changes in background lighting:

1. Decrease all overhead lighting by installing lower-wattage bulbs.
2. Keep all curtains and adjustable blinds on the south and west windows at least half-drawn, to block direct sunlight.
3. Install shades to direct the overhead light straight downward, so that it is not reflected by the screens.

Figure 10.9 Sample Recommendation Report in Memo Format.

Workstation Conditions. These are recommended changes in the workstations:

1. Reposition all screens so that light sources are at neither the front nor the back.
2. Wash the surface of each screen weekly.
3. Adjust each screen so the top is slightly below the operator's eye level.
4. Adjust all keyboards so they are 27 inches from the floor.
5. Replace all fixed chairs with adjustable, armless secretarial chairs.

Work Routines and Habits. These are recommended changes in agents' work routines and habits:

1. Allow frequent rest periods (10 minutes each hour instead of 30 minutes twice daily).
2. Provide yearly eye exams for all terminal operators as part of our routine health care program.
3. Train employees to adjust screen contrast and brightness whenever the background lighting changes.
4. Offer workshops on improving posture.

These changes will give us time to consider more complex options such as installing hoods and antiglare filters on terminal screens, replacing fluorescent lighting with incandescent, covering surfaces with nonglare paint, or other disruptive procedures.

cc.   J. Bush, Medical Director
      M. White, Manager of Physical Plant

Figure 10.9 (*Continued*)

project or task. Managers often use progress reports to evaluate projects and decide how to allocate funds. Figure 10.10 shows a progress report.

Meeting minutes. Many team or project meetings require someone to record the proceedings. Minutes are the records of such meetings. Copies of these minutes are usually distributed to all team members and interested parties. Often organizations have templates or special formats for recording minutes. Meeting minutes are often distributed via email.

Typical Components of Short Reports

Cover memo–style heading. Many short reports begin with a brief cover memo explaining what the report contains.

Headings for major sections. Use headings for the major sections. Headings allow readers to quickly scan the report before launching into the text itself, and they provide a road map for the entire document.

Body text. Use a standard font, and keep body text brief and to the point.

Bulleted lists and visuals. Use numbered or bulleted lists if the content warrants it. Lists help readers skim the document and order the information. But too many lists can be confusing, so use lists sparingly to make certain key points visible.

Usability Considerations

Use effective page layout and document design. The longer the document, the more navigation tools you should include to help readers find what they need and stay focused on the material. Even a short (two- to three-page) report of solid, unbroken text (no font changes, no headings) can quickly become hard to read. Use headings, numbered lists, page numbers, and font changes to increase readability.

Perform your best research. Make sure you've gathered the right information before you begin writing the report. For the recommendation report in Figure 10.9, the writer did enough research to rule out one problem (computer display screens as the cause of employee headaches) before settling on the actual problem (excessive glare on display screens from background lighting). Research may include interviewing people, using the library, searching for information on the Internet, and taking informal surveys (see Chapter 4).

Use visuals as appropriate. Insert visuals as needed. In a short report, you don't want to bog readers down with excessive graphic information, but a few well-chosen graphs, tables, or charts can help clarify your point (see Chapter 9).

Subject: **Progress Report: Equipment for New Operations Building**

Work Completed

Our training group has met twice since our May 12 report in order to answer the questions you posed in your May 16 memo. In our first meeting, we identified the types of training we anticipate.

Types of Training Anticipated

- Divisional Surveys
- Loan Officer Work Experience
- Divisional Systems Training
- Divisional Clerical Training (Continuing)
- Divisional Clerical Training (New Employees)
- Divisional Management Training (Seminars)
- Special/New Equipment Training

In our second meeting, we considered various areas for the training room.

Training Room

The frequency of training necessitates having a training room available daily. The large training room in the Corporate Education area (10th floor) would be ideal. Before submitting our next report, we need your confirmation that this room can be assigned to us.

　　　　To support the training programs, we purchased this equipment:

- Audioviewer
- LCD monitor
- Videocassette recorder and monitor
- CRT
- Software for computer-assisted instruction
- Slide projector
- Tape recorder

This equipment will allow us to administer training in a variety of modes, ranging from programmed and learner-controlled instruction to group seminars and workshops.

Figure 10.10 **Sample Progress Report in Memo Format.**

Work Remaining

To support the training, we need to furnish the room appropriately. Because the types of training will vary, the furniture should provide a flexible environment. Outlined here are our anticipated furnishing needs.

- Tables and chairs that can be set up in many configurations. These would allow for individual or group training and large seminars.
- Portable room dividers. These would provide study space for training with programmed instruction and allow for simultaneous training.
- Built-in storage space for audiovisual equipment and training supplies. Ideally, this storage space should be multipurpose, providing work or display surfaces.
- A flexible lighting system, important for audiovisual presentations and individualized study.
- Independent temperature control, to ensure that the training room remains comfortable regardless of group size and equipment used.

The project is on schedule. As soon as we receive your approval of these specifications, we will proceed to the next step: sending out bids for room dividers and having plans drawn for the built-in storage space.

cc. R. S. Pike, SVP
     G. T. Bailey, SVP

Figure 10.10 (*Continued*)

Address the purpose. Remember the purpose when you create the report. If your purpose is to recommend, don't take a neutral stance and simply state the facts. If your purpose is to show progress, make it clear at the outset what progress has been made. Use the direct approach (see Figure 10.6)—for example:

> Our goals for this month were to finish the Alpha project and begin planning the Beta project. We have exceeded these goals, and this report will describe our current progress.

Use appropriate headings. Use headings that make sense to your readers. The memo in Figure 10.9 is essentially an overview of a problem followed by a recommended solution, and the headings ("Cause of Agents' Discomfort" and "Recommended Changes") make this clear.

Write clearly and concisely. Get to the point quickly. Use a brief introductory paragraph that states your case or conclusion. Don't bog your reader down with unnecessary background or history sections.

Checklist for Memos and Short Reports

Ethical, Legal, and Interpersonal Considerations
- Is the information specific, accurate, and unambiguous?
- Is this the best report medium (paper, email, phone) for the situation?
- Are all appropriate parties receiving a copy?

Organization
- Is the important information in an area of emphasis?
- Is the direct or indirect pattern used appropriately to present the report's bottom line?

Format
- Does the memo have a complete heading?
- Does the subject line forecast the memo's content and purpose?
- Are paragraphs single-spaced within and double-spaced between?
- Do headings announce subtopics, as needed?
- If more than one reader is receiving a copy, does the memo include a distribution notation (cc:) to identify other readers?

Content
- Is the information based on careful research?
- Is the message brief and to the point?
- Are tables, charts, and other graphics used as needed?
- Are recipients given enough information for an *informed* decision?
- Are the conclusions and recommendations clear?

Style
- Is the writing clear and concise?
- Is the tone appropriate?
- Has the memo been carefully proofread?

Oral Communication

In addition to being good writers and designers, technical communicators need to present their ideas effectively in person. The skills required include stage presence, excellent research, and strong organization. You may be asked to make oral presentations at meetings in your department or company (status reports, team meetings, procedure updates), at professional conferences or meetings, to your community, or in the classroom.

Unlike writing, oral presentations are truly interactive. Face-to-face communication is arguably the richest form, because you can give and receive information using body language, vocal inflection, eye contact, and other physical features. In addition, there is room for give-and-take, which does not happen with traditional written documents. Oral presentations allow you to see how your audience reacts. You can get immediate feedback, and you can change or amend your ideas on the spot.

Most professionals use presentation software such as Microsoft PowerPoint when giving a presentation. But despite the colors and easy-to-use templates such products offer, you are still responsible for putting together a presentation that is well researched and professionally delivered.

Audience and Purpose Analysis

Learn about an audience's attitudes and biases toward and personal experiences with your subject, and see if you can find out exactly who will be attending and what their role is within the organization. A person's role in the organization will affect how he or she listens to your topic: Managers may care about the bottom line, while designers may care more about how much time they will have to work on the interface. Oral presentations also require you to consider the feelings of the group as a whole. When you are speaking to a live audience, people's attitudes and ideas can rub off on others. If one person raises an issue with your topic, others might be reminded that they, too, are interested in this issue. The next thing you know, your audience will become a group, not a collection of individuals.

In defining the purpose of your presentation, understand how your audience will use the information you are presenting. Do people need this information to perform tasks? What do they need to know immediately? How can you make the best use of this actual time with them, and should you save certain items for email, memos, or Web discussions? Is your purpose to inform, persuade, or train? Or is your presentation part of a larger context, such as a conference? Customize your audience and purpose analysis to address these questions, which are specific to oral presentations.

Types of Oral Presentations

Many types of oral presentations are common in science, business, and technical communication, including the following.

Informative presentations. When your audience needs factual information about products, procedures, technical topics, or other items, give an informative presentation. Informative presentations are often given at conferences, product update meetings, briefings, or class lectures. In an informative presentation, your goal is to be as impartial as possible and to provide the best information you can locate.

Training sessions. Training sessions teach audience members how to perform a specific task or set of tasks. Training can cover areas such as how to ensure on-the-job safety, how to use a specific software application, or how to exit a cap-sized kayak. Some technical communicators specialize in training.

Persuasive presentations. Persuasive presentations are designed to change an audience's opinions. For example, an engineer at a nuclear power plant may wish to persuade her peers that a standard procedure is unsafe and should be changed. In a persuasive situation, you need to perform adequate research so that you are well informed on all sides of the issue.

Action plans. A more specific form of persuasive presentations, action plans are appropriate in situations where you want your audience to take a particular action. If you not only wanted to convince other engineers about a design flaw but also wanted the company to take specific action, you would give an action plan presentation that outlined the problem, presented a specific solution, and then tried to convince your audience to take the sort of action needed to implement the solution.

Sales presentations. Sales presentations blend informative and persuasive elements. Usually, the speaker presents information about a product or service in a way that will persuade the audience to buy it. Technical sales presentations need to be well researched: At many high-tech companies, technical sales representatives are often scientists or engineers who understand the product's complexities but also have a knack for effective communication.

In addition to presenting in front of live audiences, you may be asked to present via interactive television, satellite, or a live connection via the Internet.

The more technology involved, the more complicated the presentation, so be sure you have technical experts to assist you. In particular, make sure your overhead slides or computer presentations will show up in these electronic formats.

You may also be asked to give a presentation in another person's absence; for example, a speaker suddenly falls ill or his flight gets snowbound in the airport. In these cases, get as much information as possible from the original speaker.

Typical Components of Oral Presentations

Introduction. The introduction to a presentation is your chance to set the stage. For most presentations, you have three main tasks:

1. To capture your audience's attention by telling a quick story, asking a question, or relating your topic to a current event or something else the audience cares about
2. To establish your credibility by stating your credentials or explaining where you obtained your information
3. To preview your presentation by listing the main points and the overall conclusion

An introduction following this format might sound something like this:

> How many times have you searched for medical information on the Web, only to find that after hours online, you can't locate anything useful? If you're like most Americans polled in a recent survey, you may feel that you are wasting time when it comes to Web-based medical information. My name is Travis Armstrong, and I've been researching this topic for a term paper. Today, I'd like to share my findings with you by covering three main points: how to search for medical information, how to separate good information from bad, and how to contribute to medical discussions online.

Body. Readers who get confused or want to know the scope of a written document (reports, manuals, and so on) can look back at the headings, table of contents, or previous pages. But oral presentations do not have these features. Therefore, you must give your audience a well-organized presentation that is interesting and easy to follow. Structure the material in small chunks. To signal that you are moving from one main point to another, use transition statements such as, "Now that I've explained how to separate good information from bad, let me tell you how you can contribute to medical discussions on the Internet."

Conclusion. Your conclusion should return full circle to your introduction. Remind your audience of the big picture, restate the points you've just covered, and leave listeners with some final advice or tips for locating more information. You can also distribute handouts during this time.

Good PowerPoint Slides

- Five points or fewer
- Use key words and phrases
  - Use smaller fonts for secondary points
- Have 18 point font or larger
- Use graphs over charts
- Don't have distracting images

Figure 10.11 **Sample Slide from a PowerPoint Presentation.** Don't let the software trick you into thinking you don't need to practice or do research.
Source: Reprinted with permission from Microsoft Corp.

www

10.4

Sample
PowerPoint
presentations

Computer projection software and other visual aids. Most presentations use visuals of some sort: overhead transparencies, flip charts, or computer projection software. Keep in mind that the more technology you use, the more prepared you must be. Used properly, computer software can make presentations interesting and enjoyable, because they allow the use of color, graphics, clip art, and images from the Web.

With presentation software such as PowerPoint (see Figure 10.11), you can produce professional-quality slides and then show them electronically. Here is a sampling of PowerPoint's design and display features. You can

- Create slide designs in various colors, shading, and textures
- Create drawings or graphs and import clip art, photographs, or other images
- Create animated text and images—for example, you can use bullets that flash one at a time on the screen or bars and lines on a graph that are highlighted individually, to emphasize specific characteristics of the data
- Create dynamic transitions between slides, such as having one slide dissolve toward the right side of the screen as the following slide uncovers from the left

- Amplify each slide with speaker notes that are invisible to the audience
- Sort your slides into various sequences
- Precisely time your entire presentation
- Show your presentation directly on the computer screen or large-screen projector, online via the Web, as overhead transparencies, or as printed handouts

For a step-by-step guide to getting started on PowerPoint, select "Auto-Content Wizard" from the opening screen. There you can find ideas for slide content and schemes for organizing your presentation.

The PowerPoint debate. PowerPoint advocates argue that bullet points help structure the story or the argument and help the presenter organize and stay on course. Critics argue that the mere content outline provided by the slides can oversimplify complex issues and that an endless list of bullets or animations, colors, and sounds can distract the audience from the message.

As an example of how overreliance on presentation slides can cloud the thinking process, consider the following scenario.

On February 1, 2003, the space shuttle *Columbia* burned up upon reentering the earth's atmosphere. The *Columbia* had suffered damage during launch when a piece of insulating foam broke off and damaged the wing.

While the *Columbia* was in orbit, NASA personnel tried to assess the damage and to recommend a course of action. It was decided that the damage did not seem serious enough to pose a significant threat, and reentry proceeded on schedule. (Lower-level suggestions that the shuttle fly close to a satellite that could have photographed the damage, for a clearer assessment, were overlooked and ultimately ignored by the decision makers.)

The *Columbia* Accident Investigation Board (2003) concluded that a PowerPoint presentation to NASA officials had played a role in the disaster: Engineers presented their findings in a series of confusing and misleading slides that obscured errors in their own engineering analysis. Design expert Edward Tufte points out that one especially crucial slide was so crammed with data and bullet points and so lacking in analysis that it was impossible to decipher accurately (pp. 8–9).

Here are the board's findings:

> As information gets passed up an organization hierarchy, from people who do analysis to mid-level managers to high-level leadership, key explanations and supporting information is filtered out. In this context, it is easy to understand how a senior manager might read this PowerPoint slide and not realize that it addresses a life-threatening situation.
>
> At many points during its investigation, the Board was surprised to receive similar presentation slides from NASA officials in place of technical reports. The Board views the endemic use of PowerPoint briefing slides instead of technical

papers as an illustration of the problematic methods of technical communication at NASA. (p. 191)

In the end, technological tools are merely a *supplement* to your presentation; they are no substitute for the facts, ideas, examples, numbers, and interpretations that make up the clear and complete message audiences expect.

Handouts. If you bring handouts to a presentation, consider when you want to give them to the audience. The moment you provide handouts, your audience will look at the handouts and not at you.

Time constraints. Most presentations have a time limit. If you are presenting at a conference on a panel of three or four people, you may be asked in advance to limit your talk to 15 minutes. If you are presenting at a one-hour meeting, you should consider the amount of time people are able to concentrate and remember to save time for questions. Exceeding your allotted time (usually no more than 20 minutes in most business settings) is inconsiderate of your audience and the other speakers. Practice your presentation, and make it fit the time allowed.

Usability Considerations

Maintain confidence, and project a professional persona. Fear of public speaking is very common, even for the most skilled speakers. The best way to avoid nervousness is to perform solid research on the topic, prepare well, and practice. Deep breathing and positive thinking also help with unsteady nerves. The more confident you appear, the more credible your message.

Be ready to adapt to your audience. Speaking to a live audience means you may need to adapt on the spot. If you start your talk but quickly realize that your audience does not understand some of the technical terms, you need to be ready to stop, explain some of the terms in simpler language, and perhaps even reconsider whether to do certain parts of your presentation at all. The more experience you gain with giving presentations, the better you will become at learning to "read" your audience.

Prepare for your technology to fail. No matter how many disk copies you brought, how fast the Internet connection, or how great the technical support staff, always be prepared for your technology to fail. Computer presentation software is dynamic and professional, but it does not always work. Overhead projectors are excellent for presenting outlines of your talk, visuals, and other material, but what do you do if the bulb burns out? Always have a backup plan—paper handouts (and a spare bulb) are a good idea.

Get a sense of the physical layout of the room. Make sure you know the size and layout of the room before you show up. Is it a conference room or a large lecture hall? The type size you choose for slides to be shown in a conference room may not be large enough for a lecture hall. If you can, visit the space in advance.

Spell-check your slides. Even though most people spell-check documents, for some reason they often forget to spell-check their presentation slides. You don't want the audience distracted by misspellings on the screen when you are speaking.

Use your memory, and practice your delivery. Don't read your presentation from note cards or from a prepared speech. Instead, seek a style that is professional but natural. Memorize the key phrases or concepts in your presentation, and use these key terms to jog your memory about the other items you wish to mention. Figure 10.12 shows an outline for an oral presentation. Use bullet points on your overheads or slides to help guide you. Practice until you can speak with confidence. You should practice in front of friends or sample audience members and ask for their feedback. (See the oral presentation checklist.) Alternatively, tape or video yourself, and use this to help improve your style.

Medical Information on the Web
Oral Presentation by Travis Armstrong

Outline

Introduction

    Ask questions (How many times have you searched . . . ?)
    Introduce myself
    Outline main points
        Searching
        Separating good from bad
        Contributing to discussions online

Body

    Searching for medical information
    Separating good from bad information
    Contributing to discussions online

Conclusion

    Restate my main points
    Give sources for more information and handout

Figure 10.12 **Sample Outline for a Presentation.** Make sure you practice and know your subject well. Use the main points to guide you along.

Checklist for Oral Presentations

Presentation Evaluation for (name/topic) _____

Content   *Comments*

- Stated a clear purpose.   _____
- Created interest in the topic.   _____
- Showed command of the material.   _____
- Supported assertions with evidence.   _____
- Used adequate and appropriate visuals.   _____
- Used material suited to this audience's   _____
  needs, knowledge, concerns, and interests.
- Acknowledged opposing views.   _____
- Gave the right amount of information.   _____

Organization

- Began with a clear overview.   _____
- Presented a clear line of reasoning.   _____
- Moved from point to point effectively.   _____
- Stayed on course.   _____
- Used transitions effectively.   _____
- Avoided needless digressions.   _____
- Summarized before concluding.   _____
- Was clear about what the listeners   _____
  should think or do.

Style

- Dressed appropriately.   _____
- Seemed confident, relaxed, and likable.   _____
- Seemed in control of the speaking situation. _____
- Showed appropriate enthusiasm.   _____
- Pronounced, enunciated, and spoke well.   _____
- Used no slang whatsoever.   _____
- Used appropriate gestures, tone, volume,   _____
  and delivery rate.
- Had good posture and eye contact.   _____
- Interacted with the audience.   _____
- Kept the audience actively involved.   _____
- Answered questions concisely and   _____
  convincingly.

Exercises

The Web site for this textbook (http://www.ablongman.com/gurak) contains links to sample documents online as well as exercises related to different document types.

1. **FOCUS on WRITING.** People regularly contact your organization (your company, agency, or college department) via email, letter, or your Web site to request information. To answer these many inquiries, you decide to prepare a frequently asked questions (FAQ) list in response to the ten most asked questions about products, services, specific concentrations within the major, admission requirements, or the like. In addition to being posted on your Web site, this list can be sent as an email attachment or mailed out as hard copy, depending on your readers' preferences.

   After analyzing your specific audience and purpose and doing the research, prepare your list in short report format, paying careful attention to the usability considerations in Chapter 3.

2. **FOCUS on WRITING.** Your boss or college dean wants recommendations about whether to begin electronic monitoring of email correspondence and Internet use at your company or your school. A few of your audience's major questions: What are the pros and cons? What are the ethical considerations? Should we do it routinely? Should we do it selectively? Should we rule it out? Is more inquiry needed? Should we allow the entire organization to share in the decision?

   Do the research, and prepare a recommendation memo that makes your case reasonably and persuasively (review Chapter 6 for ethical considerations).

3. Write an actual letter to a business about one of its products following the format described in this chapter. Exchange letters with another student, and check each other's letters using the rules from this chapter. Rewrite and send the letter; if you get a response, share it with the class.

4. Make up a scenario related to your current or future career about an oral presentation you may have to make. Make sure you give all related background information about your job. For example, you are a health care retailer who sells medical equipment. You need to present a new type of clamp designed by your company that you hope the hospital administrators and doctors will want to purchase at the workshop they are attending. Describe what type of oral presentation you would give, do an audience and purpose analysis, and tell what you would use to enhance your presentation. Compare your scenario with those of other students in your class.

The Collaboration Window

Writing, especially in the workplace, is not done in isolation. Even when you are the main author of a memo or report, you will work with others to gather information, analyze findings, learn about user tasks, and so on. First, with your profession or major in mind, choose one form of communication described in this chapter (letter, short report, oral presentation), and analyze how you will need to work with others in your field when composing such a document. Second, research what additional steps you will need to take to adapt your document in order to post it on a Web site. You can research what's involved in converting printed documents to Web presentation by exploring some of the links you find at http://www.refdesk.com/html.html, a reference list of 70 Internet sites related to creating Web sites.

Once you have determined how you will need to work with others at each stage of the document development process, summarize your conclusions in a brief descriptive memo or email to your professor.

The Global Window

Interview a person whose work takes him or her to one or more countries outside the United States, and ask the person to describe for you which document types are used in which situations in different countries and settings. For example, is a paper letter always considered formal? Is letterhead paper the same size around the world? In the United States, email seems to be replacing the paper memo. Is this true in other countries as well? If you have trouble locating someone to interview, try asking your instructor for the name of someone who hires interns from your program. You could also ask your instructor for the names of faculty members who travel abroad.

CHAPTER 11

Product-Oriented Communication Situations

Specifications

Airplanes, bridges, computer software, and nearly everything else in the modern world are produced according to specifications. Specifications ("specs") prescribe standards for performance, safety, and quality. Specifications describe features such as methods for manufacturing, building, or installing a product; materials and equipment used; and size, shape, and weight. Specifications are often used to ensure compliance with a particular safety code, engineering standard, or government or other ruling. Because specifications define an "acceptable" level of quality, any product that fails to meet these specs may provide grounds for a lawsuit. When injury or death results (as in a bridge collapse or an airline accident), the device is usually checked to be sure it was built and maintained according to the appropriate specifications. If not, the contractor, manufacturer, or supplier may be liable.

Specifications are called for in situations where a technology or procedure must be executed in a precise manner. For example, the Institute of Electrical and Electronics Engineers (IEEE) issues a series of specifications (called "standards") that prescribe the technical format and specs for a range of devices, including circuits, electrical insulation, and telecommunications. Engineers are obligated to follow these standards if they want their products to be both safe and compatible with others in that field. Specifications are also important in situations where many professionals from different backgrounds work together on a project. These specs help ensure that contractors, architects, landscapers, and others have a master plan and use the same parts, materials, and designs. Software developers also follow specifications when creating computer programs.

Audience and Purpose Analysis

Specifications may be written for a wide range of readers, including customers, designers, contractors, suppliers, engineers, programmers, and inspectors. An audience analysis will help you determine who will be reading the specs. If your audience consists primarily of technical experts (such as engineers who use the IEEE standards), you can use specialized language and succinct explanations (see Figure 11.1). But if your audience is a mixed group, you may need to include more detail, or you may need to refer readers to other sources of information (a glossary, Web site, or attachment).

In terms of purpose, specifications are useful when your audience needs to understand and agree on what is to be done and how it is to be done. In addition to guiding how a product is designed and constructed, specifications can also help people use and maintain a product. For instance, specifications for a color ink-jet printer (see Figure 11.2) include the product's power requirements, noise emissions, and weight and size of paper. Product support literature for appliances, power tools, and other items often contains specifications so that

IEEE C62.1-1989 - Description

IEEE
*Networking
the World*™

IEEE C62.1-1989 - revision of ANSI/IEEE C62.1-1984
IEEE Standard for Gapped Silicon-Carbide Surge Arresters for AC Power Circuits

Abstract: IEEE C62.1-1989, *IEEE Standard for Gapped Silicon-Carbide Surge Arresters for AC Power Systems,* describes the service conditions, classifications and voltage ratings, design tests with corresponding performance characteristics, conformance tests, and certification test procedures for station, intermediate, distribution and secondary class arresters. Terminal connections, housing leakage distance, mounting and identification requirements are defined. Definitions are provided to clarify the required test procedures and other portions of the text.

Contents

1. Scope

2. Definitions

3. References

4. Service Conditions
       4.1   Usual Service Conditions
       4.2   Unusual Service Conditions

5. Classification and Voltage Rating of Arresters
       5.1   Voltage Ratings
       5.2   Test Requirements

Voltage Withstand Tests
Power-Frequency Sparkover Test

Figure 11.1 Sample from an IEEE Standard for Surge Protectors.
Source: IEEE Std. C62.1-1989, IEEE Standard for Capped Silicon-Carbide Surge Arresters for AC Power Circuits Abstract. Copyright © 1969 IEEE. All rights reserved.

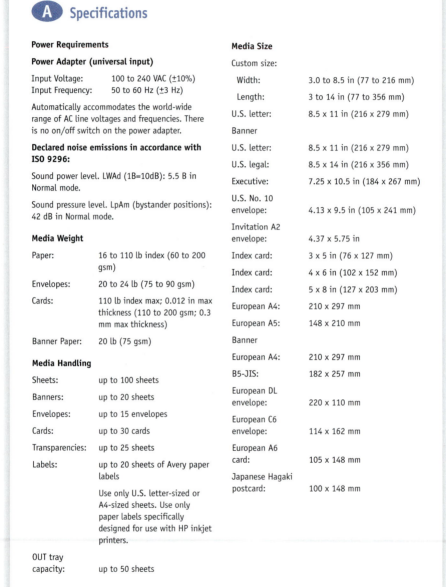

A   Specifications

Power Requirements

Power Adapter (universal input)

Input Voltage: 100 to 240 VAC (±10%)
Input Frequency: 50 to 60 Hz (±3 Hz)

Automatically accommodates the world-wide range of AC line voltages and frequencies. There is no on/off switch on the power adapter.

Declared noise emissions in accordance with ISO 9296:

Sound power level. LWAd (1B=10dB): 5.5 B in Normal mode.

Sound pressure level. LpAm (bystander positions): 42 dB in Normal mode.

Media Weight

Paper:	16 to 110 lb index (60 to 200 gsm)
Envelopes:	20 to 24 lb (75 to 90 gsm)
Cards:	110 lb index max; 0.012 in max thickness (110 to 200 gsm; 0.3 mm max thickness)
Banner Paper:	20 lb (75 gsm)

Media Handling

Sheets:	up to 100 sheets
Banners:	up to 20 sheets
Envelopes:	up to 15 envelopes
Cards:	up to 30 cards
Transparencies:	up to 25 sheets
Labels:	up to 20 sheets of Avery paper labels
	Use only U.S. letter-sized or A4-sized sheets. Use only paper labels specifically designed for use with HP inkjet printers.
OUT tray capacity:	up to 50 sheets

Media Size

Custom size:

Width:	3.0 to 8.5 in (77 to 216 mm)
Length:	3 to 14 in (77 to 356 mm)
U.S. letter:	8.5 x 11 in (216 x 279 mm)

Banner

U.S. letter:	8.5 x 11 in (216 x 279 mm)
U.S. legal:	8.5 x 14 in (216 x 356 mm)
Executive:	7.25 x 10.5 in (184 x 267 mm)
U.S. No. 10 envelope:	4.13 x 9.5 in (105 x 241 mm)
Invitation A2 envelope:	4.37 x 5.75 in
Index card:	3 x 5 in (76 x 127 mm)
Index card:	4 x 6 in (102 x 152 mm)
Index card:	5 x 8 in (127 x 203 mm)
European A4:	210 x 297 mm
European A5:	148 x 210 mm

Banner

European A4:	210 x 297 mm
B5-JIS:	182 x 257 mm
European DL envelope:	220 x 110 mm
European C6 envelope:	114 x 162 mm
European A6 card:	105 x 148 mm
Japanese Hagaki postcard:	100 x 148 mm

Figure 11.2 Specifications for a Color Ink-Jet Printer.
Source: Hewlett-Packard Development Co. Reprinted with permission.

users can select an appropriate operating environment or replace worn parts. Specifications can also be important in technical marketing material (discussed later in this chapter) by helping potential customers see the details of the product.

Types of Specifications

Industry standards. Many industries issue specifications and standards for products in the field. The IEEE, for example, issues standards for electrical and electronic devices.

Government standards. Government organizations, such as the Food and Drug Administration (FDA) and the Consumer Product Safety Commission, produce guidelines and standards for a multitude of items. The FDA, for example, regulates the production and sale of food products and vitamin supplements.

Functional specs. Functional specs are used in the private sector to outline exactly what needs to be done on a project (see Figure 11.3). A functional spec does not always indicate how certain parts of the project will be implemented, however. For example, a functional spec for a software product may indicate that the software should allow users to log in, enter data, and move between screens. Software development teams use this functional spec to guide them as they write and test the computer code.

Internet specs. The World Wide Web consortium (http://www.w3c.org) is an industry and university organization that develops common protocols (technical standards) for Web page design and development. These protocols provide standards for Web development in areas such as graphics, hypertext markup language (HTML), and other technical aspects that allow the Web to function across a variety of platforms, countries, and browsers.

Typical Components of Specifications

As noted, there are many types of specifications. The components of the document will often be dictated by the industry or organization. The IEEE surge protector standard (see Figure 11.1) follows the format for all similar IEEE documents. In general, specifications include the following parts.

11.1

Sample specifications

Brief introduction or description. Most specs include some kind of overview section, be it a one- or two-sentence introduction, an abstract, or a similarly brief description of the document. If your audience is completely familiar with the material, a title can serve this purpose.

List of component parts or materials. Specifications that deal with devices or hardware often list the individual parts. For example, if you purchase a new

Ruger, Filstone, and Grant Architects

SPECIFICATIONS FOR THE POWNAL CLINIC BUILDING

Foundation
> footings: 8" x 16" concrete (load-bearing capacity: 3,000 lbs. per sq. in.)
> frost walls: 8" x 4' @ 3,000 psi
> slab: 4" @ 3,000 psi, reinforced with wire mesh over vapor barrier

Exterior Walls
> frame: eastern pine #2 timber frame with exterior partitions set inside posts
> exterior partitions: 2" x 4" kiln-dried spruce set at 16" on center
> sheathing: 1/4" exterior-grade plywood
> siding: #1 red cedar with a 1/2" x 6' bevel
> trim: finished pine boards ranging from 1" x 4" to 1" x 10"
> painting: 2 coats of Clear Wood Finish on siding; trim primed and finished
> with one coat of bone white, oil base paint

Roof System
> framing: 2" x 12" kiln-dried spruce set at 24" on center
> sheathing: 5/8" exterior-grade plywood
> finish: 240 Celotex 20-year fiberglass shingles over #15 impregnated felt
> roofing paper
> flashing: copper

Windows
> Anderson casement and fixed-over-awning models, with white exterior
> cladding, insulating glass and screens, and wood interior frames

Landscape
> driveway: gravel base, with 3" traprock surface
> walks: timber defined, with traprock surface
> cleared areas: to be rough graded and covered with wood chips
> plantings: 10 assorted lawn plants along the road side of the building

Figure 11.3 Specifications for a Building Project.

power tool, you will probably find a list of parts somewhere in the instruction manual.

Reference to other documents or specs. Often one set of specifications refers to another. For example, a functional spec for a software product may refer readers to an earlier document. If you put your spec on a Web site, you can easily create links from the new document to the old one.

Usability Considerations

Understand how people will use the document. Will readers use the specs to build something (a bridge, a software product)? If so, they will need detailed information. But what if they need to refer to the specs only on occasion, say, if a part is needed? In this case, a spec can be shorter, for example, a list of parts with order numbers and brief descriptions.

Use the same terms to refer to the same parts or steps. If the specs list indicates "ergonomic adapter" in one section but then uses the term "iMac mouse adapter" in a later section, users may become frustrated and confused.

Use adequate retrieval aids. Especially in longer documents, some audience members may be interested in only one aspect of the spec. For example, a programmer working on a subset of the entire project may want to look up the technical details for her part of the project. If you use clear headings and a table of contents, people can find the parts they need.

Follow a standard format. If the organization follows a standard format for specs, use it. If not, you may want to create a template and suggest that the entire company use it. Standard formats help users find what they need, because each document created with a template will contain similar sections and subsections.

Keep it simple. People look at specs because they want quick access to items, parts, technical protocols, and so on. These users are not interested in reading a novel. If you can, keep your specs limited to short lists, using prose only as necessary.

Check your use of technical terms. Make sure your technical terms are standard for the industry. Be sure you have spelled these terms correctly or used the standard abbreviations. Remember that your spell-checker won't find some technical terms, so you may wish to create a new dictionary within your word-processing software just for this project.

When giving instructions, use active voice. If the specs require you to instruct your audience, use active voice and imperative mood. For example, "Insert the bolt" or "Remove the wiring insulation."

Checklist for Specifications

- Are the specifications appropriately detailed for the audience?
- Do they address all the tasks required of the user?
- To avoid excessive detail for a mixed audience, do you refer readers to other sources of information?
- Do the specs begin with a brief overview of the document?
- For hardware and mechanism specs, is each part listed and described?
- Are other/earlier specs referred to, as needed?
- Is the terminology for parts or steps consistent throughout the document?
- Are all technical terms standard for the industry?
- Are the specs easy to navigate, with clear headings and other retrieval aids?
- Do the specs follow a standard format whenever possible?
- Is the writing concise and clear, with lists preferred to paragraphs?
- Are all instructions phrased in the active voice?

Brief Instructions

Surrounded as we are by technology, we are quite naturally also surrounded by instructions. Brief, to-the-point instructions are called for when you want to provide users with information on how to assemble, connect, or use a product. Even a product as simple as a build-it-yourself bookshelf requires clear, simple instructions. Brief instructions often appear as part of a larger set of instructions and procedures to help users get started immediately. Figure 11.4 is an example— it lists six steps users need to connect their drives to their computers. Users can refer to the Quick Install brochure to get started immediately, and they can read the more extensive User's Guide later.

Audience and Purpose Analysis

Consider how much experience your audience has with the technology or task. If someone already owns a Zip drive at work, for example, and has purchased a new one for home, that person will need only a brief reminder of how to set up and operate the device. Users who are new to this technology, on the other hand, will need more information.

In terms of purpose, instructions are almost always written to help users perform a task or series of tasks. During your analysis, you need to discover what these tasks are and in what order people should perform them. For more about task-oriented communication, see Chapter 3.

Types of Brief Instructions

Quick reference brochures or cards. Figure 11.4 shows a quick reference brochure. The instructions contain only the basic steps necessary for the task.

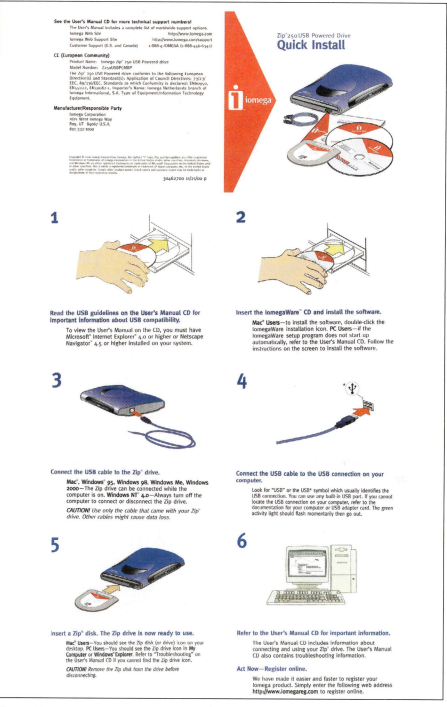

Figure 11.4 **A Quick Install Brochure.** This quick reference guide is printed as a 5-by-8-inch brochure (shown folded open in this figure). It lists the six steps users need to perform in order to connect their new drives to their computers. Note the use of action verbs (*insert, connect*) and the smart use of diagrams.

Source: Courtesy of Iomega Corp.

The brochure is designed to be used during an installation process. Some quick reference cards, such as the kind you carry in your wallet with bank ATM instructions, are designed to be used over and over as needed.

Assembly instructions. These are the instruction sheets that come with most build-it-yourself devices or products. Assembly instructions usually contain numbered steps, a parts list, and diagrams.

Wordless instructions. In a global marketplace, it's important to have instructions that can be understood across language barriers. Translating instructions into dozens of languages is expensive and leads to bulky, cumbersome materials. Many companies have turned to wordless instructions, which use diagrams and arrows to explain a procedure (see Figure 11.5).

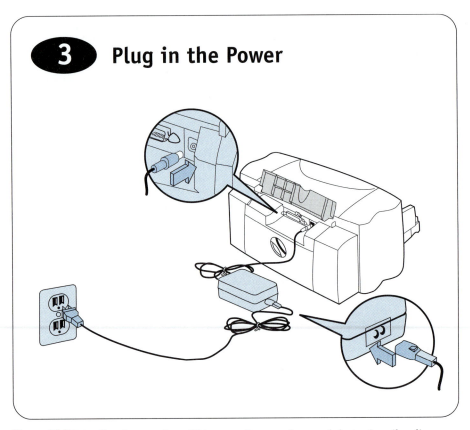

Figure 11.5 Wordless Instructions. This example uses a few words but primarily relies on an exploded diagram to explain the procedure.
Source: Hewlett-Packard Co. Reproduced with permission.

Typical Components of Instructions

Title. Most instructions, brief or extended, have a short title, such as "Quick Setup Instructions for the Printer." Keep the title brief and to the point.

11.2
Sample
instructions

Quick overview of the task. In cases where the instructions will take more than a few steps, you can create a quick overview of the entire process, such as this:

> To use your new SCSI adapter cable, you will first need to install the software and then connect the cable.

Your instructions would then be divided into two parts: installing the software and connecting the cable. Overviews help users see the big picture before they embark on the detailed actions.

Step-by-step instructions. Most instructions are written in a numbered list format so users know the sequence of the tasks and can remember where they left off.

Diagrams. Diagrams can be extremely helpful, because they allow users to see the process or the parts to be assembled. Diagrams are especially important when you are creating a document for an international audience.

Follow-up information. It is a good idea to provide an address, phone number, Web site, and email address where users can obtain assistance.

Usability Considerations

Define the task your users need to perform. Experts at writing instructions always perform a task analysis, which focuses on tasks users will need to perform in particular situations. For example, the main tasks on users' minds when they open the box for a new computer component, such as a printer, are how to set it up and use it.

Determine the size of the final document. Brief instructions are intended to help users perform tasks quickly. The final document should not be bulky or cumbersome. It should be easy to use and, if possible, printed on a single page. The quick reference brochure shown in Figure 11.4 is a good example.

Use the same terms to refer to the same parts or steps. Readers may be confused by instructions that use terms inconsistently. For example, be sure your instructions don't say to connect the "SCSI printer cable" in one step but then refer to the "peripheral cable" in a later step.

Test your instructions. Most technical communication products should be proofread or tested by real audience members, and this usability concern is especially important with instructions. You won't know if the instructions work unless you watch a group of users try them out.

Use imperative voice and action verbs. Imperative sentences leave out the word *you* and begin with the verb. Use these sentences with strong action verbs when listing tasks. For example:

> Connect the cable.
> Insert the disk.
> Open the hatch.

See Chapter 3 and Appendix A for more information on this subject.

Keep it simple. Brief instructions should be simple and to the point. Include only the information that the user needs to perform that particular task. But direct the user to other sources (online help, Web site, manual) for further information if needed.

Procedures

Procedures are documents that provide information, steps, and guidelines for completing a task. Longer than brief instructions, some procedures are used to instruct and train employees. Others are used to meet legal requirements and ensure safety. For example, the Occupational Safety and Health Administration (OSHA) requires employees in certain workplaces (factories, construction sites, hospitals) to follow strict safety procedures. These procedures must be updated according to new laws and policies, and the written procedures must be available for employees to read.

Procedures are also useful in situations where you want to standardize a task. If your company has several employees all performing the same task but doing so with different computers, different software, or different styles, it may be necessary to standardize these procedures so that everyone's work is compatible. A written document, called a standard operating procedure (SOP), becomes the formal explanation of how a particular task is done at that company.

Procedures are also part of the documentation and manuals that accompany new software, hardware, home appliances, and so on. Often these procedures will be written as brief instructions. Other times, they are more elaborate, depending on the audience's technical background, experience, and needs.

Audience and Purpose Analysis

Determine what knowledge your readers already have about the procedure. In a manufacturing plant, for example, many workers may be extremely familiar with the tasks they perform on a daily basis. But if a team that normally works with extruding equipment is asked to take over on the mixing machines, those workers would need to be trained according to the standard procedures for that equipment. Your readers in this case would know the basics, because they've worked at the plant for years, but they would need detailed information on the specific machines, amounts of chemicals, and so on.

You may learn that the procedures will be used by multiple audiences, such as longtime employees, new trainees, and so on. In this case, you should consider using the *layered* approach (see Chapter 3): a quick reference procedure for those who need to refresh their memories and a more detailed document for new workers.

In terms of purpose, you need to determine how your readers will use these procedures. Will they use them to assemble a new computer or install software? Will the procedures be used on the factory floor to remind workers of the safest way to perform a task? Can your audience access the procedures on a computer (online help or the Web), or do you need to create a paper document? Which medium is likely to be more effective in this situation? Once you know exactly how the procedures will be used, you can make decisions about the document's length, format, level of detail, and medium.

Types of Procedures

Standard operating procedures (SOPs). Figure 11.6 illustrates a standard operating procedure for using a special microscope in video-enhanced microscopy. This SOP is for students and researchers who wish to use the equipment. Because the procedure is lengthy, the document is broken into smaller chunks, easily accessible through a hyperlink (note that in a paper document, a table of contents would serve the same purpose). The procedures for each section are written in clear steps using imperative verbs such as *turn on, place,* and *focus.*

Instructions (long). Some procedures are written in the form of long instructions. For situations where your audience needs detailed material (a procedure with many parts and steps, such as assembling and starting up a new computer), you would want to create long instructions. These instructions might be turned into a manual (see "Documentation and Manuals" later in this chapter), a Web site, or a CD-ROM. Figure 11.7 is a portion of a set of long instructions on installing glass block. Note the use of bullets to list the parts users will need, the list of steps, and the clear illustrations.

Typical Components of Procedures

Title. Create a brief, succinct title that clearly states what this procedure is about; for example, "Setting Up Your IBM Thinkpad X41."

Sample procedures

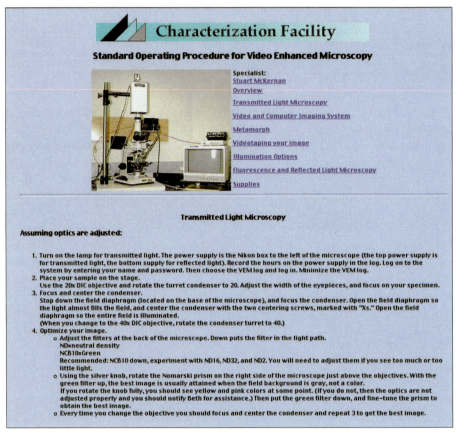

Figure 11.6 A Standard Operating Procedure. This document is part of a set of instrument instructions for the University of Minnesota's Center for Interfacial Engineering. This SOP is available on a Web site, which makes it readily accessible to readers at different physical locations.

Source: Reprinted with the permission of the Regents of the University of Minnesota.

Overview. For longer procedures or those designed for audiences who are new to the task, provide a brief overview of how to use the document and what the document contains.

List of steps. With few exceptions, procedures require audiences to follow explicit steps. Make your steps clear, and number them with large enough type so readers can easily return to a particular step if they look away from the document.

Warnings and cautions. Procedures routinely include advice about avoiding injury or equipment damage. In technical writing, safety information is gener-

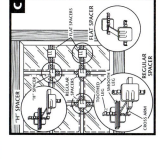

MORTAR I SYSTEM

Introduction

The Mortar I System utilizes Pittsburgh Corning perimeter channels for all four sides. You'll also use VeriTru® Spacers and glass block mortar to produce clean, consistent $^1/_4$″ joints and a traditional grid look.

Pittsburgh Corning offers an easy to follow Glass Block Installation Video. This video is available for purchase where glass block is sold or can be ordered with your VISA or MasterCard by phoning 1-800-624-2120. Looking for glass block ideas? "A Touch of Glass" idea book can also be ordered by calling the above number.

1. General Information

- The installation recommendations presented here are for small residential panels of 25 ft² or less.

- Designed for use with Pittsburgh Corning **Premiere** (4″ thick) and **Thinline**™ (3″ thick) **Series** Glass Block walls.

- Not for use in constructing curved glass block walls.

- Interior and exterior panels must be framed on all four sides.

- All glass block panels are non-load bearing, so adequate provisions must be made for support of construction around the panel.

2. Tools Required

- Margin trowel, mortar pan, polyfoam brush, sponge, tin snips, screwdriver, fine tooth saw, caulking gun, utility knife, metal file, measuring tape, $^1/_8$″ to $^1/_2$″ striking tool and a two foot level.

3. Materials Required

- The Pittsburgh Corning Glass Block Project Planner is available where glass block is sold or on our website at **www.pittsburghcorning.com**. This is a step by step guide you can use to determine the exact amount of materials required for your project.

Materials Required Include:

- Pittsburgh Corning Premiere or Thinline™ Series Glass Block.

- VeriTru® Spacers which support, align and speed installation.

- Pittsburgh Corning Perimeter Channels must be applied on all four sides of your opening and are available in 48″ lengths.

- Expansion Strips are used at the head and are available in 24″ legnths.

- #6 zinc-plated, one inch, flat head screws (approx. three per lineal foot of perimeter channel).

- Mortar: Glass Block white premixed mortar, or you can mix your own using white portland cement, powdered hydrated lime and white sand.

- Pittsburgh Corning Glass Block Sealant.

4. Preparation

- Prepare the rough opening where the panel will be located. To determine the width of your rough opening, multiply the number of glass block horizontally, times the nominal width of the glass block, and to that sum, add $^1/_2$″. To determine the height of your rough opening, multiply the number of glass block vertically, times the nominal height of the glass block, and to that sum, also add $^1/_2$″.

- Cut the perimeter channels to length to fit the bottom, top, and both sides of the opening (Illus. A). These may be cut square or mitered. Screw channels to the bottom and two sides of opening with #6 zinc-plated, one inch, flat head screws, using the holes provided. Use two screws to fasten each end. If you cut off the predrilled holes when trimming the legth, simply drill new ones at each end of the cut piece. Paint the screw heads white to reduce visibility.

- So that the last row of Pittsburgh Corning Glass Block units can be installed easily, cut the top

perimeter channel in half lengthwise with a utility knife. Install half of the channel at the top of opening (Illus. B).

- VeriTru® Spacers are sold in bags of 25. Roughly, you'll need 50% more spacers than the number of glass block being used. Where four block come together spacers are used as supplied. These are called "REGULAR" spacers (Illus. C). Where glass block meet the curb and framework, spacers are modified using tin snips. Clip off both sets of smooth legs forming a flat spacer. Twist-off tabs remain in place (Illus. C). File off any remaining burrs so that the spacer will lay flat. These spacers are called "FLAT" spacers. The spacers for the top row of glass block are called "H" spacers and should be modified by clipping off one upper toothed leg and then cutting the twist-off tab in half (Illus. C).

- Expansion Strip will be used along the entire width of the head and should be cut to a $1^1/_2$″ width for both Premiere and Thinline™ Series glass block.

Mortar Preparation

WHITE PREMIXED GLASS BLOCK MORTAR

The following gives an idea of the number of block that can be installed per 50 pound bag of mortar:

Block Sizes (Nominal)	4″x8″	6″x6″	6″x8″	8″x8″	12″x12″
*No. of Premiere Series (4″ thick)	34	34	30	26	18
*No. of Thinline™ Series (3″ thick)	42	42	36	32	N/A

*Based on $^1/_2$″ mortar joints.

- Follow instructions on the premix mortar bag. Be sure to read and understand all precautions outlined by the mortar manufacturer. Freshly mixed mortar may cause skin irritation. **Avoid direct contact where possible and wash exposed skin areas promptly with water. If any gets into eyes, rinse immediately with water and seek prompt medical attention.** Mixed mortar should be of a consistency that will allow it to stick to the edge of the glass block when the block is turned 90°. It's best to test the mortar on the block (Illus. D), and add water or mortar to the mix as needed.

Mortar I & Mortar II Systems with VeriTru® Spacers

Figure 11.7 Long Instructions for Installing Glass Block. These two pages are part of a ten-page document available as a PDF file from the manufacturer's Web site. Note the detailed step-by-step information, the use of white space and bullets to organize the information, and the clear, simple illustrations.

Source: Used by permission of Pittsburgh Corning Corp.

239

ally conveyed through the following four types of information, listed in order from least to most serious.

Note. Clarifies a point, emphasizes vital information, or describes options or alternatives.

> NOTE: If you don't name a newly initialized disk, the computer automatically names it "Untitled."

Caution. Indicates possible mistakes that could result in injury or equipment damage.

> CAUTION: A momentary electrical surge could erase the contents of your working document, so make sure you back up your data.

Warning. Alerts users to potential hazards to life or limb.

> WARNING: To prevent electrical shock, always disconnect your printer from its power source before you clean any internal parts.

Danger. Identifies an immediate hazard to life or limb.

> DANGER: The red canister contains DEADLY radioactive material. Do not break the safety seal under any circumstances.

You can visually emphasize these items with hazard symbols like these:

| Warning | Do not enter | Radioactivity | Fire Danger |

Procedure number and revision dates. Many procedures, especially SOPs, are given procedure numbers so that users can refer to a particular document. Instead of asking for "the SOP about waste disposal" (which could mean one of many documents), an engineer can ask for SOP 35.2. The number before the period (35) indicates the SOP itself, and the number after the period (2) indicates the revision. Many SOPs also list the revision date somewhere on the document itself.

Usability Considerations

Understand the physical location where people will use the information. Will people use the procedures out on the factory floor? If so, your materials may need to be in large type to allow for less than perfect lighting. You may also need to think about using plastic-coated pages in a binder or other ways to protect the material in certain settings. If users of the document are located in an office, working at a computer, for example, you may want to design a document that stays open easily (by using a comb binding, for example) so that people can read and type at the same time. In other cases, you may want to put the instructions directly on the equipment.

Understand the purpose and tasks for this document. Go back to your audience and purpose analysis and make sure you are clear on how and why your audience will use this document. If workers need to refer to the standard operating procedures while in the middle of a task, they won't want to search for the information. Therefore, headings should be clear, steps should be listed in order, and each page should be visually accessible.

Understand the technical expertise of your audience. How much background do your users have? Experienced users need only new information, whereas novice users need help getting started. In addition, individual readers may scrutinize the document more carefully, while teams may pass the document back and forth, jumping from item to item. Especially for teams, make sure your document is easy to read and steps are clearly numbered.

Test your documents. Make sure you test the usability of your procedures on a small group of users. Procedures often address serious safety issues, so test your document to be sure people are using it as you intended. (See Chapter 3 for more information on usability testing.)

Use active voice. For the parts of the procedures that give specific instructions, use active voice and imperative mood. For example, write "Insert the bolt," "Remove the wiring insulation," or "Insert the floppy disk."

Organize content chronologically. List the steps in the order you want users to perform them. Number the steps, and refer to individual steps by number, not by content ("Return to Step 4 and repeat this function.")

Documentation and Manuals

Documentation and manuals are used in many of the situations and document types described here and in Chapter 10. Documentation may include brief instructions, procedures, or descriptions. It may also describe processes and provide background on the product. Some documentation comes as a set of manuals. In a large sense, documentation is meant to do what its name implies: to *document* (provide all the supporting information for) a scientific or technical product, suite of products (such as a multimedia system consisting of many pieces of hardware and software), or services.

Documentation is called for when you have a product that is complex and requires users to have a broad range of information. Often documentation is written in a *layered* format: a large manual with all the technical details for programmers and high-end users, a quick reference card for those who just need reminders of the main keys and tasks, and a "getting started" brochure for people who want to jump right in.

More and more, documentation is produced online. If you buy a new computer, it often comes with a thin instruction manual, which contains just enough information to get you started. Once you have the machine up and running, you can access the entire library of information through the system's online help screens. Electronic documentation and manuals can be superior to paper because users can search for terms quickly without paging through an index or table of contents. In addition, online information is often *context-sensitive:* If you need help in the middle of a task (trying to save a file, for example), you can often get help with that task as you are attempting to perform it (see Chapter 3).

Although the term *documentation* refers to many types of documents, our discussion here focuses on manuals.

Audience and Purpose Analysis

Determine the audience's technical background and level of familiarity with the product. Often a company may choose to produce a manual as part of a library of information products to accompany the main product. For example, if your company writes business software for networked computers, your audience is vast. You may discover that your audience includes the following groups:

- *Network administrators,* who need to know the product's technical specifications
- *Managers,* who need to understand the bottom-line, business details of the software
- *Sales representatives,* who need a more detailed understanding of the product so they can use it to generate quotes and keep track of customers

Your first task would be to determine which of these users requires which type of documentation. Network administrators may need the largest manual, because they will need to troubleshoot an entire range of problems, from user errors to system crashes.

In terms of purpose, learn all you can about how your audience will use the document and what tasks people need to perform. After conducting interviews and studying the daily activities of network administrators, for example, you may discover that they spend 50 percent of their time looking up user errors, 10 percent checking out potential system errors, and 40 percent updating the system and running reports. This analysis should guide you in creating a manual that focuses on user errors, followed in importance by system issues.

Types of Manuals

A complete manual contains background information, specifications, descriptions, and procedures, all in one document. This type of manual is appropriate for a situation or product that is not very complex—a home appliance, a computer peripheral (scanner or printer), or a simple software application. For more complex products or services, a single document that contained all information would be too large and would be hard for mixed audiences to access: Novices would find leafing through the specifications frustrating, and experts would find all the getting-started information superfluous.

Increasingly common, especially for computer equipment, is a more concise type of manual. Often printed in small-book format, the concise manual might offer computer startup instructions, brief specifications, and basic operating tips. The more lengthy and helpful information is contained within the computer software (online help), and users can access this information once they've started up the machine.

Typical Components of Manuals

Overview. Because manuals are often large documents, it is important to provide your readers with a road map before they get started. An overview section can be brief, and it should outline what the manual contains and how users should approach the document.

Access points. Users may only need to find one piece of information in a large manual, so make sure your access points—table of contents (see Figure 11.8), running heads, index—are well developed and easy to use. Test them to see if users can actually find what they are looking for.

Chapters. In longer manuals, divide the material into chapters. Each chapter contains a logical grouping of information: "Getting Started," "Installing the Printer," "Connecting to the Network," and so on. Order chapters in the sequence you want users to encounter the information. If the manual contains more than roughly ten chapters, you might group the chapters into sections: "Section One: Getting Started," "Section Two: For Network Administrators," "Section Three: Specifications." Each section would then contain approximately three to six chapters.

Reference information. No manual can contain everything every user will need. So make sure you provide a Web address, email address, and phone number for users to contact someone if they get stuck or need more information.

CONFLICT CATCHER TABLE OF CONTENTS v

CONTENTS

Figure 11.8 **An Effective Table of Contents.**
Source: Courtesy of Casady and Greene.

Usability Considerations

Determine the appropriate medium. For large-scale computer systems, documentation may be delivered in many ways. For example, it may be printed and bound into several volumes, often in three-ring binders. Each binder may contain a specific category of information: user error codes, system messages, and so on. In addition, this information may also be delivered via the Web or on a CD. If you can, use the document type that is most familiar to the audience. And if you need to upgrade (for example, if your company determines that the printed format becomes outdated too quickly and the information should be delivered entirely via the Web), make sure you provide plenty of transition time for the users. Allow users to have their paper manuals and the new electronic information at the same time until they become familiar with the new medium.

Also, if you intend to use both paper and electronic documentation, plan them at the same time to make sure the terminology and information are consistent.

Understand what information your audience does and doesn't need. In the old days of writing manuals, writers tended to include every detail about the product. Often manual writers were engineers who worked closely on the project and were eager to explain all the technical details, the history of the project, and so on. Although this might be interesting to some readers, it is not the sort of information end users generally need.

Understand the physical location where people will use the information. If users of the document are working at a computer in an office, for example, you may want to design a manual that stays open easily so people can read and type at the same time. If your audience is network administrators, who are usually able to access the system when they encounter a problem, consider placing the information online.

Write from the user's point of view. Manuals are for users, and they should be written to reflect user needs. Instead of headings that are abstract, such as "Installation of the Microprocessor," try writing from the user's point of view. Headings in the form of questions that a user might actually ask, such as "How do I install the microprocessor?" can be very helpful. Also, make sure your material reflects what users really *care* about. If a long history of the product is not appropriate for this audience, omit it.

Include diagrams, screen samples, and illustrations. Because manuals can be long documents, it's helpful to break up the text with visuals (see Figure 11.9). Visuals can also provide users with a clearer idea of what to do or what to look for on the screen.

Adopt a style that is appropriate for your audience. Most of the time, a neutral, informative style is most appropriate for a manual. However, for certain subjects, a more informal, energized style may be useful. Consider the following examples from the Conflict Catcher user manual. (Conflict Catcher software

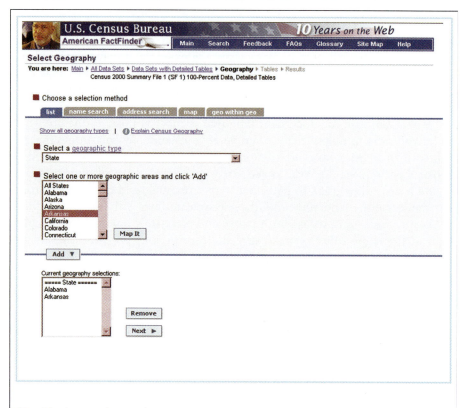

Now it's time to choose the geographic areas for which data are available:

- **Choose a selection method** from one of the five tabs across the page. For now, just leave the **list** tab selected.
- **Select a geographic type.** Click on the drop-down menu and choose the geographic type that best suits your needs (e.g., Nation, State, Census Tract, ZIP Code). Each selection will prompt you a bit differently; e.g., for a county, you must first select the state, then the county.
- **Select one or more geographic areas and click Add.** Your selection(s) will appear in the **Current geography selections** box.

Figure 11.9 Page from a U.S.Census Bureau Manual that Combines Both Text and Visuals.
Source: "4 easy steps to Census 2000 data on American FactFinder."
http://www.census.gov/prod/www/abs/4easysteps.pdf

helps Macintosh users solve problems with system crashes, freeze-ups, and other technical difficulties.)

> "Conflict Catcher's ability to *tame these little programs* can have considerable impact on your daily Macintosh life." (p. 3)

> "On the other hand, there's *no need for paranoia.* When a System Folder is truly corrupted, the problematic file is frequently the System Suitcase file." (p. 96)

Checklist for Instructions, Procedures, and Manuals

Content

- Is the material based on a prior task analysis?
- Does the title promise exactly what the instructions deliver?
- Is the background adequate for the intended audience?
- Is all needless information omitted?
- Do notes, cautions, or warnings appear whenever needed, before the step?
- Are visuals adequate for clarifying the steps?
- Has the document been tested for usability by actual audience members?
- Is follow-up/contact information provided for users to obtain assistance?
- Is the user directed to other sources (online help, Web site, manual) for further information if needed?

Organization

- Does the introduction provide a brief overview of the task?
- Do the instructions follow the exact sequence of steps?
- Is all the information for a particular step close together?
- Are visuals beside or near the step, and set off by white space?

Style

- Do steps generally have short sentences?
- Does each step begin with an action verb?
- Are all steps in the active voice and imperative mood?
- Are the terms used for specific parts/steps consistent throughout?
- Is the style appropriate for the audience?

Page Design

- Do white space and highlights set off discussion from steps?
- Are the steps in a numbered list?
- Are notes, cautions, or warnings set off or highlighted?
- Is the design based on the physical location where people will use the information?
- For a long document, are there enough access points for users to find what they are looking for—including chapter divisions if needed?

Note the upbeat, almost comic ring to these sentences. "Tame these little programs" and "no need for paranoia" are not standard phrases in technical writing. But in the case of this software, the writer probably knew that users who need Conflict Catcher are already in a bad mood because of computer trouble. The casual tone is designed to calm users down and get them to focus on the material so they can solve the problem.

Technical Marketing Material

Technical marketing material is designed to persuade an audience to purchase a product or service. Unlike proposals (see Chapter 12), which are also used to sell a product or service, technical marketing materials tend to be less formal and more dynamic, colorful, and varied. A typical proposal is tailored to one client's specific needs and follows a fairly standard format; marketing literature, by contrast, seeks to present the product in its best light for a broad array of audiences and needs. And unlike nontechnical sales material, technical marketing documents are designed for science and technology products and are often aimed at knowledgeable readers. A team of scientists looking to purchase a new electron microscope wants marketing material that provides specific technical information. Even for a general audience (for example, home computer users), technical marketing material must deal with specialized concepts not ordinarily found in nontechnical sales materials.

Technical communicators with a flare for the creative are often hired as technical marketing specialists. Some situations that call for technical marketing material include the following:

- *Cold calls*—sales representatives sending material to a range of potential new customers
- *On-site visits*—sales representatives and technical experts visiting a customer to see if a new product or service might be of interest
- *Display booths*—booths at industry trade shows displaying engaging, interesting material that people can take away to read at their leisure
- *Web information*—Web pages serving as the primary place users go to find information on a technical product or service

Audience and Purpose Analysis

When creating marketing materials, you need a clear sense of your audience. Who are the readers of these materials: managers? technical experts? purchasing agents? The level of technical language you use will be based on the answers. Also, make sure you know how audiences will use the documents. The main purpose of most marketing materials is to make potential customers aware of your product or service and to sell them your particular company, brand, or model. Marketing materials are essentially persuasive documents.

Types of Technical Marketing Material

Brochures. The term *brochure* covers many types of documents. A typical brochure is a standard-size piece of paper ($8^1/_2$ by 11 inches) folded in thirds, but a brochure can be designed in many sizes, depending on purpose, audience, and budget. Brochures are used to introduce a product or service, provide pricing information, and explain how customers can contact the company.

Web pages. Many companies are using the Web for their marketing materials. The advantage of a Web page (see Figure 11.10) over a printed document is that

Figure 11.10 Web-Based Marketing Material. Most companies have detailed marketing material about products and services available on their Web sites. Web information can be easily updated when features, versions, products, or prices change. Most marketing Web sites are interactive, letting users search for prices and store locations.

Source: http://www.apple.com/ipodshuffle/

if you change the price, specifications, version, look and feel, or other features of the product, you can easily make immediate changes to the Web site. Web pages also allow you to build in interactivity: Customers can give you feedback, request additional information, or place orders.

Letters. Letters can also be used for technical marketing. If a potential customer requests details about a product or service, you may send this information along with a brief cover letter. The letter should not only thank the customer for his or her interest but also point out the specific features of your product or service that match this customer's needs.

Large color documents. Some companies produce technical marketing material that is far more comprehensive than a typical brochure. If you've ever looked at the glossy booklets for a new car, you've seen how these large color documents serve to market a product. The high-quality photography, slick color printing, and glossy feel are designed to evoke the feeling of owning a new car. These booklets also include technical specifications, such as engine horsepower and wheelbase size.

Typical Components of Technical Marketing Material

Name of product. Most technical marketing material is designed to explain a product, so the name of this product should be clear and prominent.

Category or type of product or service. It's important to situate your product in relation to others of its class. For example, a brochure for a pacemaker will explain that this product is a medical device and will compare the pacemaker to other similar medical devices.

Features. Technical marketing material should describe the product's main features and explain the distinguishing features of this specific product.

Technical specifications. Many types of technical marketing materials provide specifications: product size, weight, electrical requirements, and so on.

Visuals. Visuals, especially diagrams and color photographs, are extremely effective in marketing materials. On the Web, you can use color easily and efficiently: Four-color brochures are expensive to print, but color on the Web is simply a matter of using the correct HTML tag.

Frequently asked questions (FAQs). Some marketing materials attempt to answer customer questions with a "frequently asked questions" (FAQ) section.

Usability Considerations

Learn as much as you can about the background and experience of decision makers. Although your materials may be read by a range of people, your main goal is to get the attention of those who make the final policy and purchasing decisions. So your brochure, Web site, or other material should be geared toward their level

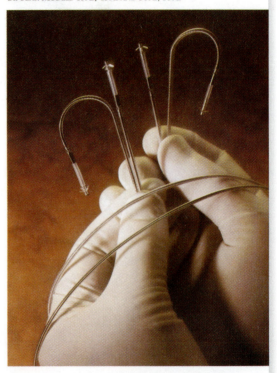

FAMILY FACT SHEET
IMPLANT GUIDELINES
SPECIFICATIONS

CapSure.SP
NOVUS

SMALL-BODIED, STEROID-ELUTING,
TINED LEAD

BIPOLAR MODELS 4092/4592 AND 5092/5592

- Proven steroid performance in more than one million leads implanted

- New silicone allows smaller size

- Medtronic offers the broadest choice of leads to meet unique patient needs and physician preferences

THE WORLD'S BEST SELLING LEAD
JUST GOT EVEN BETTER

Medtronic

Figure 11.11 A Brochure for Medical Devices. This cover photograph clearly shows the product and its size in relation to a human hand. The bullet points address the audience of medical professionals.

Source: CapSure SP Novus® Family Fact Sheet, Implant Guidelines, Specifications. Reproduced with permission of Medtronic, Inc.

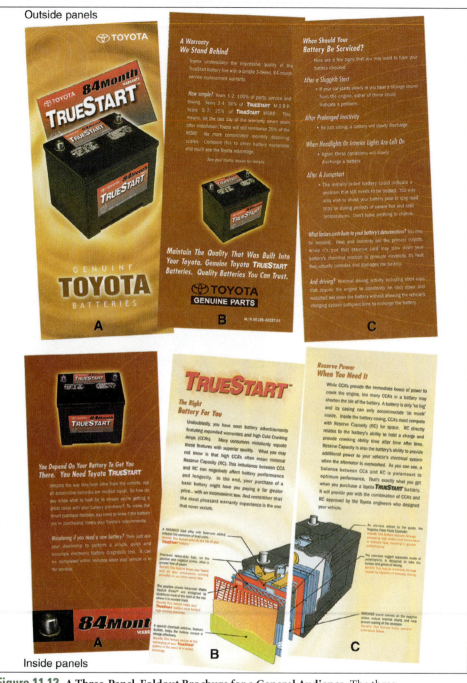

Figure 11.12 A Three-Panel, Foldout Brochure for a General Audience. The three-dimensional illustration in outside panel A enables readers to visualize the product immediately. Inside panel B—at the brochure's very center and highlighted by a yellow screen—convincingly supports panel A's claim by listing the features and specifications that make this battery special.

Source: Courtesy of Toyota Motor Sales, U.S.A., Inc.

of expertise and needs. For example, the medical device brochure in Figure 11.11 uses technical language ("steroid-eluting") for its audience of medical professionals, whereas the car battery brochure in Figure 11.12 uses simpler language for a more general audience. Also, if you know that the decision makers value a product's effectiveness over its cost, emphasize quality, not price. For example, although cost is always a factor, physicians ultimately want medical devices to work properly.

Use upbeat, dynamic language. Be careful not to overdo it, though. Technical people tend to dislike an obvious sales pitch.

Use visuals and color. Color images can accurately convey the shape and feel of the item; also, color can add excitement and visual interest to your materials (see Figure 11.10). If you create both print and Web material, make sure your color choices are consistent so that you convey an overall look and feel for your company and product.

Emphasize the special appeal of this product or service. Briefly explain how this product or service fits the reader's exact needs, and provide solid evidence to support your claim.

Checklist for Technical Marketing Material

- Is the document based on a detailed audience and purpose analysis?
- Is the material geared toward the needs and level of expertise of the ultimate decision makers?
- Is the format (brochure, Web page, letter, etc.) appropriate?
- Is the name of the product highly visible?
- Is the product clearly situated in relation to others in its class?
- Does the document describe the product's main features as well as unique features?
- Does the document emphasize the special appeal of this product or service?
- Does the document provide the product's technical specifications, as needed?
- Is a FAQ list included, as needed?
- Are visuals used extensively and effectively?
- Is color used effectively to convey an overall look and feel for the company and the product?
- Is the language dynamic and upbeat—without sounding like a sales pitch?

Exercises

1. How do specifications come into play in your workplace or even your home? Find one example of specs used in your home or workplace, and complete a usability analysis. For example, if you recently purchased an item that needed to be assembled, it probably came with a list of parts. How easily were you

able to find the parts listed in the specs? What could the writers have done to improve the usability of this document?

2. **FOCUS ON WRITING.** Find two examples of documentation, one that you consider good and one that you think is bad. These can be from any source. With one or two other students, list the features that make the good one good and the bad one bad. Then draft a memo to the writer of the bad documentation, outlining things he or she should do to improve on the next version.

The Collaboration Window

For this project, work in groups of four. Two group members will serve as marketing managers, with the task of presenting a new product to an audience of potential clients and customers. The other two group members will serve as engineering specialists, with the task of developing the specifications and technical features of the product that marketing is planning to present. Your group has been asked by the CEO to prepare a range of technical marketing materials that can be used by sales reps to sell the new product.

First, determine the product that you are going to develop marketing materials for—will it be a new piece of software? a new digital media device? a medical tool or device? Once you have decided, the engineering team should develop specifications for the new product while the marketing team decides what features should be highlighted in marketing the new product.

Working as a group, first prepare an audience and purpose analysis for your product. To whom will you primarily be selling it? What are their needs, and how are you going to meet them with your new product? How can you persuade them to purchase your product?

Once your audience analysis is complete, decide as a group what media you want to use to reach that audience: brochures? a Web site? live presentations? posters? Choose the two most effective media for your audience, and focus on them.

Working collaboratively, create draft versions of your marketing materials in the two selected media. For a more intensive project, revise your draft versions and develop finished working models of your technical marketing materials. Prepare a brief presentation to share your "sales pitch" and marketing materials with the rest of your class.

The Global Window

Assume the following scenario: Members of your environmental consulting firm travel in teams worldwide on short notice to manage various environmental emergencies (toxic spills, chemical fires, and the like). Because of the rapid response required for these assignments and the international array of clients being served, team members have little or no time to research the particular cultural values of each client. Members typically find themselves having to establish immediate rapport and achieve agreement as they collaborate with clients during highly stressful situations.

Too often, however, ignorance of cultural differences leads to misunderstanding and needless delays in critical situations. Clients can lose face when they feel they are being overtly criticized and when their customs or values are ignored. When people feel insulted, or offended by inappropriate behavior, communication breaks down.

To avoid such problems, your boss has asked you to prepare a set of brief, general instructions titled "How to Avoid Offending International Clients." For immediate access, the instructions should fit on a pocket-sized quick reference card.

Working alone or in groups, do the research and design the reference card.

Complex Communication Situations

Definitions and Descriptions

Definitions explain a term or concept that is specialized or unfamiliar to an audience. In some cases, a term may have more than one meaning, and a clearly written definition tells readers exactly how the term is being used. Such precision is important in technical fields, where terms and phrases usually have specific meanings. Engineers talk about "elasticity" or "ductility"; bankers discuss "amortization" or "fiduciary relationships." For people both inside and outside the fields, these terms must be defined.

Descriptions, like definitions, help define an idea. In addition, descriptions use words and visuals to create a picture of the product or process, such as the structure of a bicycle frame or the process of nuclear fusion. These strategies (definition and description) rely on each other and provide the basis for virtually any type of technical explanation. For example, an audience of electrical engineering students may need a description of a solenoid, turbine, or some other electrical component. You may also need to use description or definition for lay audiences, such as people who want to know what a circuit breaker is or how an automobile bumper jack works in case of a flat tire.

Audience and Purpose Analysis

Make sure your particular language and content match the audience's background and experience. For a group of electrical engineers, your definition or description of a solenoid can be brief and to the point, and you can use highly technical language. For engineering students, your definition will need more detail. For general audiences, your definition will require language they can understand. See Figure 12.1 for a definition and description that includes a diagram to help general readers understand the entire process by which chemical contaminants are removed from soil. Figure 12.2 is a brief description for nursing students.

In terms of purpose, you need to understand why a particular audience needs or wants this information. If you are describing an automobile bumper jack for a general audience (as in Figure 12.3), you may learn that your readers' main purpose is to understand how the jack works so that they can use it to change a car tire. Therefore, the description or definition should be written in clear language and should avoid highly technical terms. It should follow an outline format or other layout that uses headings and white space so that readers can get in and out of the document quickly. And it should include diagrams or drawings to help readers see the whole picture.

Types of Definitions and Descriptions

Brief. Often you can clarify the meaning of a word by using a more familiar synonym or a clarifying phrase, as in

The *leaching field* (sievelike drainage area) requires crushed stone.

Dubbed the "lasagna" process because of its layers, this technology cleans up liquid-borne organic and inorganic contaminants in dense, claylike soils. Initial work is focused on removing chlorinated solvents.

Because clay is not very permeable, it holds ground water and other liquids well. Traditional remediation for this type of site requires that the liquid in the soil (usually ground water) be pumped out. The water brings many of the contaminants with it, then is chemically treated and replaced—a time-consuming and expensive solution.

The lasagna process, on the other hand, allows the soil to be remediated *in situ* by using low-voltage electric current to move contaminated ground water through treatment zones in the soil. Depending on the characteristics of the individual site, the process can be done in either a horizontal or vertical configuration. (See figure below.)

The first step in the lasagna process is to "fracture" the soil, creating a series of zones. In a horizontal configuration, a vertical borehole is drilled and a nozzle inserted; a highly pressurized mixture of water and sand (or another water/solid mix) is injected into the ground at various depths. The result: a stack of pancake-shaped, permeable zones in the denser, contaminated soil. The top and bottom zones are filled with carbon or graphite so they can conduct electricity. The zones between them are filled with treatment chemicals or microorganisms that will remediate the contaminants.

When electricity is applied to the carbon and graphite zones, they act as electrodes, creating an electric field. Within the field, the materials in the soil migrate toward either the positive or negative electrode. Along with the migrating materials, pollutants are carried into the treatment zones, where they are neutralized or destroyed.

The vertical configuration works in much the same way, differing only in installation. Because the electrodes and treatment zones extend down from the surface, this configuration does not require the sophisticated hydraulic fracturing techniques that are used in the horizontal configuration.

Schematic Diagram of the Lasagna Process

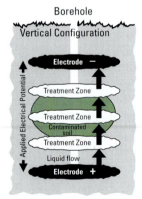

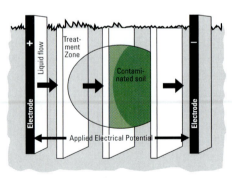

Figure 12.1 **A Definition and Description of the "Lasagna Process" for Filtering Contaminants out of Soil.**

Source: Adapted from Japikse (1994), p. 27.

A Description of the Standard Stethoscope

The stethoscope is a listening device that amplifies and transmits body sounds to aid in detecting physical abnormalities.

This instrument has evolved from the original wooden, funnel-shaped instrument invented by a French physician, R. T. Lennaec, in 1819. Because of his female patients' modesty, he found it necessary to develop a device, other than his ear, for auscultation (listening to body sounds).

This report explains to the beginning paramedical or nursing student the structure, assembly, and operating principle of the stethoscope.

The standard stethoscope is roughly 24 inches long and weighs about 5 ounces. The instrument consists of a sensitive sound-detecting and amplifying device whose flat surface is pressed against a bodily area. This amplifying device is attached to rubber and metal tubing that transmits the body sound to a listening device inserted in the ear.

The stethoscope's Y-shaped structure contains seven interlocking pieces: (1) diaphragm contact piece, (2) lower tubing, (3) Y-shaped metal piece, (4) upper tubing, (5) U-shaped metal strip, (6) curved metal tubing, and (7) hollow ear plugs. These parts form a continuous unit (Figure 1).

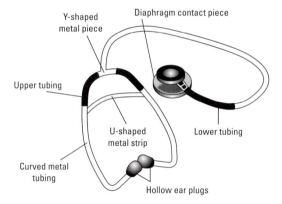

FIGURE 1 Stethoscope with Diaphragm Contact Piece (Front View)

The seven major parts of the stethoscope provide support for the instrument, flexibility of movement for the operator, and ease in use.

In an operating cycle, the diaphragm contact piece, placed against the skin, picks up sound impulses from the body's surface. These impulses cause the plastic diaphragm to vibrate. The amplified vibrations, in turn, are carried through a tube to a dividing point. From here, the amplified sound is carried through two separate but identical series of tubes to hollow ear plugs.

Figure 12.2 A Short Description of a Standard Stethoscope.

I. Introduction: General Description
   A. Definition, Function, and Background of the Item
   B. Purpose (and Audience—for classroom only)
   C. Overall Description (with general visuals, if applicable)
   D. Principle of Operation (if applicable)
   E. List of Major Parts

II. Description and Function of Parts
   A. Part One in Your Descriptive Sequence
      1. Definition
      2. Shape, dimensions, material (with specific visuals)
      3. Subparts (if applicable)
      4. Function
      5. Relation to adjoining parts
      6. Mode of attachment (if applicable)
   B. Part Two in Your Descriptive Sequence (and so on)

III. Summary and Operating Description
   A. Summary (used only in a long, complex description)
   B. Interrelation of Parts
   C. One Complete Operating Cycle

Figure 12.3 A Longer Description of an Automobile Bumper Jack. This first page provides an outline of the description.

Description of a Standard Bumper Jack

Introduction—General Description

The standard bumper jack is a portable mechanism for raising the front or rear of a car through force applied with a lever. This jack enables even a frail person to lift one corner of a 2-ton automobile.

The jack consists of a molded steel base supporting a free-standing, perpendicular, notched shaft (Figure 1). Attached to the shaft are a leverage mechanism, a bumper catch, and a cylinder for insertion of the jack handle. Except for the main shaft and leverage mechanism, the jack is made to be dismantled. All its parts fit neatly in the car's trunk.

The jack operates on a leverage principle, with the operator's hand traveling 18 inches and the car only $\frac{3}{8}$ of an inch during a normal jacking stroke. Such a device requires many strokes to raise the car off the ground but may prove a lifesaver to a motorist on some deserted road.

Five main parts make up the jack: base, notched shaft, leverage mechanism, bumper catch, and handle.

Description of Parts and Their Function

Base. The rectangular base is a molded steel plate that provides support and a point of insertion for the shaft (Figure 2). The base slopes upward to form a platform containing a 1-inch depression that provides a stabilizing well for the shaft. Stability is increased by a 1-inch cuff around the well. As the base rests on its flat surface, the bottom end of the shaft is inserted into its stabilizing well.

Shaft. The notched shaft is a steel bar (32 inches long) that provides a vertical track for the leverage mechanism. The notches, which hold the mechanism in position on the shaft, face the operator.

The shaft vertically supports the raised automobile, and attached to it is the leverage mechanism, which rests on individual notches.

Leverage Mechanism. The leverage mechanism provides the mechanical advantage needed for the operator to raise the car. It is made to slide up and down the notched shaft. The main body of this pressed-steel mechanism contains two units: one for transferring the leverage and one for holding the bumper catch.

The leverage unit has four major parts: the cylinder, connecting the handle and a pivot point; a lower pawl (a device that fits into the notches to allow forward and prevent backward motion), connected directly to the cylinder; an upper pawl, connected at the pivot point; and an "up-down" lever,

Figure 12.3 (*Continued*)

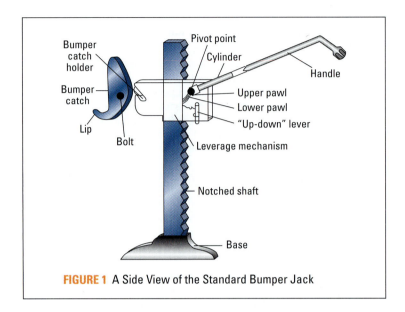

FIGURE 1 A Side View of the Standard Bumper Jack

which applies or releases pressure on the upper pawl by means of a spring (Figure 1). Moving the cylinder up and down with the handle causes the alternate release of the pawls, and thus movement up or down the shaft—depending on the setting of the "up-down" lever. The movement is transferred by the metal body of the unit to the bumper catch holder.

The holder consists of a downsloping groove, partially blocked by a wire spring (Figure 1). The spring is mounted in such a way as to keep the bumper catch in place during operation.

Bumper Catch. The bumper catch is a 9-inch molded plate that attaches the leverage mechanism to the bumper and is bent to fit the shape of the bumper. Its outer $\frac{1}{2}$ inch is bent up to form a lip (Figure 1), which hooks behind the bumper to hold the catch in place. The two sides of the plate are bent back 90 degrees to leave a 2-inch bumper contact surface, and a bolt is riveted between them. This bolt slips into the groove in the leverage mechanism and provides the attachment between the leverage unit and the car.

Jack Handle. The jack handle is a steel bar that serves both as lever and lug bolt (or lugnut) remover. This round bar is 22 inches long, $\frac{5}{8}$ inch in diameter, and is bent 135 degrees roughly 5 inches from its outer end. Its outer

Figure 12.3 (*Continued*)

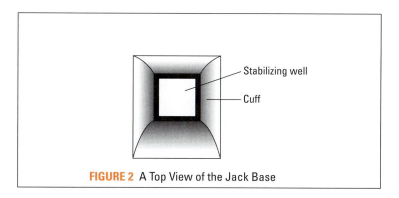

FIGURE 2 A Top View of the Jack Base

end is a socket wrench made to fit the wheel's lug bolts. Its inner end is beveled to form a bladelike point for prying the wheel covers and for insertion into the cylinder on the leverage mechanism.

Conclusion and Operating Description

One quickly assembles the jack by inserting the bottom of the notched shaft into the stabilizing well in the base, the bumper catch into the groove on the leverage mechanism, and the beveled end of the jack handle into the cylinder. The bumper catch is then attached to the bumper, with the lever set in the "up" position.

As the operator exerts an up-down pumping motion on the jack handle, the leverage mechanism gradually climbs the vertical notched shaft until the car's wheel is raised above the ground. When the lever is in the "down" position, the same pumping motion causes the leverage mechanism to descend the shaft.

Figure 12.3 (*Continued*)

In an online document, such as a Web page or online help system, short definitions such as these can easily be linked to the main word or phrase. A user who clicks on "leaching field" would be taken to a window that contains the definition and other important information.

A slightly longer way to define a phrase is to use the "term-class-features" method. You begin by stating the term. Then you indicate the broader class that this item belongs to, followed by the features that distinguish it from other items in that general grouping. Here are some examples:

Term	Class	Features
Carburetor:	A mixing device . . .	in gasoline engines that blends air and fuel into a vapor for combustion within the cylinders.
Diabetes:	A metabolic disease . . .	caused by a disorder of the pituitary gland or pancreas.

Brief definitions are fine when the audience does not require a great deal of information. For example, the sentence about the leaching field might be adequate in a progress report to a client whose house you are building. But a document that requires more detail, such as a public health report on groundwater contamination, would call for an expanded definition.

12.1

Sample expanded definitions

Expanded. Expanded definitions are appropriate when audiences require more detail. Depending on audience and purpose, an expanded definition may be a short paragraph or may extend to several pages. If a device, such as a digital dosimeter (used for measuring radiation exposure), is being introduced for the first time to an audience who needs to understand how this instrument works, your definition would require at least several paragraphs, if not pages. In such cases, your document would evolve from a simple definition to one that both defines and describes the device.

Typical Components of Definitions and Descriptions

Etymology. Sometimes a word's origin (etymology) can help users understand its meaning. *Biometrics,* for example, is derived from the Greek *bio,* meaning "life," and *metron,* meaning "measure." You can use a dictionary to learn the origins of most words.

History and background. In some cases, the history or background of a term, concept, or procedure can be useful in defining and describing it. For students or researchers who want in-depth information, history and background are appropriate. However, for users trying to perform a task, history and background can be cumbersome and unnecessary. If you wanted to install a new modem, you might be interested in a quick sentence explaining that *modem* stands for "modulator-demodulator." But you would not really care about the history of how modems were developed.

Operating principle. If part of the document's purpose is to teach people to use a product correctly, it is usually helpful for your audience to understand how a device operates. For example, a manual for a garden rototiller is intended to help people use the tiller. Therefore, users should have a sense of how the tiller operates: It uses gasoline, it needs a clean spark plug, and so on. A list of parts is another way of illustrating how a device operates.

Usability Considerations

Use appropriate levels of technicality. Your language in a definition or description needs to match the particular audience's level of experience. An audience of medical technicians will easily understand jargon related to their field, but nonexperts will need language they find familiar. For example, the sentence

> A tumor is a neoplasm.

would make sense to most medical professionals. But for an audience outside that field, you would need to unpack the term *neoplasm* and use more accessible language, as in

> A tumor is a growth of cells that occurs independently of surrounding tissue and serves no useful function.

Consider length and placement. The length of a definition or description should be appropriate for your audience and purpose. For example, if your audience needed to know only the very basics about a term (such as *tumor*), you could write a short sentence. But if your audience needed more information, you would need to amplify your definition with a description (say, of the process by which tumor cells displace healthy tissue).

Placement is also important. Each time an audience encounters an unfamiliar term or concept, it should be defined or described in the same area on the page or screen. In a printed text, you can accomplish this by placing brief definitions in an outside margin. On the screen, you would use a hypertext link. Hypertext and the Web are perhaps the best answer yet to making definitions and descriptions accessible, because readers can click on the item, read about it, and return to their original place on the page.

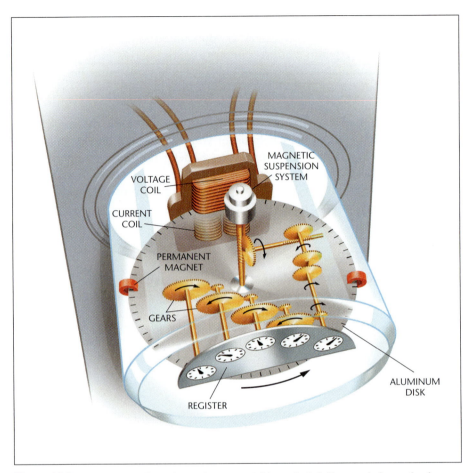

Figure 12.4 **Description of an Electricity Meter.** This exploded diagram helps make the written description it accompanies come to life.

Source: From Rosenau L. (2000, March). Working knowledge: Electric Meters, *Scientific American*, 108. Reprinted by permission of George Retseck.

Use visuals. Visuals can be very important in definitions and descriptions. You can explain as clearly as you like, but as the saying goes, a picture is worth a thousand words—even more when used with clear, accurate prose. The cutaway diagram (top view) in Figure 12.4 is a description of an electricity meter, designed for a general audience.

Use clear, concise language. Use sentences that are brief and to the point. Provide readers with the most important information quickly. If all your audience needs is a one-sentence definition, don't write a long description, no matter how interesting you think it might be.

Choose words with precision. Choose words carefully, and use the same word to refer to the same item. Is a tumor a "growth of cells" or simply "cells"? When describing fiber-optic technology, don't suddenly switch and call it "high-speed cable."

Use comparisons and examples. By comparing new information to ideas your audience already understands, you help build a bridge between people's current knowledge and the new ideas. For example, for a group of nonexperts, you could explain how earthquakes start in this manner:

> Imagine an enormous block of gelatin with a vertical knife slit through the middle of its lower half. Giant hands are slowly pushing the right side forward and the left side back along the slit, creating a strain that eventually splits the block. (Earthquake hazard analysis, 1984, p. 8.)

Use an appropriate organizational sequence. For longer descriptions, choose the organizational pattern that is most consistent with your purpose. If you want to describe how something looks or what parts it has, use a *spatial* sequence: Describe the items as your audience will see them. If you want to describe how something works, use a *functional* sequence: Describe the workings (functions) of the device. And if you want to describe how something is assembled, use a *chronological* sequence (see "Brief Instructions" and "Procedures" in Chapter 11).

Checklist for Definitions and Descriptions

- Is the length of the definition or description suited to its audience and purpose?
- Is the expanded definition adequately developed for its audience?
- Are visuals used adequately and appropriately?
- Does the definition appear in the appropriate location?
- Are comparisons and examples used to enhance understanding?
- Are any details missing, needless, or confusing for this audience?
- Does the description follow the clearest possible sequence?
- Will the level of technicality connect with the audience?
- Is the language clear and concise?
- Is the terminology precise and consistent?

Long Reports

When your purpose is to inform an audience, offer a solution to a problem, report progress, or make a detailed recommendation, you may need to write a long report. Long reports are often structured like a small book, with a table of contents, appendixes, and an index. Like short reports (see Chapter 10), long reports present ideas and facts to interested parties, decision makers, and other audiences. Technical professionals rely on reports as a basis for making informed decisions on a range of matters, from the possible side effects of a new pain medication to the environmental risks posed by a certain gasoline additive.

Long reports are called for in situations where an audience needs detailed information, statistics, and background information—the whole story. For example, your team of engineers needs to make far-reaching decisions about the best site for a toxic waste containment field. You have several months to research and make a decision, so you hire a consulting firm to report on all the relevant information. Their resulting product, a long report describing the geologic conditions of potential sites, might contain an appendix with detailed comparisons of topsoil, groundwater, and other conditions.

Audience and Purpose Analysis

Do your best to determine who will read the report. For instance, even if the report is addressed to team members, it may be sent on to other managers, the legal department, or sales and marketing. If you can learn about the actual audience members in advance, you can anticipate their various needs as you create the report. Before you start the report, be clear about its true purpose. For example, you may be under the impression that the report is intended simply to inform an audience. But after some initial research, you learn that your manager really wants you to recommend an action, not just state the facts. Recommending is different from informing, so it's important to understand the reason you are writing the report in the first place. For instance, the writers of the biodiesel report excerpted in Figure 12.5 made it clear that the audience was Georgia legislators and others making decisions whether or not to produce or use biodiesel. The document also has a clear purpose, stating clearly in the introduction, "The purpose of this report is . . ."

Types of Long Reports

Causal. Causal reports are used in situations where you need to explain what caused something to happen. For example, medical researchers may need to explain why so many apparently healthy people have sudden heart attacks. Or you might need to anticipate the possible effects of a particular decision, say, the effects of a corporate merger on employee morale.

Comparative. Comparative reports are used when you need to rate similar items on the basis of specific criteria. For example, you may need to answer questions such as "Which type of security procedure—firewall or encryption—should we install in our company's computer system?"

Feasibility. Feasibility reports are used when your purpose is to assess the practicality of an idea or plan. For example, if your company needs to know whether increased business will justify the cost of an interactive Web site, you would need to do some research and describe the results in a feasibility report.

Sometimes these categories overlap. Any single study may in fact require you to take several approaches. The sample report in Figure 12.9 is an example. The report is designed to answer the question, "Should the state of Georgia use and produce biodiesel?"

A General Model for Long Reports

After analyzing your audience and purpose, do some basic research. Then sketch a rough outline with headings and subheadings for the report.

12.2
Additional sample long reports

Introduction. The introduction engages and orients the audience and provides background as briefly as possible for the given situation. Often writers who are familiar with the product are tempted to write long introductions because they have a lot of background knowledge about the product or issue. But readers don't generally

---

Introduction

The State of Georgia faces two issues that may provide a unique opportunity for rural economic growth. The first issue is that major urban areas of the State have air quality problems that will require actions to reduce sources of pollution. One major pollution source is from exhaust emissions from cars and trucks. The use of alternative fuel sources such as biodiesel can make a significant reduction in certain exhaust emissions, thus reducing pollution and improving air quality.

The second issue facing the State is depressed crop farm incomes due to low market prices for the many oilseeds produced. Prices for soybeans, cottonseed and crush quality peanuts have been at very low levels for the last four years. These low prices have reduced farm incomes. Additionally, disposal of animal fat by-products and spent vegetable oils may become increasingly difficult in the future.

The opportunity for economic growth resides in the processing of these oilseeds and other suitable feedstocks produced within the State into biodiesel. The new fuel can be used by vehicles traversing the State, thus reducing air pollution and providing another market for Georgia produced oilseeds while creating a value added market for animal fats and spent oils. The benefits of biodiesel go far beyond the clean burning nature of the product. Biodiesel is a renewable resource helping reduce the economy's dependency on limited resources and imports. Also, biodiesel will help create a market for farmers and certain feedstocks and help reduce the amount of waste oil, fat and grease being dumped into landfills and sewers.

The purpose of this report is to provide decision makers with information on the feasibility of producing biodiesel in Georgia.

Figure 12.5 Introduction to the Biodiesel Report.
Source: From "A Study on the Feasibility of Biodiesel Production in Georgia" by Professor George A. Shumaker, et al. February 3, 2003. Reprinted by permission of George A. Shumaker.

need long history lessons about the topic. In the introduction, identify the topic's origin and significance, define or describe the problem or issue, and explain the report's purpose. Briefly identify your research methods (interviews, literature searches, and so on). List working definitions, but if you have more than two or three, place definitions in a glossary. Finally, briefly state your conclusion. Don't make readers wade through the entire report to find out what you are recommending or advising. The strength of such brevity can be seen in the introduction to the biodiesel report shown in Figure 12.5.

Body. The body describes and explains your findings. Present a clear and detailed picture of the evidence, interpretations, and reasoning on which you will base your conclusion. Divide topics into subtopics, and use informative headings as aids to navigation, as in the body section of the biodiesel report excerpted in Figure 12.6.

Potential Drawbacks to Biodiesel

Biodiesel can be corrosive to rubber materials and liner materials. Biodiesel cannot be stored in concrete lined tanks. In some cases, the fuel intake orifices may need to be reduced in size to create a higher cylinder pressure. And, given current petroleum prices, biodiesel is more costly to produce than biodiesel.

Georgia Diesel Demand

According to the Petroleum Marketing Monthly, published by the Energy Information Administration, 4.64 million gallons of diesel were sold per day in Georgia in 2000. This included all diesels, low and high sulfur, auto and farm, amounting to about 3.89% of the national annual demand.

Several institutions that are influenced or controlled by the state government are large users of diesel fuel. Demand from school districts in the metro Atlanta (21 counties) amounted to 9,702,798 gallons used in 2000. MARTA estimates using 6,644,070 gallons of diesel in 2000. Finally, the Georgia Department of Transportation used 1,521,957 gallons of diesel in 2000 statewide. These three institutions alone use close to 18 million gallons of diesel per year. Map 1 illustrates the amount of diesel used in the Metro Atlanta counties during 2000.

The Biodiesel Production Process

The technology of converting vegetable oils and animal fats into biodiesel is a well established process. The most commonly used and most economical process is called the *base catalyzed esterification of the fat with methanol*, typically referred to as "the methyl ester process". Essentially the process involves combining the fat/oil with methanol and sodium or potassium hydroxide. This process creates four main products - methyl ester (biodiesel), glycerine, feed quality fat and methanol that is recycled back through the system. The primary product, methyl ester, is better known as biodiesel. The glycerine and fats can be sold to generate added income from the process.

Figure 12.6 **Body of the Biodiesel Report.**

Source: From "A Study on the Feasibility of Biodiesel Production in Georgia" by Professor George A. Shumaker, et al. February 3, 2003. Reprinted by permission of George A. Shumaker.

The body of your report will vary greatly, depending on the audience, topic, purpose, and situation.

Conclusion. As seen in the portion of the biodiesel report excerpted in Figure 12.7, the conclusion is important because it answers the questions that originally sparked the analysis. In the conclusion, you summarize, interpret, and recommend. Although you have interpreted evidence at each stage of your analysis, your conclusion presents a broad interpretation and suggests a course of action where appropriate. Your conclusion should provide a clear and consistent perspective on the whole document. Don't introduce new ideas, facts, or statistics in the conclusion.

Conclusions

There exist a variety of potential feedstocks both in Georgia and nearby states that could be utilized to produce biodiesel. These feedstocks vary significantly in price depending on supply and demand condition as well as market structural conditions. Feedstock costs represent between 50 and 75 percent of the cost of producing biodiesel, and thus a reliable source of low priced feedstocks is critical to success. A 15 million gallon biodiesel plant would require about 27% of the vegetable and animal fats currently available within the state of Georgia. This facility would produce 750 million gallons of 2% blend for approximately twice the state demand. A 20% blend will create 75 million gallons of B20 or roughly 20% of the Georgia diesel market.

The processing technology for producing biodiesel is well established and presents little technological risk. The production of biodiesel is a very efficient process, returning about 3.2 units of energy for each unit used in production. Biodiesel is thus an excellent renewable fuel source. Biodiesel can be very easily integrated into the existing petroleum distribution system from the handling, chemical, physical and performance perspectives.

Lacking government mandates or subsidies, a feedstock cost of about 10 cents per pound or less, given current diesel fuel prices, is needed for biodiesel to be cost competitive.

Figure 12.7 Conclusion Section of the Biodiesel Report.
Source: From "A Study on the Feasibility of Biodiesel Production in Georgia" by Professor George A. Shumaker, et al. February 3, 2003. Reprinted by permission of George A. Shumaker.

Front Matter and End Matter in Long Reports

A long document must be easily accessible and must accommodate users with various interests. Preceding the report is *front matter:* the title page, letter of transmittal, table of contents, and abstract or summary of the report's content. Following the report (as needed) is *end matter:* The glossary, appendixes, and list of references cited can either provide supporting data or help users follow technical sections. Users can refer to any of these supplements or skip them altogether, according to their needs.

Title page. The title page gives the report title, the names of all authors, and their affiliations or the name of the organization that commissioned the report. The title announces the report's purpose and subject by using descriptive words such as *analysis, proposal, feasibility,* or *progress* (as in Figure 12.9).

Letter of transmittal. Many long reports include a letter of transmittal, addressed to a specific reader. This letter might

- Acknowledge individuals and organizations that helped with the report
- Refer to sections of special interest
- Discuss limitations of your study or any problems in gathering data
- Discuss possible follow-up investigations
- Offer personal (or off-the-record) observations
- Urge the recipient to immediate action

If a report is being sent to numerous people who are variously qualified and bear various relationships to you, individual letters of transmittal may vary.

Table of contents. Help readers find the information they're looking for by providing a table of contents. In designing your table, follow these guidelines:

- Number the front-matter (transmittal letter, abstract) pages with lowercase roman numerals. (The title page, though not listed, is counted as page i.) Number glossary, appendix, and endnote pages with arabic numerals, continuing the page sequence of your report proper, in which page 1 is the first page of the report text.
- Include no headings in the table of contents not listed as headings or subheadings in the report; the report may, however, contain subheadings not listed in the table of contents.
- Phrase headings in the table of contents exactly as in the report.
- List headings at various levels in varying type styles and indention.
- Use *leader lines* (. . . . .) to connect headings to page numbers. Align rows of dots vertically, each above the other.

List of tables and figures. On a separate page following the table of contents or integrated with it, list the tables and figures appearing in the report.

Abstract or executive summary. Reports are often read by many people: researchers, developers, managers, vice presidents, customers. For readers who are interested only in the big picture, the entire report may not be relevant, so most long reports are commonly preceded by an abstract (short) or an executive summary (longer). In this brief description, you explain the issue, describe how you researched it, and state your conclusion. Busy readers can then flip through the document to locate sections of importance to them.

In preparing your abstract, follow these suggestions:

- Make sure your abstract stands alone in terms of meaning.
- Write for a general audience. Readers of the abstract are likely to vary in expertise, perhaps more than those who read the report itself; therefore, translate all technical data.
- Add no new information. Simply summarize the report.
- Present your information in the following sequence:
    1. Identify the issue or need that led to the report.
    2. Offer the major findings from the body of the report.
    3. Include a condensed conclusion and recommendations, if any.

Appendixes. Add one or more appendixes to your report if you have large blocks of material or other documents that are relevant but will bog readers down if placed in the middle of the document itself. For example, if your report on the cost of electricity at your company refers to another report issued by the local utility company, you may wish to include this second report as an appendix.

Other items that belong in an appendix might include complex formulas, interview questions and responses, maps, photographs, sample questionnaires and tabulated responses, texts of laws and regulations, and the like. Do not stuff appendixes with needless information or use them unethically for burying bad or embarrassing news that belongs in the report proper. Title each appendix clearly: "Appendix A: Projected Costs." Mention the appendix early in the introduction, and refer readers to it at appropriate points in the report: "(see Appendix A)."

See, for example, Appendixes A and B in this textbook.

Glossary. Use a glossary if your report contains more than two or three technical terms that may not be understood by all audience members. Use standard definitions in your glossary: Refer to company style guides or technical dictionaries. If fewer than five terms need defining, place them in the report introduction as working definitions, or use footnote definitions. If you use a separate glossary, announce its location: "(see the glossary at the end of this report)."

List of references. List each of your outside references in alphabetical order or in the same numerical order as they are cited in the report proper.

Not all reports have all of these supplements. For example, the biodiesel report (Figure 12.9) omits the letter of transmittal because this report was presented in person. And, in that report, the introduction (Figure 12.5) also functions as the abstract. No glossary is needed because the opening pages present an expanded definition of biodiesel, its uses and production. A long appendix containing calculations and formulas has been omitted here, to save space. Finally, there is no formal list of references because the bulk of the research is based on public sources or hired consultants, each cited in the text (as on page 10, bottom, in Figure 12.9).

For examples of many of these supplements in a student-written report, see "Feasibility Analysis of a Career in Technical Marketing, " on the accompanying Web site, at www.ablongman.com/gurak.

Usability Considerations

Clearly identify the problem or goal. To address the true purpose of the situation, you must carefully identify your goal. Begin by defining the main questions involved in the report and then outlining any subordinate questions. Your legislator, for example, might pose this question: "Will producing biodiesel benefit the state of Georgia?" Answering this question is the main goal of the report; however, this question leads to others, such as "What are the drawbacks of biodiesel use?" Create a goal statement, such as "The goal of this report is to examine and evaluate claims about the production of biodiesel in the state of Georgia." (See pages 276–281 for the complete Biodiesel report.)

Provide enough information but not too much. Any usable analysis must address the needs, interests, and technical expertise of your audience. A long history of the development of the pacemaker may be interesting to you but inappropriate for your report. As you plan the report, find out how much of the information you've gathered readers need in order to make a decision. Also, make sure your technical terms are not too complex for your audience. If you have a mixed audience, provide a glossary where readers can look up unfamiliar terms. If your report is posted to a Web site, you can use hyperlinks for glossary terms.

Provide accurate information. Make sure your information is as accurate as possible and, to the best of your ability, without bias. Use reputable information sources, particularly for statistical data. Be careful when taking information from the Web; Web sites often sound credible but can be based on biased or inaccurate information (see Chapters 4 and 5). Also, make sure you interpret information fairly and provide valid conclusions based on your best research. Assume, for example, that you were writing a report to recommend the best brand of chain saw for a logging company. In reviewing test reports, you learned that one brand, Bomarc, is easiest to operate but also has the fewest safety features. Both pieces of information should be included in the report, regardless of your personal preference for this brand.

Use appropriate visuals. As discussed in Chapter 9, visual information can make complex statistics and numeric data easy to understand. Graphs are especially useful for analyzing rising or falling trends, levels, and long-term forecasts. Tables and charts are helpful for comparing data. Photographs and diagrams are an excellent way to show a component or special feature. Be sure your visual is placed near the accompanying text, and be careful not to overuse visuals. For example, the biodiesel report in Figure 12.9 makes good use of diagrams, such as the one featured in Figure 12.8.

Use informative headings. Headings and subheadings in your report announce what each section contains. The heading "Data Analysis" does not really say much, whereas the heading "Physiological Effects and Health Risks" offers a clear, informative preview of the content of a section.

Write clearly and concisely. Even readers who need every bit of information in your report don't want to be bogged down with prose that is cumbersome, long-winded, and hard to read. Keep your language crisp and clear. Use active voice whenever possible. Ask a colleague or editor to copyedit your report before it is printed.

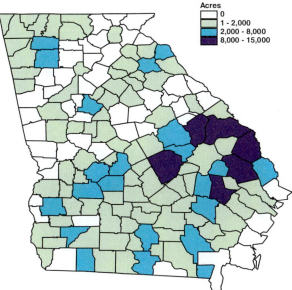

Source: Center for Agribusiness and Economic Development

Figure 12.8 **Visual from the Biodiesel Report.**

A Study on the Feasibility
of
Biodiesel Production in Georgia

by
Professor George A. Shumaker
Professor John McKissick, Director
Christopher Ferland, Research Coordinator
Bridgid Doherty, Agricultural Statistician

February 3, 2003

A Study on the Feasibility of Biodiesel Production in Georgia

Table of Contents

A Study on the Feasibility of Biodiesel Production in Georgia

George A. Shumaker, John McKissick, Christopher Ferland, and Bridgid Doherty
Professor, Professor and Director, Research Coordinator, Agricultural Statistician

Introduction

The State of Georgia faces two issues that may provide a unique opportunity for rural economic growth. The first issue is that major urban areas of the State have air quality problems that will require actions to reduce sources of pollution. One major pollution source is from exhaust emissions from cars and trucks. The use of alternative fuel sources such as biodiesel can make a significant reduction in certain exhaust emissions, thus reducing pollution and improving air quality.

The second issue facing the State is depressed crop farm incomes due to low market prices for the many oilseeds produced. Prices for soybeans, cottonseed and crush quality peanuts have been at very low levels for the last four years. These low prices have reduced farm incomes. Additionally, disposal of animal fat by-products and spent vegetable oils may become increasingly difficult in the future.

The opportunity for economic growth resides in the processing of these oilseeds and other suitable feedstocks produced within the State into biodiesel. The new fuel can be used by vehicles traversing the State, thus reducing air pollution and providing another market for Georgia produced oilseeds while creating a value added market for animal fats and spent oils. The benefits of biodiesel go far beyond the clean burning nature of the product. Biodiesel is a renewable resource helping reduce the economy's dependency on limited resources and imports. Also, biodiesel will help create a market for farmers and certain feedstocks and help reduce the amount of waste oil, fat and grease being dumped into landfills and sewers.

The purpose of this report is to provide decision makers with information on the feasibility of producing Biodiesel in Georgia.

Benefits of Biodiesel

There are several benefits to using biodiesel as a blended fuel in diesel engines: Biodiesel has a lower flash point than petroleum diesel and thus helps prevent damaging fires; biodiesel burns cleaner than petroleum diesel and thus reduces particulate matter, thus lowering emissions of nitrogen, carbon monoxide and unburned hydrocarbons; the odor of burned biodiesel fuel is considered by many to be less offensive than petroleum diesel; there are only limited or no needed modifications to current engines to use biodiesel; there would be no need to change the transportation and storage systems to handle biodiesel; biodiesel behaves similarly to petroleum for engine performance and mileage; and biodiesel dissipates engine heat better than petroleum diesel.

2

Potential Drawbacks to Biodiesel

Biodiesel can be corrosive to rubber materials and liner materials. Biodiesel cannot be stored in concrete lined tanks. In some cases, the fuel intake orifices may need to be reduced in size to create a higher cylinder pressure. And, given current petroleum prices, biodiesel is more costly to produce than biodiesel.

Georgia Diesel Demand

According to the Petroleum Marketing Monthly, published by the Energy Information Administration, 4.64 million gallons of diesel were sold per day in Georgia in 2000. This included all diesels, low and high sulfur, auto and farm, amounting to about 3.89% of the national annual demand.

Several institutions that are influenced or controlled by the state government are large users of diesel fuel. Demand from school districts in the metro Atlanta (21 counties) amounted to 9,702,798 gallons used in 2000. MARTA estimates using 6,644,070 gallons of diesel in 2000. Finally, the Georgia Department of Transportation used 1,521,957 gallons of diesel in 2000 statewide. These three institutions alone use close to 18 million gallons of diesel per year. Map 1 illustrates the amount of diesel used in the Metro Atlanta counties during 2000.

The Biodiesel Production Process

The technology of converting vegetable oils and animal fats into biodiesel is a well established process. The most commonly used and most economical process is called the *base catalyzed esterification of the fat with methanol*, typically referred to as "the methyl ester process". Essentially the process involves combining the fat/oil with methanol and sodium or potassium hydroxide. This process creates four main products - methyl ester (biodiesel), glycerine, feed quality fat and methanol that is recycled back through the system. The primary product, methyl ester, is better know as biodiesel. The glycerine and fats can be sold to generate added income from the process.

Figure 12.9 **The Biodiesel Report in Full.**

Source: From "A Study on the Feasibility of Biodiesel Production in Georgia" by Professor George A. Shumaker, et al. February 3, 2003. Reprinted by permission of George A. Shumaker.

3

Figure 1. Diesel Utilization by Metro Counties, Georgia 2000.

Diesel Utilization by Metro Counties*, Georgia 2000

Gallons Used
- 0
- 1 - 1,000,000
- 1,000,001 - 3,000,000
- 3,000,001 - 6,000,000

*Includes school districts and MARTA.

Source: Center for Agribusiness and Economic Development

4

Figure 2. Methyl Ester Process

Methyl Ester Process

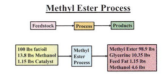

For each unit of energy used to produce biodiesel, about 3.2 units of energy are gained. Ratio for ethanol is about 1.25.

Source: Frazier, Barnes & Associates.

The methyl ester process is very energy efficient in that for each unit of energy required by the process approximately 3.2 units of energy are gained. Biodiesel is thus an excellent renewable fuel source. The ratio for ethanol production is 1.25.

Biodiesel can be produced from any type of vegetable oil or animal fat. Some of the suitable feedstocks may require some pre-processing to remove materials that reduce the yield of biodiesel. Crude or unrefined vegetable oils contain free fatty acids and gums that must be removed before entering the methyl ester process. The pre-processing can take the form of refining, degumming and/or filtering to remove the impurities. Degumming involves mixing a small amount of water (about 3-5%) with the feedstock which precipitates the gums which then can be separated by centrifuging the mixture. Refining involves adding sodium hydroxide to the feedstock to form a soap that can be separated by centrifuge from the oil. Yellow grease or spent restaurant fats must be filtered and refined to remove the free fatty acids and residual cooking fines.

Some of these impurities have market value and can be sold to other industries in or near Georgia. The fats can be used in feed rations for poultry and other livestock.

Feedstock Availability

Major feedstocks for the methyl ester process currently available in Georgia include soybean oil, cottonseed oil, peanut oil, spent restaurant fats and rendered poultry fats. Other

---

5

suitable feedstocks suitable for the methyl ester process but not currently readily available in Georgia include canola oil, beef tallow and rendered pork fat.

It appears that there is an adequate supply of oils and fats available in or near Georgia to produce biodiesel. Two existing Georgia firms, Chickasha of Georgia in Tifton and Mid Georgia Processing in Vienna produce vegetable oils. These two firms crush peanuts and cotton seed and produce an estimated 9.6 million gallons of vegetable oil per year. A proposed farmer owned cooperative, Farmers Oilseed Cooperative, Inc, if developed could produce an additional 13 million gallons of vegetable oil from primarily soybeans and canola. A large soybean crushing facility in Southeast South Carolina also could be a supply of soybean oil with an annual output of about 17 million gallons per year.

Poultry is the leading agricultural commodity in the state. Thus, the volume of broiler fat produced in Georgia is high. On an annual basis, it is estimated that 7.2 billion pounds of birds are slaughtered in Georgia (Georgia Department of Agriculture). Roughly 12 to 15 percent of a bird is fat, thus, a maximum of 1.08 billion pounds of fat is available in Georgia annually. However, of this total pounds of fat, half is estimated to be edible fat and will remain on the market as chicken skin on wings or fryers, thus reducing the pounds of available fat to 540 million pounds. The integrators own approximately 80-85% of the processing of poultry. Currently, integrators such as Cargill import oil and other feeds from outside the state via railways. These integrated firms have been using 99% of their poultry fat rendered into their feed production. The fat serves multiple purposes as : anitdust, milling, nutritional and energy value, and an anti-caking agent in the poultry feed. The poultry industry has spent numerous dollars formulating a feed to raise a 1.5 ounce egg into a 6-pound bird in roughly 42 days. This highly researched diet has been proven and substituting anything into the diet will cost money and be highly questionable. Thus the researcher assumes that little poultry fat will be released from the integrators for use as biodiesel. This leaves 15-20% of the rendered poultry fat, 105 million pounds, available for use in a biodiesel facility or approximately 14 million gallons of marketable fat per year.

6

Figure 3. County Distribution of Soybean Production in Georgia.

Soybean Production in Georgia: 2001

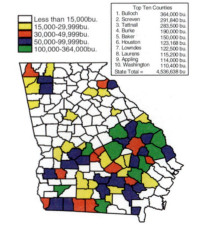

Less than 15,000bu.
15,000-29,999bu.
30,000-49,999bu.
50,000-99,999bu.
100,000-364,000bu.

Top Ten Counties	
1. Bulloch	364,000 bu.
2. Screven	291,840 bu.
3. Tattnall	283,500 bu.
4. Burke	190,000 bu.
5. Baker	150,000 bu.
6. Houston	123,168 bu.
7. Lowndes	122,500 bu.
8. Laurens	115,200 bu.
9. Appling	114,000 bu.
10. Washington	110,400 bu.
State Total =	4,536,638 bu.

Figure 12.9 (*Continued*)

7

Figure 4. Poultry Fat Production by County, Georgia 2000

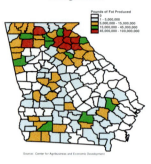

Poultry Fat Production by County, Georgia 2000

Pounds of Fat Produced
- 0
- 1 - 5,000,000
- 5,000,000 - 15,000,000
- 15,000,000 - 45,000,000
- 45,000,000 - 100,000,000

Source: Center for Agribusiness and Economic Development

8

Figure 5. County Distribution of Soybean Production in South Carolina in 1999.

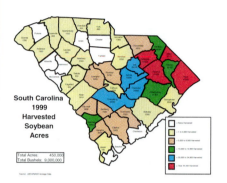

South Carolina
1999
Harvested
Soybean
Acres

| Total Acres: | 450,000 |
| Total Bushels: | 9,000,000 |

- None Harvested
- 1 to 4,999 Harvested
- 5,000 to 9,999 Harvested
- 10,000 to 19,999 Harvested
- 20,000 to 34,999 Harvested
- Over 35,000 Harvested

Source: USDA/NASS Acreage Data

Another potential feedstock is spent fats or yellow grease. Yellow grease is inedible fat, oil and grease used and removed from the food service industry. Fryolators, grills, and water-to-oil separators are the major producers of yellow grease. Handling of yellow grease begins at the source, the food service industry. Most grease will be placed into a closed container waiting for disposal from a rendering service.

Most of the yellow grease produced in Georgia is collected by renderers who clean the grease and prepare it for other use in chemicals, soap, cosmetics, plastics, lubricants, and livestock and poultry feeds. Recent concerns about BSE in the beef industry may lead to reduced use of the rendered yellow grease as a feed ingredient, potentially making it available for biodiesel. The Agricultural and Bioengineering Department at the University of Georgia estimates that 95% of the yellow grease produced by the food service industry in Georgia is

---

9

currently used in animal feeds.

Across the United States, another large market for yellow grease is the export market accounting for 35% of disappearance. It is estimated that this will continue to rise, absent other emerging domestic markets. A study done at the University of Georgia mentions that the high value of yellow grease has made it a target for theft in certain areas. Yellow grease has been used in the commercial food production industry where petroleum lubricants cannot come in contact with food.

It is difficult to get an exact estimate of the volume of rendered yellow grease availability in Georgia. While there is a significant volume handled, the amount available for sale is not yet determined. It is estimated that given a profitable return from biodiesel production, rendered yellow grease could be a good feedstock source.

Historical Feedstock Costs

Vegetable and animal fat prices vary depending upon supply and demand for each of the products and also upon the overall supply and demand situation for the entire fat/oil complex due to substitutability between products in some uses. In general, the vegetable oils have a higher unit value than do the animal fats. The following table shows the recent historical range of prices for some of the leading potential feedstock sources.

Table 1. Historical Feedstock Cost Ranges, 1996-2000.

Feedstock	Price Range Per Pound	Pre-processing Cost Per Pound	Feedstock Cost Per Pound
Crude Soy Oil	$0.15-0.27	$0.005-0.01	$0.16-0.28
Refined Cottonseed Oil	$0.15-0.28	suitable as is	$0.15-0.28
Crude Canola Oil	$0.12-019	$0.05-0.01	$0.13-0.20
Crude Corn Oil	$0.15-0.29	$0.005-0.01	$0.16-0.30
Crude Peanut Oil	$0.20-0.50	$0.005-0.01	$0.21-0.51
Yellow Grease	$0.08-0.14	$0.02-0.025	$0.105-0.165
Poultry Fat	$0.06-0.12	$0.005-0.10	$0.07-0.13

Feedstock Conclusion

It appears that only a limited supply of viable feedstocks exist in Georgia for a large-scale biodiesel operation. One of the problems is the high concentration in the poultry industry in Georgia demanding similar feedstock for poultry feed. Another problem is the other

---

10

uses for recycled oil and beef tallow existing in the Southeast with soap, lubricant, cosmetics, and further processing of poultry.

Regional vegetable oil sites which use their oil production internally were not counted. Those oil sites available totaled 26.9 million gallons.

Table 2 provides the apparent quantities available of the feedstock investigated along with the prices paid for as indicated in the Feedstock publication.

Table 2. Availability and Prices of Feedstock in Georgia

Feedstock	Quantity (7.5lbs=gallon)	Price (Raw)	Price Per Gallon	Total Gallons
Beef Tallow	Limited	$.13-.17	$.97-1.27	N/A
Poultry Fat	Est. 105 million lbs	$.06-.12	$.45-.90	14 million
Recycled Oil	Est. 27 million lbs	$.08-.14	$.60-1.05	2.7 million
Oilseed	Est. 202 million lbs	$.15-.29	$1.12-2.17	26.9 million
Total Available	Est. 334 million lbs			**43.6 million**

The proposed biodiesel production facility would be capable of using any or all of the above feedstocks. Obviously, it would be in the best interest to secure as much feedstock as possible at the least cost in order to reduce the cost to the consumer of the biodiesel product. However, it is unlikely that enough yellow grease and poultry fat could be secured to run the plant full time so that other oils would also be needed. The most likely other higher valued oils would be soybean oil, cottonseed oil and peanut oil.

In summary, it appears that there is currently an adequate volume of feedstock produced in the State to meet the needs of a medium sized biodiesel production facility. The facility would need approximately 115 million pounds of feedstock or 1/3 of the estimated available market. The question yet to be answered is whether or not sufficient feedstock can be purchased at a price that would make biodiesel production economically feasible.

The Economics of Biodiesel Production

The Center for Agribusiness and Economic Development at the University of Georgia secured the services of Frazier, Barnes & Associates (FBA) of Memphis, TN, a consulting firm specializing in vegetable oil processing, to assess the capital cost of various sized biodiesel production facilities. Each of the plant cost estimates are for a facility capable of handling a wide variety of feedstocks for biodiesel production. The capital cost estimates include the cost of facilities needed to pre-process any feedstock such that it could be converted to biodiesel using the methyl ester process described earlier. FBA evaluated four different sized biodiesel site

---

Figure 12.9 (*Continued*)

11

production plants, looking closely at estimated construction and operating costs. Tables 3 and 4 present a summary of the findings:

Table 3. Estimated Capital Cost Comparison of Various Plant Sizes.

Plant Size (million gallon/yr)	.5	3	15	30
Capital Cost	$950,000	$3.4 mill.	$9.6 mill.	$15 mill.
Feedstock Needed Pounds Gallons	3.75 mill. 500,000	22.5 mill. 3 mill.	112.5 mill. 15 mill.	225 mill. 30 mill.

Source: Frazier, Barnes & Associates
Assumes a green field site. Estimated Accuracy +/- 25%. Total includes capital cost for pre-processing feedstock

The capital cost ranges from $950,000 to $15 million depending on the capacity of the operation. The feedstock needed to run at full capacity ranged from 3.75 million pound at the smallest level of production to 225 million pounds at the highest level of production.

Table 4. Production Cost Sensitivity to Feedstock Cost by Plant Size, Dollars per Gallon of Biodiesel.

Plant Size (million gallon/yr)	.5	3	15	30
$0.10 per lb cost	$1.96	$1.33	$1.11	$1.10
$0.15 per lb cost	$2.34	$1.70	$1.48	$1.48
$0.20 per lb cost	$2.72	$2.08	$1.85	$1.85
$0.25 per lb cost	$3.09	$2.46	$2.21	$2.21

Based on the data provided in Tables 3 and 4, it appears the most appropriate size facility for Georgia is the one that produces about 15 million gallons of biodiesel per year with a capital cost of about $9.6 million. In Table 3 we see that most of the economies of scale are realized in a 15 million gallon plant. Unit costs of production do not appear to fall by doubling the size to 30 million gallons. Therefore, the remainder of this report will focus on a plant size of 15 million gallon capacity.

Capital Costs for the 15 Million Gallon Biodiesel Facility

The following table presents a breakdown of the capital cost components of a 15 million gallon per year capacity biodiesel production facility. The cost estimates represent a 'turn-key' facility placed upon a green site near transportation access.

12

Table 5. Estimated Biodiesel Capital Cost Details for a 15 Million Gallon Capacity Plant.

Equipment	$3,600,000
Buildings	$1,200,000
Utilities	$720,000
Civil/Mechanical/Electrical	$2,736,000
Land/Prep/Trans Access	$192,000
Engineering/Permitting	$192,000
Set-up Consulting	$3,000
Contingency (10%)	$960,000
Total Installed Cost	$9,603,000

Source: Frazier, Barnes & Associates

The physical plant would require approximately 7 to 10 acres for the building, tank farm and transportation areas. A buffer zone may require more land depending upon the surrounding level of development. The building needed to house the plant would be approximately 5,000 square feet and about 60 feet in height. It would contain all the processing equipment plus a laboratory for quality control and offices. The processing area would use about 3,400 square feet. The tank farm may utilize about 20,000 square feet and would contain tanks totaling 650,000 gallon capacity divided between both holding tanks for feedstock and finished product. This plant would operate continuously and stop production only for maintenance and repair. It would require an operating employment force of eight people plus six people in management, sales, accounting and clerical.

Sensitivity to Feedstock Costs

The actual physical costs of production of biodiesel is a relatively small proportion of the total production costs (see Table 6). Costs of feedstocks are the dominant factor in determining final production cost. In the 15 million gallon per year plant, total annual operating costs would be about $22.947 million. Actual estimated operating costs are about 25 percent of total cost while feedstock acquired at $0.15 per pound average cost would represent about 75 percent of total cost. Clearly, the ability to acquire low priced feedstocks is imperative to minimize the cost of biodiesel production.

Biodiesel Production Costs

The cost of producing a gallon of methyl ester is highly dependent upon the average cost of the feedstocks used to produce it. The following table presents a detailed breakdown of

13

biodiesel production costs for a 15 million gallon facility with average feedstock costs of 15 cents per pound.

Table 6. Breakeven for Biodiesel Production for a 15 Million Gallon per Year Facility with Feedstock Cost Averaging 15 Cents per Pound.

Item	Total	Per Gallon
Income	$18,123,000	$1.21*
Feedstock & Direct	$20,213,640	$1.35
Labor	$722,500	$.05
Variable Cost	$678,043	$.05
Fixed Cost	$1,332,780	$.09
Total Cost	$22,947,363	$1.48
Profit/Loss	**($4,824,362)**	**($.032)**

* includes glycerin & feed fat by-products

Table 6 exhibits that the greatest portion of the cost in manufacturing biodiesel is the feedstock and direct cost. The direct cost consists of the catalyst and methanol. These costs total $1.35 or 90% of the total cost when the feedstock is purchased for $.15 per gallon.

Table 7. Total Production Cost per Gallon of 100% Biodiesel at Various Average Feedstock Costs from a 15 Million Gallon per Year Plant.

Average Feedstock Cost	Total Production Cost Per Gallon
$0.10	$1.11
$0.15	$1.48
$0.20	$1.85
$0.25	$2.21
$0.30	$2.58
$0.35	$2.94

The results in Table 7 reveal the strong relationship between the final product cost and the feedstock cost. If Georgia wishes to compete and produce biodiesel, a relatively cheap ($.10 to $.15) feedstock needs to be used in the biodiesel production.

14

Sensitivity to Changes in Budgeted Costs

Sound analysis of a proposed project calls for a look at what would happen if the assumed production cost structure changes. The following chart demonstrates the impact of both higher and lower costs of production upon the net returns of the operation. As one might expect, net return increases with lower costs and decreases with higher costs. The point to be made is not that relationship but rather the magnitude of changes in net return given various changes in costs.

Graph 1. Profit/Loss versus Change in Budgeted Costs

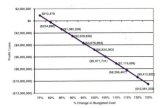

Graph 1 indicates the 15 million gallon facility needs to reduce cost by 22% to breakeven. This may be achievable with a subsidy on the feedstock.

Breakeven Feedstock Cost

The following graph clearly illustrates the relationship between the profitability or loss of a 15 million gallon facility as feedstock costs change. The breakeven cost of feedstock, assuming all other costs remain constant it is about $0.108 per pound. Returns above costs would obtain if average feedstock cost is below $0.108 per pound while operating losses would result if average feedstock cost is above $0.108 per pound.

Figure 12.9 (*Continued*)

15

Graph 2. Profit/Loss versus Feedstock Costs

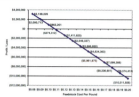

Graph 2 exhibits the strong relationship between the feedstock and breakeven. When the feedstock price approaches $.10 per pound the facility creates a positive net return.

Sensitivity to Changes in Selling Price

Another source of risk involves changes in the selling price of the methyl ester product. The following chart illustrates the relationship between net returns and differing methyl ester sales prices. The breakeven selling price of methyl ester is about $1.48 per gallon when feedstock costs average 15 cents per pound.

Graph 3. Profit/Loss versus Change in Sales Price

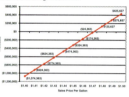

Graph 3 shows a sales price of $1.48 is needed to create a positive return.

16

The Bottom Line - Can Biodiesel from the Proposed Facility Compete with Regular Diesel?

Perhaps the question is a bit misleading. The cost of producing biodiesel given current average feedstock costs of about $0.15 a pound is about $1.56 per gallon (see Table 6). This value should be compared to the wholesale price of diesel fuel to get a proper comparison. Wholesale Diesel Prices can be estimated by the following formula:

$$\text{WDP} = \text{Crude Oil Price per Barrel} / 42 \text{ gallons} + \text{Processing } (\$0.05/\text{gal}) + \text{Transportation } (\$0.02) + \text{Profit } (\$0.05)$$

$$\text{WDP} = \$25.11 \text{ (March 19, 2002)} /42 + \$.12 = \$0.72 \text{ per gallon}$$

Current early 2002 estimated wholesale diesel fuel prices are about $0.72 per gallon. Thus it appears biodiesel is not competitive at current prices.

However, biodiesel is used primarily as a fuel additive and is seldom used in 100% form. Most commonly it is mixed as either 2 or 20 percent blends. When you look at the added cost of the blended product, then the question becomes more appropriate, especially in light of the challenges facing Georgia in terms of both the environmental impact and low farm incomes.

Tables 8 and 9 illustrate the added cost to the retail price of fuel when biodiesel is blended at 2 and 20 percent levels. The point to gain from the tables is that the added cost to the retail price is relatively small from blending in biodiesel, especially with 2% biodiesel. Furthermore, at higher fuel prices, similar to what we have seen during early 2001, biodiesel can even reduce the retail price.

Table 8. Added Cost to Retail Price of Diesel Fuel When Blended with 2 Percent Biodiesel.

	Retail Diesel Prices Per Gallon						
	$0.60	$0.75	$0.90	$1.05	$1.20	$1.35	$1.50
Biodiesel Cost 100%	Added Cost in Cents per Gallon						
$1.25	0.013	0.010	0.007	0.004	0.001	(0.002)	(0.005)
$1.50	0.018	0.015	0.012	0.009	0.006	0.003	
$1.75	0.023	0.020	0.017	0.012	0.011	0.008	0.005
$2.00	0.028	0.025	0.022	0.019	0.016	0.013	0.010
$2.25	0.033	0.030	0.027	0.024	0.021	0.018	0.015

17

Table 9. Added Cost to Retail Price of Diesel Fuel When Blended with 20 Percent Biodiesel.

	Retail Diesel Prices Per Gallon						
	$0.60	$0.75	$0.90	$1.05	$1.20	$1.35	$1.50
Biodiesel Cost 100%	Added Cost in Cents per Gallon						
$1.25	0.130	0.100	0.070	0.040	0.010	(0.020)	(0.050)
$1.50	0.180	0.150	0.120	0.090	0.060	0.030	
$1.75	0.230	0.200	0.170	0.140	0.110	0.080	0.050
$2.00	0.280	0.250	0.220	0.190	0.160	0.130	0.100
$2.25	0.330	0.300	0.270	0.240	0.210	0.180	0.150

Biodiesel can be produced and marketed in a 2% blend formulation at competitive price if

1. Feedstock costs are near 10 cents per pound and retail diesel prices near $1.15 per gallon.
2. Retail diesel prices are above $1.25 per gallon with feedstock costs of 15 cents per pound.
3. There is a tax reduction (State or Federal or both) that would make up the difference between the delivered cost of the biodiesel and diesel.

Biodiesel Products and Handling Considerations

The methyl ester from the plant can be used directly to run a diesel engine. However, in most cases, the product is blended with regular diesel fuel. The most commonly used blends are 2 and 20 percent blends where either 2 or 20 percent of the blend is the methyl ester and the dominant remainder is regular diesel fuel. These products are easily mixed and require no special equipment to accomplish the blending process. Typically the methyl ester is placed in a container and the diesel fuel is then poured into the methyl ester and 'splash blended'. No further stirring is needed to accomplish blending. Once blended the two products are reported to remain stable.

According to the National Biodiesel Board in Jefferson, MO, biodiesel can be stored in the same containers as petroleum diesel, however concrete storage tanks should not be used. Biodiesel is non-toxic and biodegradable. If stored above ground in a blended form the requirements are the same as for petroleum. When held as 100% methyl ester, it should be handled similar to vegetable oils.

Biodiesel can gel in cold weather conditions similar to diesel. This problem is solved either through storage in heated environments or by the addition of additives that inhibit gelling.

18

Gelling of biodiesel varies depending upon the chemical composition of the feedstock used in its production. The higher the saturated fat of the feedstock, such as in animal fats, the higher the temperature at which gelling occurs. The converse is also true. Canola oil, with low levels of saturated fats, derived biodiesel provides the lowest gelling temperature biodiesel. Pure biodiesel should be stored and transported at temperatures above 50 F and blending temperatures should be above 40 F.

Environmental Impacts of Biodiesel Use

Studies completed by the Environmental Protection Agency (NREL/TP 2001) state that a 20% blend is "basically a trade off between cost, emissions, cold weather, material compatibility and solvency issues". Researchers believe the 20% blend to be the best blend for general use without encountering major issues. Higher blends often cause problems in winter and with nitrogen oxide emissions.

Table 10. Emission Changes with Biodiesel Fuels.

Emission	100% Biodiesel*	20% Biodiesel Blend*
Carbon Monoxide	-43.2%	-12.6%
Hydrocarbons	-56.3%	-11%
Particulates	-55.4%	-18%
Nitrogen Oxides	+5.8%	+1.2%
Air Toxics	-60% to -90%	-12% to -20%
Mutagenicity	-80% to -90%	-20%
Carbon Dioxide**	-78.3%	-15.7%

* Average of data from 14 EPA FTP Heavy duty test cycle tests, variety of stock engines
** Life Cycle Emission

It would appear that the use of biodiesel can be an effective means for reducing exhaust emissions. The relevant question becomes, how does the cost of reducing emission using biodiesel compare to other means of obtaining the same level of emission reduction? The answer to that question is beyond the scope of this inquiry.

Impact Analysis

Impact analysis is a key component of any feasibility study. An impact analysis indicates the effect of a new venture on the economy. Building a new biodiesel facility in Georgia will impact the economy on two levels. The new plant will generate output as it begins selling biodiesel and its by-products. These sales will, in turn, generate additional sales as the plant purchases inputs. The suppliers to the plant will increase the purchase of their inputs, thus

---

Figure 12.9 (*Continued*)

19

increasing demand for those items. These increased sales will ripple through the economy. An input-output model will capture and quantify these effects.

The input-output model, IMPLAN (IMpact Analysis for PLANning, Minnesota IMPLAN Group 1999) was utilized for this project. IMPLAN can predict the effects of a new venture on output (sales), employment and tax revenue. IMPLAN models can be constructed for a state, a region or a county. Input-output models work by separating the economy into its various sectors, such as agriculture, construction, manufacturing, and so on. An IMPLAN model will show each sector and industry in the specific region's economy. The model can capture how a change in one industry (for example, biodiesel) will change output and employment in other industries.

A new sector was developed in IMPLAN to represent the biodiesel industry. The production function was created from the cost estimates provided by the research team. The production function was assumed to remain constant over the sizes of the plant. This may or may not hold true as returns to scale dictate.

The changes in the initial industry (biodiesel) are labeled direct effects and the changes in the other industries and household spending are called indirect effects. The direct and indirect effects are summed to give the total economic impact. Direct impacts are those at the plant. For instance, direct output is equal to total sales of the plant. Direct employment equals the number of people working at the plant. Indirect impacts are those that exist due to the plant's functioning. This would include people such as chemical suppliers, oil refiners, feedstock producers, and so forth.

Direct output of the 15 million gallon plant is $17.4 million annually. This leads to indirect sales in the Georgia economy of $16.9 million. In total, the economic impact of sales of the plant will be $34.3 million. Fourteen jobs will be created at the plant. The operation of the plant will cause another 119 jobs to be developed in Georgia, thus total employment creation will be up 132 jobs. State and local non-education tax revenues will increase by $2 million per year.

Table 11. Economic Impact on Sales, Employment and Revenue of a 15 Million Gallon Biodiesel Plant in Georgia.

	Direct	Indirect	Total
Sales (Output)	$17,373,000	$16,899,714	$34,272,716
Employment	14	119	132
Tax Revenue	NA	NA	$2,116,870

The job creation is a one-time occurrence in that it indicates the total number of jobs created by the project. However, those jobs remain year-after-year. The money flows indicated by the economic impact and the tax revenues are recurring events year-after-year. This project

20

has an economic lifetime of about 25 years, thus one can expect a total economic impact over the twenty five year period of about $858 million dollars. The total tax flows over the twenty five year period would be about $52.75 million.

This study focused upon the 15 million gallon plant size as it was felt it was the most appropriately scaled facility. One final summary table presents the IMPLAN results for each of the four plant sizes that were evaluated.

Table 12. Comparison of Total Impacts by Plant Size.

	Total Output	Total Employment	Total Tax Revenue
500,000 Gallons	$1,495,955	18	$205,656
3 Million Gallons	$7,982,526	53	$806,029
15 Million Gallons	$34,272,716	132	$2,116,870
30 Million Gallons	$76,838,499	364	$4,561,222

Conclusions

There exist a variety of potential feedstocks both in Georgia and nearby states that could be utilized to produce biodiesel. These feedstocks vary significantly in price depending on supply and demand condition as well as market structural conditions. Feedstock costs represent between 50 and 75 percent of the cost of producing biodiesel, and thus a reliable source of low priced feedstocks is critical to success. A 15 million gallon biodiesel plant would require about 27% of the vegetable and animal fats currently available within the State of Georgia. This facility would produce 750 million gallons of 2% blend for approximately twice the state demand. A 20% blend will create 75 million gallons of B20 or roughly 20% of the Georgia diesel market.

The processing technology for producing biodiesel is well established and presents little technological risk. The production of biodiesel is a very efficient process, returning about 3.2 units of energy for each unit used in production. Biodiesel is thus an excellent renewable fuel source. Biodiesel can be very easily integrated into the existing petroleum distribution system from the handling, chemical, physical and performance perspectives.

Lacking government mandates or subsidies, a feedstock cost of about 10 cents per pound or less, given current diesel fuel prices, is needed for biodiesel to be cost competitive.

21

Figure 6. Cotton Acreage by County, Georgia, 2000

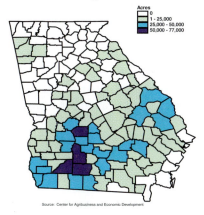

Cotton Acreage, by County, Georgia 2000

Acres
- 0
- 1 - 25,000
- 25,000 - 50,000
- 50,000 - 77,000

Source: Center for Agribusiness and Economic Development

22

Figure 7. Peanut Acreage by County, Georgia 2000

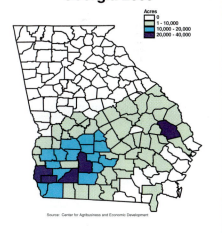

Peanut Acreage, by County, Georgia 2000

Acres
- 0
- 1 - 10,000
- 10,000 - 20,000
- 20,000 - 40,000

Source: Center for Agribusiness and Economic Development

Figure 12.9 (*Continued*)

Use action verbs. Especially when recommending a plan of action, use action verbs such as *examine, evaluate, determine,* or *recommend.* Avoid nominalizations: Don't use *determination* when you mean *determine,* for example.

Checklist for Long Reports

- Does the report grow from a clear audience and purpose analysis?
- Does the report address a clearly identified problem or goal?
- Is the report's length and information adequate and appropriate for the subject?
- Is the information accurate and unbiased?
- Is there enough information for readers to make an informed decision?
- Are all necessary components (including front and end matter) provided?
- Are visuals used whenever possible to aid communication?
- Are headings informative and adequate?
- Are action verbs used generously?
- Is the level of technicality appropriate for the intended audience?
- Is the language clear and concise?

Proposals

Proposals encourage an audience to take some form of direct action: to authorize a project, purchase a service or product, or otherwise support a specific plan for solving a problem. Although proposals often contain the same basic elements as reports, they have one specific purpose: to propose an action or series of actions. This purpose differs from more generic reports, which can be used for other purposes, as noted earlier. Proposals can be called for in a variety of situations: a request to fund a training program for new employees, a suggestion to change the curriculum in your English or biology department, a bid to the U.S. Defense Department on a missile contract. Depending on the situation, proposals may be short or long and may be written in the form of a report, a letter, or a memo.

Audience and Purpose Analysis

In science, business, industry, government, and education, proposals are written for any number of audiences: managers, executives, directors, clients, board members, or community leaders. Inside or outside the organization, these people review various proposals and then decide whether the plan is worthwhile, whether the project will materialize, and whether the service or product is useful. At the most general level, the purpose is to persuade your audience. More specifically, proposals often answer questions about the nature of the problem or product, the benefits of your proposed plan, cost, completion dates, schedules, and so on.

Types of Proposals

Proposals may be solicited or unsolicited. Solicited proposals are those that have been requested by a client or customer. For example, if you represent an engineering firm specializing in highway construction, you may receive a request for proposal (RFP) from a local township asking you to bid on a road project. Typically, an RFP is issued to numerous companies, and your proposal will need to stack up against all the others. Unsolicited proposals have not been specifically requested. If you are a new advertising agency in town, you may send out short proposals to local radio stations suggesting that they use your agency for their advertising needs.

Because the audience for a solicited proposal has made the request, you may not need to spend as much time introducing yourself or providing background on the product or service. For an unsolicited proposal (sometimes called a "cold call" in sales), you will need to catch your readers' attention quickly and provide incentives for them to continue reading: perhaps by printing a price comparison of your fees on the first page, for example.

Both solicited and unsolicited proposals can take the following forms.

Planning proposal. A planning proposal offers solutions to a problem or suggestions for improvement. It might be a request for funding to expand the campus newspaper, an architectural plan for new facilities at a ski area, or a plan to develop energy alternatives to fossil fuels. Figure 12.10 is a short planning proposal that was solicited and will be used internally within the company. The XYZ Corporation has contracted a team of communication consultants to design inhouse writing workshops, and the consultants must convince the client that their methods will succeed. After briefly introducing the problem, the authors develop their proposal under three headings and two subheadings, making the document easy to read and to the point.

Research proposal. Research (or grant) proposals request approval and funding for research projects. A chemist at a university might address a research proposal to the Environmental Protection Agency for funds to identify toxic contaminants in local groundwater. Research proposals are solicited by many agencies, including the National Science Foundation and the National Institutes of Health. Each agency has its own requirements and guidelines for proposal format and content. Successful research proposals follow these guidelines and carefully articulate the goals of the project. In these cases, proposal readers will generally be other scientists, so writers can use language that is appropriate for other experts. Other research proposals might be submitted by students requesting funds for undergraduate research projects. In Figure 12.11, the writer used the prescribed form and was careful to relate his research to the goals of the program.

Dear Mary:

Thanks for sending the writing samples from your technical support staff. Here is what we're doing to design a realistic approach.

Assessment of Needs
After conferring with technicians in both Jack's and Terry's groups and analyzing their writing samples, we identified this hierarchy of needs:

• improving readability
• achieving precise diction
• summarizing information
• organizing a set of procedures
• formulating various memo reports
• analyzing audiences for upward communication
• writing persuasive bids for transfer or promotion
• writing persuasive suggestions

Proposed Plan
Based on the needs listed above, we have limited our instruction package to eight carefully selected and readily achievable goals.

Course Outline. Our eight, two-hour sessions are structured as follows:

1. achieving sentence clarity
2. achieving sentence conciseness
3. achieving fluency and precise diction
4. writing summaries and abstracts
5. outlining manuals and procedures
6. editing manuals and procedures
7. designing various reports for various purposes
8. analyzing the audience and writing persuasively

Classroom Format. The first three meetings will be lecture-intensive with weekly exercises to be done at home and edited collectively in class. The remaining five weeks will combine lecture and exercises with group editing of work-related documents. We plan to remain flexible so we can respond to needs that arise.

Limitations
Given our limited contact time, we cannot realistically expect to turn out a batch of polished communicators. By the end of the course, however, our students will have begun to appreciate writing as a deliberate process.

If you have any suggestions for refining this plan, please let us know.

Figure 12.10 Planning Proposal.

To: Dr. John Lannon
From: T. Sorrells Dewoody
Date: March 16, 2006
Subject: *Proposal for Determining the Feasibility of Marketing*
         Dead Western White Pine

Introduction
Over the past four decades, huge losses of western white pine have occurred in the northern Rockies, primarily attributable to white pine blister
rust and the attack of the mountain pine beetle. Estimated annual mortality
is 318 million board feet. Because of the low natural resistance of white
pine to blister rust, this high mortality rate is expected to continue indefi-
nitely.

If white pine is not harvested while the tree is dying or soon after death,
the wood begins to dry and check (warp and crack). The sapwood is dis-
colored by blue stain, a fungus carried by the mountain pine beetle. If the
white pine continues to stand after death, heart cracks develop. These
factors work together to cause degradation of the lumber and consequent
loss in value.

Statement of Problem
White pine mortality reduces the value of white pine stumpage because the
commercial lumber market will not accept it. There are two major implications of this problem: First, in the face of rising demand for wood, vast
amounts of timber lie unused; second, dead trees are left to accumulate in
the woods, where they are rapidly becoming a major fire hazard here in
northern Idaho and elsewhere.

Proposed Solution
One possible solution to the problem of white pine mortality and waste is to
search for markets other than the conventional lumber market. The last
few years have seen a burst of popularity and growing demand for weath-
ered barn boards and wormy pine for interior paneling. Some firms around
the country are marketing defective wood as specialty products. (These
firms call the wood from which their products come "distressed," a term I
will use hereafter to refer to dead and defective white pine.) Distressed
white pine will quite possibly find a place in such a market.

Scope
To assess the feasibility of developing a market for distressed white pine, I
plan to pursue six areas of inquiry:

1. What products are presently being produced from dead wood, and
   what are the approximate costs of production?

Figure 12.11 Undergraduate Research Proposal.

2. How large is the demand for distressed-wood products?
3. Can distressed white pine meet this demand as well as other species meet it?
4. Does the market contain room for distressed white pine?
5. What are the costs of retrieving and milling distressed white pine?
6. What prices for the products can the market bear?

Methods
My primary data sources will include consultations with Dr. James Hill, Professor of Wood Utilization, and Dr. Sven Bergman, Forest Economist—both members of the College of Forestry, Wildlife, and Range. I will also inspect decks of dead white pine at several locations and visit a processing mill to evaluate it as a possible base of operations. I will round out my primary research with a letter and telephone survey of processors and wholesalers of distressed material.

Secondary sources will include publications on the uses of dead timber and a review of a study by Dr. Hill on the uses of dead white pine.

My Qualifications
I have been following Dr. Hill's study on dead white pine for two years. In June of this year, I will receive my B.S. in forest management. I am familiar with wood milling processes and have firsthand experience at logging. My association with Dr. Hill and Dr. Bergman gives me the opportunity for an in-depth feasibility study.

Conclusion
Clearly, action is needed to reduce the vast accumulations of dead white pine in our forests. The land on which they stand is among the most productive forests in northern Idaho. By addressing the six areas of inquiry mentioned earlier, I can determine the feasibility of directing capital and labor to the production of distressed white pine products. With your approval, I will begin research at once.

Figure 12.11 (*Continued*)

Sales proposal. Sales proposals offer services or products and may be solicited or unsolicited. If solicited, several firms may be competing for the contract, so your proposal may be ranked by a committee against several others. Sales proposals can be cast as letters if the situation calls for them to be brief. If the situation requires a longer proposal, you follow the guidelines for writing a report: Use a title page, make sure you have clear headings, and so on. A successful sales proposal persuades customers that your product or service surpasses those of any competitors. In the sample sales proposal in Figure 12.12, the writer explains why his machinery is best for the job, what qualifications his company can offer, and what costs are involved. What you include in a sales proposal is determined by the guidelines from the client or by a thorough analysis of the kinds of information your audience needs.

Typical Components of Proposals

After conducting your audience and purpose analysis, you should perform some basic research. For example, you might look into the very latest technology for solving the problem or doing the project; compare the costs, benefits, and drawbacks of various approaches; contact others in your field for their suggestions; and so on. Then generate a rough outline with headings and subheadings for the proposal. The outline in Figure 12.13 is general enough to adapt to your specific situation.

12.3
Additional
sample
proposals

As noted, proposals can be short (letter or memo format) or long (report format). For a long proposal, include the components and supplements ordinarily contained in a long report: abstract, introduction, body, conclusion, and appendixes. Include a letter of transmittal, especially if your proposal is unsolicited.

Background. A background section (sometimes used as an introduction) can be brief or long. In Figure 12.10, the writer's opening sentence ("Thanks for sending the writing samples from your technical support staff") provides a quick reminder of the context for the project. This sentence is brief because the writer correctly assumes that the reader is very familiar with the project. For a new audience, this single sentence might need to be expanded into a longer paragraph of background on the project. The background section may contain a statement of the problem or issue. If the topic warrants it, the background section may take up several pages.

Objective. If your audience needs this information spelled out, you may wish to provide a clear statement of the proposal's objectives: "Our objective is to offer a plan to make areas of the library quiet enough for serious study."

Clear statement of what is being proposed. Whether your proposal is short or long, make it easy for your audience to locate the exact details of what you are

Subject: *Proposal to Dig a Trench and Move Boulders at Bliss Site*

Dear Mr. Haver:

I've inspected your property and would be happy to undertake the landscaping project necessary for the development of your farm.

The backhoe I use cuts a span 3 feet wide and can dig as deep as 18 feet—more than an adequate depth for the mainline pipe you wish to lay. Because this backhoe is on tracks rather than tires and is hydraulically operated, it is particularly efficient in moving rocks. I have more than twelve years of experience with backhoe work and have completed many jobs similar to this one.

After examining the huge boulders that block access to your property, I am convinced they can be moved only if I dig out underneath and exert upward pressure with the hydraulic ram while you push forward on the boulders with your D-9 Caterpillar. With this method, we can move enough rock to enable you to farm that now inaccessible tract. Because of its power, my larger backhoe will save you both time and money in the long run.

This job should take 12 to 15 hours, unless we encounter subsurface ledge formations. My fee is $200 per hour. The fact that I provide my own dynamiting crew at no extra charge should be an advantage to you because you have so much rock to be moved.

Please phone me anytime for more information. I'm sure we can do the job economically and efficiently.

Figure 12.12 Sales Proposal.

I. **Introduction**
   A. Statement of Problem and Objective
   B. Background
   C. Need
   D. Benefits
   E. Qualifications of Personnel
   F. Data Sources
   G. Limitations and Contingencies
   H. Scope

II. **Body**
   A. Methods
   B. Timetable
   C. Materials and Equipment
   D. Personnel
   E. Available Facilities
   F. Needed Facilities
   G. Cost
   H. Expected Results
   I. Feasibility

III. **Conclusion**
   A. Summary of Key Points
   B. Request for Action

Figure 12.13 A General Proposal Outline That You Can Adapt to Your Situation.

proposing. In the research proposal shown in Figure 12.11, the third heading, "Proposed Solution," is the obvious place for readers to turn if they want to see the details of the solution.

Budget and costs. If your proposal involves financial costs, make sure your cost and budget section is accurate and easy to understand. If you work with an accountant or other financial specialist, ask that person to check your figures. If the proposal is solicited, make sure you follow the client's guidelines for establishing a budget.

Usability Considerations

Understand the audience's needs. The proposal audience wants specific suggestions to meet their specific needs. Their biggest question is "What will this plan do for me?" Make your proposal demonstrate a clear understanding of the client's problem and expectations, and then offer an appropriate solution. In the planning proposal in Figure 12.10, the writer begins with a clear assessment of needs and then moves quickly into a proposed plan of action.

Maintain a clear focus on benefits. Show your readers that you understand what they will gain by adopting your plan. The planning proposal in Figure 12.10 includes a numbered list of exactly what tasks will be accomplished after the technical support staff takes the instruction courses.

Use honest and supportable claims. Because they typically involve large sums of money as well as contractual obligations, proposals require a solid ethical and legal foundation. False promises not only damage the writer's or company's reputation but also invite lawsuits. If the solutions you offer have certain limitations, make sure you say so. For example, if you are proposing to install a new network server, make it clear what capabilities this server has, as well as what it cannot do under certain circumstances.

Use appropriate visuals. See Chapter 9 for a discussion of visuals.

Write clearly and concisely. Make sure your document is easy to read, uses action verbs, and avoids puffed-up language or terms that are too technical for your audience. If necessary for a mixed audience with differing technical levels, include a glossary.

Use convincing language. There is no need to be coy when writing a proposal. You are trying to sell yourself or your ideas. So be sure to write a document that will move people to action. Use statistics ("for the third year in a row, our firm has been ranked as the number 1 architecture firm in the Midwest") and direct sentences ("We know you will be satisfied with the results").

Checklist for Proposals

- Are all required proposal components included?
- Is the problem clearly identified?
- Is the objective clearly identified?
- Is the proposed plan, service, or product stated clearly and prominently?
- Does the proposal demonstrate a clear understanding of the client's problem and expectations?
- Is the background section appropriate for this audience's needs?
- Does the proposal maintain a clear focus on benefits?
- Is the proposed solution appropriate and realistic?
- Is the cost and budget section accurate and easy to understand?
- Are the claims honest and supportable?
- Are all foreseeable limitations identified?
- Are visuals used effectively?
- Is the language convincing and precise?
- Does the tone encourage acceptance of the proposal?

Exercises

1. **FOCUS ON WRITING.** Choose a situation and an audience, and prepare an expanded technical definition specifically designed for this audience's level of technical understanding. In addition to the usability considerations on pages 265–267, use these guidelines:

   - *Decide on the level of detail.* Definitions vary greatly in length and detail, from a few words in parentheses to a complete essay. How much does this audience need in order to follow your explanation or grasp your point?
   - *Classify the term precisely.* The narrower your class, the clearer your meaning. *Stress* is classified as an applied force; saying that stress "is what . . ." or "takes place when . . ." fails to reflect a specific classification. *Diabetes* is precisely classified as a metabolic disease, not as a medical term.
   - *Differentiate the term accurately.* If the distinguishing features are too broad, they will apply to more than this one item. A definition of *brief* as a "legal document used in court" fails to differentiate a brief from all other legal documents (wills, affidavits, and so on).
   - *Avoid circular definitions.* Do not repeat, as part of the distinguishing feature, the word you are defining. "*Stress* is an applied force that places stress on a body" is a circular definition.
   - *Expand your definition selectively.* Begin with a one-sentence definition, and select from a combination of development strategies.
   - *Use negation to show what a term does not mean.* For example, *raw statistics* are not "information"; data become information only after they have been evaluated, interpreted, and applied.

2. **FOCUS ON WRITING.** Choose another situation and audience, and prepare a technical description for this audience's level of technical understanding. As you prepare your description, refer to the usability considerations on pages 265–267 and to these guidelines:

   - *Always begin with some type of orienting statement.* Descriptions rarely call for a standard topic or thesis statement, because their goal is simply to catalog the details that readers can visualize. Any description, however, should begin by telling readers what to look for.
   - *Choose descriptive details to suit your purpose and the reader's needs.* Select only details that advance your meaning. Use objective details to provide a picture of something exactly as a camera would record it. Use subjective details to convey your impressions—to give readers a new way of seeing or appreciating something, as in a marketing brochure (see Figure 11.12).

- *Select details that are concrete and specific enough to convey an unmistakable picture.* Most often, description works best at the lowest levels of abstraction and generality.

Vague	Exact
at high speed	80 miles per hour
a tiny office	an 8-by-10-foot office
the seal	the rubber O-ring

- *Use sensory details as needed.* Allow readers to see, hear, and feel. Let readers touch and taste. Use vivid comparisons to make the picture come to life. Rely on action verbs to convey the energy of movement.
- *Order details in a clear sequence.* Descriptions generally follow a spatial or general-to-specific order—whichever parallels the angle of vision readers would have if viewing the item. Details may also be arranged according to the dominant impression desired.

3. **FOCUS ON WRITING.** Choose a specific situation and audience, and prepare a long report that documents a causal, comparative, or feasibility analysis—or some combination of these types. As you prepare your report, refer to the usability considerations on pages 274–282 and the following guidelines:

For Causal Analysis

- *Be sure the cause fits the effect.* Keep in mind that faulty causal reasoning is extremely common, especially when people ignore other possible causes or confuse mere coincidence with causation.
- *Make the links between cause and effect clear.* Identify the immediate cause (the one most closely related to the effect) as well as the distant causes (the ones that precede the immediate cause). For example, the immediate cause of a particular airplane crash might be a fuel tank explosion, caused by a short circuit in frayed wiring, caused by faulty design or poor quality control by the manufacturer. Discussing only the immediate cause often only scratches the surface of the problem.
- *Clearly distinguish among possible, probable, and definite causes.* Unless the cause is obvious, limit your assertions by using *perhaps, probably, maybe, most likely, could, seems to, appears to,* or similar qualifiers that prevent you from making an unsupportable claim.

For Comparative Analysis

- *Rest the comparison on a clear and definite basis.* Make comparisons on the basis of costs, uses, benefits and drawbacks, appearance, or results. In evaluating the merits of competing items, identify your specific criteria and rank them in order of importance.
- *Give both items balanced treatment.* Discuss points for each item in identical order.

- *Support and clarify the comparison or contrast through credible examples.* Use research, if necessary, to find examples that readers can visualize.
- *Follow either a block pattern or a point-by-point pattern.* In the block pattern, first one item is discussed fully and then the next. Choose a block pattern when the overall picture is more important than the individual points.

    In the point-by-point pattern, one point about both items is discussed, then the next point, and so on. Choose a point-by-point pattern when specific points might be hard to remember unless placed side by side.

Block pattern	**Point-by-point pattern**
Item A	First point of item A
First point	First point of item B
Second point	
Third point, etc.	
Item B	Second point of item A
First point	Second point of item B
Second point	etc.
Third point	
etc.	

- *Order your points for greatest emphasis.* Try ordering your points from least to most important, dramatic, useful, or reasonable. Placing the most striking point last emphasizes it best.
- *If you are writing an evaluative comparison, offer your final judgment.* Base your judgment squarely on the criteria presented.

For Feasibility Analysis

- *Consider the strength of supporting reasons.* Decide carefully which are the best reasons supporting the action or decision being considered, based on solid evidence.
- *Consider the strength of opposing reasons.* Remember that people usually see only what they want to see. Avoid the temptation to overlook or downplay opposing reasons, especially for an action or decision that you have been promoting. Consider alternative points of view, and examine all the evidence.
- *Recommend a realistic course of action.* After weighing all the pros and cons, make your recommendation—but be prepared to backtrack if you discover that what seemed like the right course of action turns out to be wrong.

The Collaboration Window

Working in groups of four, develop an unsolicited proposal for solving a problem, improving a situation, or satisfying a need in your school, community, or workplace. Begin by brainstorming as a group to come up with a list of possible issues or problems to address in your proposal. Narrow your list, and work as a group to focus on a specific issue or idea that you think will work well as the topic for a persuasive proposal (review pages 283–287 for details on the different types of proposals and the components of each).

Your proposal should address a clearly identified audience of decision makers and stakeholders on the issue you are discussing. Conduct an audience and purpose analysis to define the characteristics of the audience you are trying to persuade.

As you develop and revise your proposal, keep the following guidelines in mind:

- *Spell out the problem (and its causes) clearly and convincingly.* Give enough detail for your audience to appreciate the problem's importance. Answer the implied question "Why is this such a big deal?"
- *Point out the benefits of solving the problem.* Answer the implied question "Why should we spend time, money, and effort to do this?"
- *Offer a realistic solution.* Stick to claims or assertions you can support. Answer the implied question "How do we know this will work?"
- *Address anticipated objections to your solution.* Consider carefully the audience's skepticism on this issue. Answer the implied question "Why should we accept the things that seem wrong with your plan?"
- *Induce readers to act.* Decide exactly what you want readers to do, and give reasons why they should be the ones to act. Answer the implied question "What action am I supposed to take?"

 ## The Global Window

Compare the sorts of proposals regularly done in the United States with those created in other countries. For example, is the format the same? Are there more proposals for certain purposes in the United States than in another country? You can learn about this topic by interviewing an expert in international business (someone you meet on the job, during an internship, or through your adviser). You can also search the Web for information on international business communication. Describe your findings in a short memo that you will share with your classmates.

Grammar

Punctuation

Lists

Avoiding Sentence Fragments and Run-On Sentences

Usage (Commonly Misused Words)

Subject-Verb and Pronoun Antecedent Agreement

Faulty Modification

Mechanics

Punctuation

A.1

Exercises
on
punctuation

Punctuation Mark	How It's Used	Examples
Period (.) For more on the period, see sentence fragments and run-on sentences on pages 300, 301.	A period is used at the end of a complete idea to signal the end of a sentence.	*Use of white space is an important consideration when designing documents. However, there are no strict rules about how much white space should be on a page.*
Semicolon (;) For more on the semicolon, see sentence fragments and run-on sentences on pages 300, 301.	A semicolon is used at the end of a complete idea to signal a pause but not the end of the sentence. A semicolon is always followed by another complete idea that is closely related to the one before it.	*Use of white space is an important consideration when designing documents; however, there are no strict rules about how much white space should be on a page.*
	A semicolon can also be used between items in a series when the items themselves contain commas.	*This summer we plan to visit relatives in Milwaukee, Wisconsin; Indianapolis, Indiana; and Des Moines, Iowa.*
Colon (:) For more on the colon, see lists on page 298.	Like the semicolon, a colon is used at the end of a complete idea to signal a pause. However, a colon doesn't need to be followed by another complete idea. Usually, the information that follows the colon explains or clarifies the information that comes before the colon. Often a colon is used at the end of a *complete sentence* to introduce a list.	*We can't reopen for business this week: The renovation work is not yet complete.* *Before we can reopen for business, we will need to order the following supplies: printer paper, printer cartridges, envelopes, and postage stamps.*
	A colon is not used to introduce a list after *including* or *such as.*	*We will need to order office supplies, including printer paper, printer cartridges, envelopes, and postage stamps.*
Comma (,) For more on the comma, see sentence fragments and run-on sentences on pages 300, 301.	Commas are used to set off an appositive—words that identify or explain someone or something that's already been stated.	*Sue Jones, the first person we interviewed, was the most qualified candidate.*
	A comma is used between two complete ideas connected with a coordinating conjunction *(and, but, for, or, nor, yet).*	*We interviewed Sue Jones first, and she turned out to be the most qualified candidate.*
	A comma is used to separate an incomplete idea from a complete idea when the incomplete idea comes first.	*Because she has the most experience, we all agreed that Sue Jones was the most qualified candidate.*

Punctuation Mark	How It's Used	Examples
	When the incomplete idea comes after the complete idea, no comma should be used.	*We all agreed that Sue Jones was the most qualified candidate because she has the most experience.*
Apostrophe (')	Use an apostrophe to form possessives. For singular words, even those that end in *s*, use an apostrophe followed by *s* to form the possessive. For plurals that end in *s*, use only the apostrophe.	*When you design a document, the user's needs should always come first.* *When you design documents, users' needs should always come first.*
	Also use apostrophes to form contractions.	*Can't, shouldn't, wouldn't, won't, etc.*
Quotation Marks ("")	Use quotation marks around words that are spoken.	*Many survey respondents replied, "That's none of your business!"*
	Use quotation marks around the titles of songs, stories, poems, and parts of longer works, such as chapter titles.	*"When is our next deadline?" she asked.* *I found the lyrics to "Over the Rainbow" in Chapter 7, "Hits of the 1930s and 1940s."*
	NOTE: Periods and commas belong inside quotation marks. Colons and semicolons belong outside quotation marks. Question marks belong inside quotation marks if they are part of the material being quoted. Otherwise they belong outside.	
Italics/Underlining	Use italics or underlining for titles of books, journals, magazines, films, and newspapers. Also use them for foreign words, technical terms, or words highlighted as words. Use italics *sparingly* for special emphasis.	*Star Wars is still my favorite movie.* *The word khaki was misspelled throughout the catalog.* *Do not leave your child unsupervised in the infant swing.*
Parentheses ( )	Use parentheses to set off explanatory material that could be deleted without altering the meaning of the sentence.	*In general, the survey indicates that people are satisfied with the current document (see Appendix B for complete survey results).*
Dashes (—)	Use a dash to set off explanatory material that you want to emphasize.	*Storyteller—a collection of short stories by Leslie Marmon Silko— is an excellent book for use in introductory literature classes.*

Lists

Lists of items can be treated in one of two ways: as part of the text (embedded lists) or displayed with one item on each line (vertical lists).

Embedded Lists

On an embedded list, a series of items is integrated into a sentence, as here:

> The file menu allows you to perform the following tasks: create a new file, open an existing file, and save a current file.

Embedded lists can be numbered, as in the next example. To number an embedded list, use parentheses around the numerals and either commas or semicolons between the items.

> If you wish to apply for admission to the program, you must (1) submit official transcripts of all previous academic work, (2) complete a department application form, (3) submit at least three letters of recommendation from former employers or teachers, and (4) submit GRE scores.

Vertical Lists

Embedded lists are appropriate when you only need to list a few short items. Vertical lists, with numerals, letters, or bullets, are more appropriate than embedded lists when you need to list several items. Use numerals or letters if the items in the list belong in a particular order (steps in a procedure, for example) and bullets if the order of items is unimportant. Listing items vertically is also a way to increase the white space on a page and to draw a reader's attention to the content of the list. The following examples show how to introduce and punctuate vertical lists.

You can introduce a vertical list with a sentence that contains "the following" or "as follows." End the introductory sentence with a colon.

> Before the second week of class, students must purchase *the following:*
>
> - Printer card
> - Three-ring notebook
> - Course packet
> - Writing handbook

You can also introduce a vertical list with a sentence that ends with a noun. Again, end the introductory sentence with a colon.

> Before the second week of class, students must purchase *four items:*
>
> **1.** Printer card
> **2.** Three-ring notebook
> **3.** Course packet
> **4.** Writing handbook

You can also introduce a vertical list with a sentence that is not grammatically complete without the list items.

> To adjust the volume of sound input devices:
>
> **1.** Choose Control Panels from the main menu.
> **2.** Open the Sound Control panel.
> **3.** Select Volumes from the pop-up menu.
> **4.** Drag the sliders up and down to achieve the desired volume.

Do not use a colon to introduce a list with a sentence that ends with a verb, a preposition, or an infinitive. Either remove the colon or revise the sentence.

Incorrect because the introductory sentence ends with a verb.

> Before the second week of class, students *need:*
>
> • A printer card
> • An activated university email account
> • A course packet

Incorrect because the introductory sentence ends with a preposition.

> Before the second week of class, students need *to:*
>
> • Purchase a printer card
> • Activate a university email account
> • Purchase a course packet

Incorrect because the introductory sentence ends with an infinitive.

> Before the second week of class, students need *to buy:*
>
> • A printer card
> • A three-ring notebook
> • A course packet
> • A writing handbook

If another sentence comes after the sentence that introduces a list, use periods after both sentences. **Do not** use a colon to introduce the list.

> The next step is to configure the following fields. Consult Chapter 3 for more information on each field.
>
> - Serial port
> - Baud rate
> - Data bits
> - Stop bits

Note that some of the preceding examples use a period after each list item and some do not. As a general rule, use a period after each list item if any of the items contains a complete sentence. Do not use a period if none of the list items contains a complete sentence. Also note that items included in a list should be grammatically parallel and comparable. For more on parallelism, see page 306.

Avoiding Sentence Fragments and Run-On Sentences

A.2
Exercises in revising sentences

Two of the most common writing errors involve punctuating strings of words as sentences when they are in fact not sentences. *Sentence fragments* contain too few grammatical elements, and *run-on sentences* contain too many.

Avoiding Sentence Fragments

A sentence fragment is a grammatically incomplete sentence. A grammatically complete sentence consists of at least one subject-verb combination and expresses a complete thought. It might include more than one subject-verb combination, and it might include other words or phrases as well. All the following examples are grammatically complete sentences because they all contain at least one subject-verb combination and they all express complete thoughts.

> This   book   summarizes   recent   criminal   psychology   research.
>   Subject   Verb
>
> The   smudge   tool   creates   soft   effects.
>   Subject   Verb
>
> The   table   of   contents   is   still   incomplete.
>   Subject   Verb

A sentence fragment might contain a subject-verb combination but fail to express a complete idea. The following example is a fragment. Even though it contains a subject-verb combination, it doesn't express a complete thought.

> Although the report was not yet complete.
> Subject   Verb

This wording leaves a reader waiting for something to complete the thought. To make the sentence grammatically complete, add another subject-verb combination that completes the thought.

> Although the report was not yet complete, I began editing.
> Subject   Verb   Subject Verb

Watch out for *although* and other words like it, including *because, if, while, since, when,* and *unless*. These are called subordinating conjunctions: When any of these words is combined with a subject-verb combination, it produces a subordinate clause (a clause that expresses an incomplete idea). This incomplete idea can be turned into a complete sentence only if another subject-verb combination that does express a complete idea is added on.

There are various other kinds of sentence fragments as well. For example, this next group of words is a fragment because it contains no verb.

> DesignPro, a brand-new desktop publishing program.

It can be turned into a complete sentence in a couple of ways.

> DesignPro, a brand-new desktop publishing program, will be available soon.

> DesignPro is a brand-new desktop publishing program.

Watch out for sentences that seem to contain a subject-verb combination but actually do not. Verb forms that end in *-ing*, such as *being* in the next phrase, are not complete verbs.

> Dale being a document design expert.

This fragment can be turned into a complete sentence by substituting the verb *is* for *being*.

> Dale is a document design expert.

Avoiding Run-On Sentences

Whereas a sentence fragment is a grammatically incomplete sentence, a run-on sentence suffers from the opposite problem: It contains too many grammatically complete sentences joined together as one. For example, the following run-on sentence contains two subject-verb combinations, each of which expresses a complete thought:

> For emergencies, we dial 911 for other questions, we dial 088.
> Subject Verb   Subject Verb

This sentence can be repaired in various ways. One possibility is to divide it into two sentences.

> For emergencies, we dial 911. For other questions, we dial 088.

Another possibility is to use a semicolon to join the two parts of the sentence. This option indicates a break that is not quite as strong as the period and therefore signals to the reader that the two items are closely related.

> For emergencies, we dial 911; for other questions, we dial 088.

Another possibility is to add a coordinating conjunction (*and, but, for, or, nor, yet*).

> For emergencies, we dial 911, but for other questions, we dial 088.

One **unacceptable** repair would be to add a comma. Doing so would produce a comma splice, which is another kind of run-on sentence.

> For emergencies, we dial 911, for other questions, we dial 088.

Another **unacceptable** repair would be to add a transitional word such as *however, consequently,* or *therefore.* These words alone or with a comma are not appropriate for joining two complete sentences.

> For emergencies, we dial 911, however, for other questions, we dial 088.

Instead, words such as *however, consequently,* and *therefore* (conjunctive adverbs) must be used with a semicolon or period.

> For emergencies, we dial 911; however, for other questions, we dial 088.
>
> For emergencies, we dial 911. However, for other questions, we dial 088.

Usage (Commonly Misused Words)

Be aware of the following pairs of words, which are commonly confused with each other in speech and in writing.

Word Pair	*Examples*
Affect means "to influence."	Sleep deprivation negatively *affects* driving ability.
Effect used as a noun means "a result."	Sleep deprivation has a negative *effect* on driving ability.
Effect used as a verb means "to cause" or "to bring about."	Management believes that the new policy will *effect* an increase in productivity.
Among is used with three or more people or items.	We can now divide the work *among* the three of us.
Between is used with two people or items.	We used to have to divide all of our work *between* the two of us.
Continually means "repeatedly."	Most young children need to be *continually* reminded to brush their teeth after meals.
Continuously means "nonstop."	The whole time I was driving, it rained *continuously*.
Disinterested means "neutral" or "objective."	Scientists are expected to be *disinterested* in their subject matter.
Uninterested means "bored" or "unconcerned."	Most of the students were *uninterested* in memorizing the grammar rules they were supposed to know for the quiz.
Farther refers to physical distances that can be measured.	I now live *farther* from the grocery store than I used to.
Further refers to abstract distances that can't be measured.	If you have any *further* questions, you'll need to speak with a supervisor.
Fewer refers to quantities that can be counted.	Most students like to take *fewer* credit hours in the spring quarter than they do in the winter quarter.
Less refers to quantities that cannot be counted.	The teacher was *less* concerned than usual about attendance this week.
Infer means "to guess" or "to speculate."	Several people who heard the victim's story were able to *infer* who committed the crime.
Imply means "to insinuate."	Her remarks *implied* that I was at fault.
Lay means "to put down" or "to set down." It requires a direct object.	Please *lay* all your books on the floor during the exam.
Lie means "to recline." It does not require a direct object. (Note that the past tense of *lie* is *lay*.)	Dentists usually advise their patients to *lie* down for several hours after any kind of dental work that requires anesthesia.
Like should be followed by a noun, not by a subject-verb combination.	You look *like* a million bucks.
As if should be followed by a subject-verb combination.	You look *as if* you could use a couple more hours of sleep.

(continued)

Word Pair	Examples
Percent should be used with a specific number to represent a figure.	Only two *percent* of survey respondents approve of the current system.
Percentage should be used to refer to an unspecified amount.	Only a small *percentage* of survey respondents approve of the current system.
Principle means "a fundamental rule or guideline."	Sometimes employees must choose whether to act in accordance with their own personal *principles* or those of the corporation.
Principal, when used as a noun, means "the chief person."	The school *principal* had to call several parents to let them know about the incident.
Principal, when used as an adjective, means "chief."	Her *principal* goal in seeking a new job is to earn more money.

Subject-Verb and Pronoun-Antecedent Agreement

Grammatical agreement involves number (singular or plural), person (first, second, or third), case (nominative or objective), and gender (male, female, or neither).

Subject-Verb Agreement

- Make the verb agree with its subject, not with a word that comes between.

  > The *tulips* in the pot on the balcony *need* watering.

  > The *teacher,* as well as his assistant, *was* reprimanded for his behavior.

- Treat compound subjects connected by *and* as plural.

  > *Terry and Julie enjoy* collaborating on writing projects.

- With compound subjects connected by *or* or *nor,* make the verb agree with the part of the subject nearer to the verb.

  > If my parents or *sister calls,* tell her I will be right back.

  > Neither the professor nor *the students were* able to figure out what was going on.

- Treat most indefinite pronouns (*anybody, each, everybody,* etc.) as singular.

  > Almost *everybody* who registered for the class *was* there on the first day.

- Treat collective nouns as singular unless the meaning is clearly plural.

> The *group respects* its leader.
>
> The *team were* debating among *themselves.*

- Make the verb agree with its subject even when the subject follows the verb.

> At the back of the room *were a stereo and a small chair.*

Pronoun-Antecedent Agreement

- Make pronouns and the words they refer to agree with each other.

> *Everyone* should proceed at *his or her* own pace.
>
> The *committee* finally decided to proceed with *its* building plan.
>
> The *committee* put *their* signatures on the final draft of the report.

Faulty Modification

Faulty modification occurs either when a phrase has no word to modify or when the position of a phrase within a sentence makes it difficult to determine which word the phrase is supposed to modify. For example, the following sentence makes no sense because the phrase "taking a shower" has no word to modify: This phrase is a *dangling modifier.*

> Taking a shower, the baby crawled out of his crib.

Revised as follows, the meaning of the sentence is clear:

> While I was taking a shower, the baby crawled out of his crib.

Here are some additional examples of sentences containing dangling modifiers.

> Faulty   *Dialing the phone,* the cat ran out the open door.
>
> Revised   As Joe dialed the phone, the cat ran out the open door.
>
> Faulty   *After completing the student financial aid application form,* the Financial Aid Office will forward it to the appropriate state agency.
>
> Revised   After you complete the student financial aid application form, the Financial Aid Office will forward it to the appropriate state agency.

The next sentence is unclear because the phrase "that was really boring" is supposed to modify "a weekend." Because of the position of this phrase in the sentence, a reader would mistakenly think it was the cabin, rather than the weekend, that was boring: This phrase is a *misplaced modifier.*

| We spent a weekend at the cabin that was really boring.

Revised as follows, the meaning of the sentence is much clearer.

| We spent a really boring weekend at the cabin.

Here are some additional examples of sentences containing misplaced modifiers.

Faulty   Joe typed another memo on our computer *that was useless.*

Revised   Joe typed another useless memo on our computer.

Faulty   He read a report on the use of nonchemical pesticides *in our conference room.*

Revised   In our conference room, he read a report on the use of nonchemical pesticides.

Faulty   She volunteered to deliver the radioactive shipment *immediately.*

Revised   She immediately volunteered to deliver the radioactive shipment.

Parallel Structure

Parallel structure is a fancy way of saying that similar items should be expressed in similar grammatical form. For example, the following sentence is not parallel:

| She enjoys many outdoor activities, including *running, kayaking,* and *the design of new wilderness trails.*

This sentence is essentially a list of items. The first two items, *running* and *kayaking,* are expressed as gerunds with *-ing* endings. The third item, *the design of new wilderness trails,* is not a gerund; it is a nominalization. To make this sentence parallel, you would revise as follows:

| She enjoys many outdoor activities, including *running, kayaking,* and *designing new wilderness trails.*

Items on bulleted and numbered lists must also be parallel. (For more on bulleted and numbered lists, see pages 298–300.) For example, on the list included in the following paragraph, the first two items are parallel, but the third is not.

As the enclosed résumé illustrates, I have held several jobs relevant to the security management position your company is currently attempting to fill:

- Park ranger for the city of Minneapolis
- Security guard at the Mall of America
- I also worked as a part-time bouncer at Pete's Tavern, a local bar

To make the third item parallel with the first two, revise it as follows:

- Bouncer at Pete's Tavern, a local bar

Other places to look for series of items that should be parallel include outlines, procedures, and sequences of subheadings within the same document.

Transitions Within and Between Paragraphs

You can choose from three techniques to achieve smooth transitions within and between paragraphs.

1. Use transitional expressions. These are words such as *again, furthermore, in addition, meanwhile, however, also, although, for example, specifically, in particular, as a result, in other words, certainly, accordingly, because,* and *therefore.* Such words serve as bridges between ideas.

2. Repeat key words, phrases, and concepts. Begin a sentence or paragraph by referring to something that was mentioned in the previous sentence or paragraph. The following paragraphs provide examples.

Original paragraph

> Breast cancer is a leading cause of death for women over 50. All women should learn to do monthly breast self-examinations. Doctors can easily teach women how to do these examinations, and public health organizations publish pamphlets to teach women how to do them. Many women think breast cancer will never happen to them, so they don't do self-examinations.

Revised paragraph

> Breast cancer is a leading cause of death for women over 50. *Because breast cancer is so common and so deadly,* all women should learn to do monthly breast self-examinations. *Women* can easily *learn* to do these *examinations* from doctors or from pamphlets published by public health organizations. However, *even though breast self-examinations are easy to learn,* many women don't do them because they think breast cancer will never happen to them.

The italicized words in the revised paragraph indicate places where key information from one sentence is repeated in the sentence that follows. (Also note that the transitional word *however* is inserted at the beginning of the last sentence.)

3. Use forecasting statements to tell the reader where you are going next. The following list provides examples of forecasting statements.

> The next step is to further examine Johnson's points. (*The writer would then proceed to examine Johnson's points.*)
>
> Of course we can also explore other avenues. (*The writer would then proceed to explore these avenues.*)
>
> There are at least two reasons why affirmative action as we know it will never improve racial relations in the United States. (*The writer would then proceed to list and explain these reasons.*)

Use these methods as revision guidelines, but remember that they will not solve every organizational problem that occurs in real-life writing situations. If you encounter a situation where you think you need a better transition but none of these methods seems appropriate, it may be that you need to delete or move some information. Sometimes writers include information that is irrelevant to their topic, and sometimes information in one paragraph would tie in more easily with a different paragraph. In these situations, better transitions are not possible without doing some major renovation first.

Mechanics

The mechanical aspects of writing a document include abbreviation, hyphenation, capitalization, use of numbers, and spelling. (Keep in mind that not all of these rules are hard and fast; some may depend on style guides used in your field or your company.)

Abbreviations

The following should *always* be abbreviated:

- Titles such as *Ms., Mr., Dr.,* and *Jr.* when they are used before or after a proper name.
- Time designations that are specific (400 BCE, 5:15 A.M.).

The following should *never* be abbreviated:

- Military, religious, or political titles (*Reverend, President*).
- Time designations that are used without actual times (*Sarah arrived early in the morning*—not "early in the A.M.").

Avoid abbreviations whose meanings might not be clear to all readers. Units of measurement can be abbreviated if they appear frequently in your report. However, a unit of measurement should be spelled out the first time it is used. Avoid abbreviations in visual aids unless saving space is absolutely necessary.

Hyphenation

Hyphens divide words at line breaks and join two or more words used as a single adjective if they precede the noun (but not if they follow it):

> Com-puter (at a line break)
>
> The rough-hewn wood
>
> An all-too-human error
>
> The wood was rough hewn
>
> The error was all too human

Other commonly hyphenated words include the following:

- Most words that begin with the prefix *self-* (*self-reliance, self-discipline*—see your dictionary for exceptions).
- Combinations that might be ambiguous (*re-creation* versus *recreation*).
- Words that begin with *ex* when *ex* means "past" (*ex-faculty member* but *excommunicate*).
- All fractions, along with ratios that are used as adjectives and that precede the noun, and compound numbers from twenty-one through ninety-nine (*a two-thirds majority, thirty-eight windows*).

Capitalization

Capitalize the first words of all sentences as well as titles of people, books, and chapters; languages; days of the week; months; holidays; names of organizations or groups; races and nationalities; historical events; important documents; and names of structures or vehicles. In titles of books, films, and the like, capitalize the first and last words and all others except articles, short prepositions, and coordinating conjunctions (*and, but, for, or, nor, yet*).

Do not capitalize the seasons (*spring, winter*) or general groups (*the younger generation, the leisure class*).

Capitalize adjectives derived from proper nouns (*Chaucerian English*).

Capitalize words such as *street, road, corporation, university,* and *college* only when they accompany a proper noun (*High Street, Rand Corporation, Bob Jones University*).

Capitalize *north, south, east,* and *west* when they denote specific regions (*the South, the Northwest*) but not when they are simply directions (*turn east at the light*).

Use of Numbers

Numbers expressed in one or two words can be written out or written as numerals. Use numerals to express larger numbers, decimals, fractions, precise technical figures, or any other exact measurements.

543	2,800,357
3.25	15 pounds of pressure
50 kilowatts	4,000 rpm

Use numerals for dates, census figures, addresses, page numbers, exact units of measurement, percentages, times with A.M. or P.M. designations, and monetary and mileage figures.

page 14	1:15 P.M.
18.4 pounds	9 feet
12 gallons	$15

Do not begin a sentence with a numeral. If the figure needs more than two words, revise your word order.

Six hundred students applied for the 102 available jobs.

The 102 available jobs attracted 650 applicants.

Do not use numerals to express approximate figures, time not designated as A.M. or P.M., or streets named by numbers less than 100.

About seven hundred fifty

Four fifteen

108 East Forty-Second Street

In contracts and other documents in which precision is vital, a number can be stated both in numerals and in words:

The tenant agrees to pay a rental fee of three hundred seventy-five dollars ($375.00) monthly.

Spelling

Always use the spell-check function in your word-processing software. However, don't rely on it exclusively. Take the time to use your dictionary for all writing assignments. And if you are a poor speller, ask someone else to proofread every document before you present it to your primary audience.

Documenting Sources

Quoting the Words of Others

You must place quotation marks around all exact wording you borrow, whether the words were written, spoken (as in an interview or presentation), or posted electronically. Even a single borrowed sentence or phrase, or a single word used in a special way, needs quotation marks, with the exact source properly cited. These sources include people with whom you collaborate.

If your notes don't identify quoted material accurately, you might forget to credit the source. Even when this omission is unintentional, you face the charge of *plagiarism* (misrepresenting someone else's words or ideas as your own). Possible consequences of plagiarism include expulsion from school, loss of a job, and lawsuits.

Research writing is a process of independent thinking in which you work with the ideas of others in order to reach your own conclusions; unless the author's exact wording is essential, try to paraphrase instead of quoting borrowed material.

Paraphrasing the Words of Others

Paraphrasing means more than changing or shuffling a few words; it means restating the original idea in your own words—sometimes in a clearer, more direct, and emphatic way—and giving full credit to the source.

To borrow or adapt someone else's ideas or reasoning without properly documenting the source is plagiarism. To offer as a paraphrase an original passage that is only slightly altered—even when you document the source—is also plagiarism. Equally unethical is offering a paraphrase, although documented, that distorts the original meaning.

What You Should Document

Document any insight, assertion, fact, finding, interpretation, judgment, or other "appropriated material that readers might otherwise mistake for your own" (Gibaldi & Achtert, 1988, p. 155)—whether the material appears in published form or not. Specifically, you must document

- Any source from which you use exact wording
- Any source from which you adapt material in your own words
- Any visual illustration: charts, graphs, drawings, or the like (see Chapter 9 for documenting visuals)

In some instances, you might have reason to preserve the anonymity of unpublished sources ("A number of employees expressed frustration with . . .")—for example, to allow people to respond candidly without fear of reprisal (as with employee criticism of the company) or to protect their privacy (as with certain material from email inquiries or electronic newsgroups). You must still document the fact that you are not the originator of this material by providing a general acknowledgment in the text ("Interviews with Polex employees, May 2005") but not in your list of references.

You don't need to document anything that is considered *common knowledge:* material that appears repeatedly in general sources. In medicine, for instance, it has become common knowledge that foods containing animal fat contribute to higher blood cholesterol levels. So in a report on fatty diets and heart disease, you would probably not need to document that well-known fact. But you would document information about how the fat-cholesterol connection was discovered, what subsequent studies have found (say, the role of saturated versus unsaturated fats), and any information for which some other person or group could claim specific credit. If the borrowed material can be found in only one specific source, not in multiple sources, document it. When in doubt, document the source.

How You Should Document

Cite borrowed material twice: at the exact place you use that material and at the end of your document. Documentation practices vary widely, but all systems work almost identically. A brief reference in the text names the source and refers readers to the complete citation, which allows readers to retrieve the source.

Many disciplines, institutions, and organizations publish their own style guides or documentation manuals. Here are a few:

> *Geographical Research and Writing*
>
> *Style Manual for Engineering Authors and Editors*
>
> *IBM Style Manual*
>
> *NASA Publications Manual*

Three common documentation styles are those of the Modern Language Association (MLA), used mostly in the humanities; the American Psychological Association (APA), used mostly in the social sciences; and the Council of Science Editors (CSE), used mostly in the physical and applied sciences. Consult the most recent edition of the *MLA Handbook for Writers of Research Papers,* the *Publication Manual of the American Psychological Association,* or the CBE manual, *Scientific Style and Format,* for guidance on documenting sources according to these systems. For information on a documentation style designed specifically for electronic and Internet sources, see *The Columbia Guide to Online Style* (1998) by Janice R. Walker and Todd Taylor.

MLA Documentation Style

In MLA style, in-text parenthetical references briefly identify each source. Full documentation then appears in a Works Cited section at the end of the document. The parenthetical reference usually includes the author's surname and the exact page number where the borrowed material can be found:

```
One notable study indicates an elevated risk of leukemia for
children exposed to certain types of electromagnetic fields
(Bowman et al. 59).
```

Readers seeking the complete citation for Bowman can refer easily to the Works Cited section, listed alphabetically by author:

```
Bowman, J. D., et al. "Hypothesis: The Risk of Childhood Leukemia
        Is Related to Combinations of Power-Frequency and Static
        Magnetic Fields." Bioelectromagnetics 16.1 (1995): 48-59.
```

This complete citation includes page numbers for the entire article.

MLA Parenthetical References

For clear and informative parenthetical references, observe these rules:

- If your discussion names the author, do not repeat the name in your parenthetical reference; simply give the page number:

```
Bowman et al. explain how their recent study indicates an elevated
risk of leukemia for children exposed to certain types of
electromagnetic fields (59).
```

- If you cite two or more works in a single parenthetical reference, separate the citations with semicolons:

```
(Jones 32; Leduc 41; Gomez 293-94)
```

- If you cite two or more authors with the same surnames, include the first initial in your parenthetical reference to each author:

```
(R. Jones 32)
```

```
(S. Jones 14-15)
```

- If you cite two or more works by the same author, include the first significant word from each work's title, or a shortened version:

```
(Lamont, Biophysics 100-01)
```

```
(Lamont, Diagnostic 81)
```

- If the work is by an institutional or corporate author or if it is unsigned (that is, the author is unknown), use only the first few words of the institutional name or the work's title in your parenthetical reference:

```
(American Medical Assn. 2)
```

```
("Distribution Systems" 18)
```

To avoid distracting the reader, keep each parenthetical reference brief. The easiest way to keep parenthetical references brief is to name the source in your discussion and place only the page number in parentheses.

For a paraphrase, place the parenthetical reference *before* the closing punctuation mark. For a quotation that runs into the text, place the reference *between* the final quotation mark and the closing punctuation mark. For a quotation set off (indented) from the text, place the reference one space *after* the closing punctuation mark.

MLA Works Cited Entries

The Works Cited list includes each source that you have paraphrased or quoted in your document. In preparing the list, type the first line of each entry flush with the left margin. Indent the second and subsequent lines five spaces. Double-space within and between each entry. Use one character space after any period, comma, or colon.

Following are examples of complete citations as they would appear in the Works Cited section of your document. Shown after each citation is the corresponding parenthetical reference as it would appear in the text.

MLA Works Cited entries for books.   Any citation for a book should contain the following information: author, title, editor or translator, edition, volume number, and facts about publication (city, publisher, date).

1. Book, Single Author—MLA

```
Kerzin-Fontana, Jane B. Technology Management: A Handbook. 3rd ed.
    Delmar: American Management Assn., 2005.

Parenthetical reference: (Kerzin-Fontana 3-4)
```

If several cities of publication are listed on the title page, give only the first. For U.S. cities, omit the state. For unfamiliar cities in Canada, include the two-letter postal abbreviation for the province. For unfamiliar cities in other countries, include an abbreviation of the country name.

2. Book, Two or Three Authors—MLA

```
Aronson, Linda, Roger Katz, and Candide Moustafa. Toxic Waste
    Disposal Methods. New Haven: Yale UP, 2004.

Parenthetical reference: (Aronson, Katz, and Moustafa 121-23)
```

Shorten publisher's names—"Simon" for Simon & Schuster, "GPO" for Government Printing Office, "Yale UP" for Yale University Press. For page numbers with more than two digits, give only the final digits for the second number.

3. Book, Four or More Authors—MLA

Santos, Ruth J., et al. <u>Environmental Crises in Developing
Countries</u>. New York: Harper, 1998.

Parenthetical reference: (Santos et al. 9)

Et al. is the abbreviated form of the Latin *et alia*, meaning "and others."

4. Book, Anonymous Author—MLA

<u>Structured Programming</u>. Boston: Meredith, 2005.

Parenthetical reference: (<u>Structured</u> 67)

5. Multiple Books, Same Author—MLA

Chang, John W. <u>Biophysics</u>. Boston: Little, 1999.

---. <u>Diagnostic Techniques</u>. New York: Radon, 1994.

Parenthetical reference: (Chang, <u>Biophysics</u> 123-26); (Chang,
<u>Diagnostic</u> 87)

When citing more than one work by the same author, do not repeat the author's name; type three hyphens followed by a period. List the works alphabetically by title.

6. Book, One or More Editors—MLA

Morris, A. J., and Louise B. Pardin-Walker, eds. <u>Handbook of New
Information Technology</u>. New York: Harper, 1996.

Parenthetical reference: (Morris and Pardin-Walker 34)

For more than three editors, name only the first, followed by *et al.*

7. Book, Indirect Source—MLA

Kline, Thomas. <u>Automated Systems</u>. Boston: Rhodes, 1992.

Stubbs, John. <u>White-Collar Productivity</u>. Miami: Harris, 1999.

Parenthetical reference: (qtd. in Stubbs 116)

When your source has quoted or cited another source, list each source in its appropriate alphabetical place on your Works Cited page. Use the name of the original source (here, Kline) in your text and precede your parenthetical reference with "qtd. in," or "cited in" for a paraphrase.

8. Anthology Selection or Book Chapter—MLA

```
Bowman, Joel P. "Electronic Conferencing." Communication and
        Technology: Today and Tomorrow. Ed. Al Williams. Denton:
        Assn. for Business Communication, 1994. 123-42.

Parenthetical reference: (Bowman 129)
```

The page numbers in the complete citation are for the selection cited from the anthology.

MLA Works Cited entries for periodicals. A citation for an article should give this information (as available): author, article title, periodical title, volume or number (or both), date (day, month, year), and page numbers for the entire article—not just the pages cited. List the information in this order, as in the following examples.

9. Article, Magazine—MLA

```
DesMarteau, Kathleen. "Study Links Sewing Machine Use to
        Alzheimer's Disease." Bobbin Oct. 1994: 36-38.

Parenthetical reference: (DesMarteau 36)
```

No punctuation separates the magazine title and date. Nor is the abbreviation *p.* or *pp.* used to designate page numbers.

If no author is given, list all other information:

```
"Distribution Systems for the New Decade." Power Technology
        18 Oct. 2000: 18+.

Parenthetical reference: ("Distribution Systems" 18)
```

This article begins on page 18 and continues on page 21. When an article does not appear on consecutive pages, give only the number of the first page, followed immediately by a plus sign. Use a three-letter abbreviation for any month spelled with five or more letters.

10. Article, Journal with New Pagination for Each Issue—MLA

```
Thackman-White, Joan R. "Computer-Assisted Research." American
        Library Journal 51.1 (2005): 3-9.

Parenthetical reference: (Thackman-White 4-5)
```

Because each issue in a given year will have page numbers beginning with 1, readers need the issue number. The 51 denotes the volume number; 1 denotes the issue number. Omit *The, A,* or *An* if it is the first word in a journal or magazine title.

11. Article, Journal with Continuous Pagination—MLA

```
Barnstead, Marion H. "The Writing Crisis." Journal of Writing
        Theory 12 (2004): 415-33.
```

Parenthetical reference: (Barnstead 415-16)

When page numbers continue from one issue to the next for the full year, readers won't need the issue number because no other issue in that year repeats these same page numbers. (Include the issue number, however, if you think it will help readers retrieve the article.) The 12 denotes the volume number.

12. Article, Newspaper—MLA

```
Baranski, Vida H. "Errors in Technology Assessment." Boston Times
        15 Jan. 2005, evening ed., sec. 2: 3.
```

Parenthetical reference: (Baranski 3)

When a daily newspaper has more than one edition, cite the edition after the date. Omit any introductory article in the newspaper's name (not *The Boston Times*). If no author is given, list all other information. If the newspaper's name does not include the city of publication, insert it, using brackets: *Sippican Sentinel* [Marion, MA].

MLA Works Cited entries for other sources. Miscellaneous sources range from unsigned encyclopedia entries to conference presentations to government publications. A full citation should give this information (as available): author, title, city, publisher, date, and page numbers.

13. Encyclopedia, Dictionary, or Other Alphabetical Reference—MLA

```
"Communication." The Business Reference Book. 1998 ed.
```

Parenthetical reference: ("Communication")

Begin a signed entry with the author's name. For any work arranged alphabetically, omit page numbers in the citation and the parenthetical reference. For a well-known reference book, include only an edition (if stated) and a date. For other reference books, give the full publication information.

14. Report—MLA

```
Electrical Power Research Institute (EPRI). Epidemiologic Studies
        of Electric Utility Employees. (Report No. RP2964.5). Palo
        Alto: EPRI, Nov. 1994.
```

Parenthetical reference: (Electrical Power Research Institute
        [EPRI] 27)

If no author is given, begin with the organization that sponsored the report.

For any report or other document with group authorship, include the group's abbreviated name in your first parenthetical reference, and then use only that abbreviation in any subsequent reference.

15. Conference Presentation—MLA

Smith, Abelard A. "Radon Concentrations in Molded Concrete."

First British Symposium in Environmental Engineering.

London, 11-13 Oct. 1998. Ed. Anne Hodkins. London:

Harrison, 1999. 106-21.

Parenthetical reference: (Smith 109)

This citation is for a presentation that has been included in the published proceedings of a conference. For an unpublished presentation, include the presenter's name, the title of the presentation, and the conference title, location, and date, but do not underline or italicize the conference information.

16. Interview, Personally Conducted—MLA

Nasser, Gamel. Chief Engineer for Northern Electric. Personal

interview. Rangeley, ME. 2 Apr. 2006.

Parenthetical reference: (Nasser)

17. Interview, Published—MLA

Lescault, James. "The Future of Graphics." Executive Views of

Automation. Ed. Karen Prell. Miami: Haber, 2000. 216-31.

Parenthetical reference: (Lescault 218)

The interviewee's name is placed in the entry's author slot.

18. Letter, Unpublished—MLA

Rogers, Leonard, Letter to the author. 15 May 2006.

Parenthetical reference: (Rogers)

19. Questionnaire—MLA

Taylor, Lynne. Questionnaire sent to 612 Massachusetts business

executives. 14 Feb. 2000.

Parenthetical reference: (Taylor)

20. Brochure or Pamphlet—MLA

Investment Strategies for the 21st Century. San Francisco: Blount
    Economics Assn., 1999.

Parenthetical reference: (Investment)

If the work is signed, begin with its author.

21. Lecture—MLA

Dumont, R. A. "Managing Natural Gas." Lecture. U of Massachusetts
    Dartmouth. 15 Jan. 2006.

Parenthetical reference: (Dumont)

If the lecture title is not known, write simply *Address, Lecture,* or *Reading.*
Include the sponsor and the location if available.

22. Government Document—MLA

Virginia. Highway Dept. Standards for Bridge Maintenance.
    Richmond: Virginia Highway Dept., 1997.

Parenthetical reference: (Virginia Highway Dept. 49)

If the author is unknown (as here), list the information in this order: name of the
government, name of the issuing agency, document title, place, publisher, and date.

For any congressional document, identify the house of Congress (Senate or House of
Representatives) before the title and the number and session of Congress after the title:

United States. Cong. House. Armed Services Committee. Funding for
    the Military Academies. 105th Cong., 2nd sess. Washington:
    GPO, 1998.

Parenthetical reference: (U.S. Cong. 41)

GPO is the abbreviation for the U.S. Government Printing Office. For an entry
from the *Congressional Record,* give only date and pages:

Cong. Rec. 10 Mar. 1999: 2178-92.

Parenthetical reference: (Cong. Rec. 2184)

23. Document with Corporate Authorship—MLA

Hermitage Foundation. Global Warming Scenarios for the Year 2030.
    Washington: Natl. Res. Council, 2000.

Parenthetical reference: (Hermitage Foundation 123)

24. Map or Other Visual—MLA

> Deaths Caused by Breast Cancer, by County. Map. Scientific
>
>   American Oct. 1995: 32D.
>
> Parenthetical reference: (Deaths Caused)

If the creator of the visual is listed, give that name first. Identify the type of visual (*Map, Graph, Table, Diagram*) immediately following the title.

25. Unpublished Dissertation, Report, or Miscellaneous Items—MLA

> Author (if known). "Title." Sponsoring organization or publisher,
>
>   date. Page numbers.

For any work that has group authorship (corporation, committee, task force), cite the name of the group or agency in place of the author's name.

MLA Works Cited entries for electronic sources. Citation for an electronic source with a printed equivalent should begin with that publication information (see relevant sections above). But whether or not a printed equivalent exists, any citation should enable readers to retrieve the material electronically.

The Modern Language Association recommends the following general conventions.

Publication Dates: For sources taken from the Internet, include the date the source was posted to the Internet or last updated or revised as well as the date you accessed the source.

Uniform Resource Locators (URLs): Include a full and accurate URL (electronic address) for any source taken from the Internet (with access mode identifier—*http, ftp, gopher,* or *telnet*). Enclose URLs in angle brackets (< >). When a URL continues from one line to the next, break it only after a slash. Do not add a hyphen.

Page Numbering: Include page or paragraph numbers when given by the source.

26. Online Database—MLA

> Sahl, J. D. "Power Lines, Viruses, and Childhood Leukemia."
>
>   Cancer Causes Control 6.1 (Jan. 1995): 83. MEDLINE. Online.
>
>   DIALOG. 7 Nov. 1995.
>
> Parenthetical reference: (Sahl 83)

For entries with a printed equivalent, begin with publication information, then the database title (underlined or italicized), the "Online" designation to indicate the medium, and the service provider (or URL or email address) and the date of access. The access date is important because frequent updatings of databases can produce different versions of the material.

For entries with no printed equivalent, give the title and date of the work in quotation marks, followed by the electronic source information:

> Argent, Roger R. "An Analysis of International Exchange Rates for
>   2004." Accu-Data. Online. Dow Jones News Retrieval. 10 Jan.
>   2005.
>
> *Parenthetical reference:* (Argent 4)

If the author is not known, begin with the work's title.

27. Computer Software—MLA

> Virtual Collaboration. Diskette. New York: Harper, 1994.
>
> *Parenthetical reference:* (Virtual)

Begin with the author's name, if known.

28. CD-ROM—MLA

> Cavanaugh, Herbert A. "EMF Study: Good News and Bad News."
>   Electrical World Feb. 1995: 8. ABI/INFORM. CD-ROM.
>   Proquest. Sept. 1995.
>
> *Parenthetical reference:* (Cavanaugh 8)

If the material is also available in print, begin with the information about the printed source, followed by the electronic source information: name of the database (underlined), CD-ROM designation, vendor name, and electronic publication date. If the material has no printed equivalent, list its author (if known) and title (in quotation marks), followed by the electronic source information.

If you are citing an abstract of the complete work, insert *Abstract,* followed by a period, immediately after the work's page numbers.

For CD-ROM reference works and other material not routinely updated, give the title of the work, followed by the CD-ROM designation, place, electronic publisher, and date:

> Time Almanac. CD-ROM. Washington: Compact, 1994.
>
> *Parenthetical reference:* (Time Almanac 74)

Begin with the author's or editor's name, if known.

29. Listserv—MLA

Korsten, A. "Major Update of the WWWVL Migration and Ethnic
      Relations." Online posting. 7 Apr. 1998. ERCOMER News.
      8 Apr. 1998 <http://www.ercomer.org/archive/ercomer-
      news/0002.html>.

Parenthetical reference: (Korsten)

Begin with the author's name (if known), followed by the title of the work (in quotation marks), the *Online posting* designation, publication date, name of discussion group, date of access, and the URL. The parenthetical reference includes no page number because none is given in an online posting.

30. Usenet—MLA

Dorsey, Michael. "Environmentalism or Racism." Online posting.
      25 Mar. 1998. 1 Apr. 1998 <news:alt.org.sierra-club>.

Parenthetical reference: (Dorsey)

31. Email—MLA

Wallin, John Luther. "Frog Reveries." Email to the author. 12
      Oct. 2006.

Parenthetical reference: (Wallin)

Cite personal email as you would printed correspondence. If the document has a subject line or title, enclose it in quotation marks.

For publicly posted email (say, a newsgroup or discussion list) include the address and date of access.

32. Web Site—MLA

Dumont, R. A. "An Online Course in Technical Writing." 10 Dec.
      2004. U of Massachusetts Dartmouth Online. 6 Jan. 2006

<http://www.umassd.edu/englishdepartment.html>.

Parenthetical reference: (Dumont 7-9)

Begin with the author's name (if known), followed by title of the work (in quotation marks), posting date, name of Web site, date of access, and Web address (in angle brackets). Note that a Web address that continues from one line to the next is broken only after a slash. No hyphen is added.

33. Article in an Online Periodical—MLA

```
Jones, Francine L. "The Effects of NAFTA on Labor Union

      Membership." Cambridge Business Review 2.3 (1999): 47-64.

      4 Apr. 2000 <http://www.mun.ca/cambrbusrev/1999vol2/

      jones2.html>.
```

Parenthetical reference: (Jones 48-49)

Information about the printed version is followed by the date of access to the Web site and the electronic address.

34. Real-Time Communication—MLA

Synchronous communication occurs in a "real time" forum and includes MUDs (multiuser dungeons), MOOs (MUD object-oriented software), IRC (Internet relay chat), and FTPs (file transfer protocols). The message typed in by the sender appears instantly on the screen of the recipient, as in a personal interview.

```
Mendez, Michael R. Online debate. "Solar Power Versus Fossil Fuel

      Power." 3 Apr. 1998. College TownMOO. 3 Apr. 1998

      <telnet://next.cs.brc.edu.777>.
```

Parenthetical reference: (Mendez)

Begin with the name of the communicator, and indicate the type of communication (personal interview, online debate, and so on), topic title, posting date, name of forum, access date, and electronic address.

MLA Works Cited Page

Place your Works Cited section on a separate page at the end of the document. Arrange entries alphabetically by author's surname. When the author is unknown, list the title alphabetically according to its first word (ignoring introductory articles). For a title that begins with a numeral, alphabetize the entry as if the numeral were spelled out.

APA Documentation Style

One popular alternative to MLA style is set out in the *Publication Manual of the American Psychological Association.* APA style is useful when writers wish to emphasize the publication dates of their references. A parenthetical reference in the text briefly identifies the source, date, and page numbers:

```
In a recent study, mice continuously exposed to an electromagnetic
field tended to die earlier than mice in the control group (de
Jager & de Bruyn, 1994, p. 224).
```

The full citation then appears in the alphabetical listing of references, at the report's end:

```
de Jager, L., & de Bruyn, L. (1994). Long-term effects of a 50-Hz
    electric field on the life expectancy of mice. Review of
    Environmental Health, 10, 221-224.
```

Because it emphasizes the date, APA style (or some similar author-date style) is preferred in the sciences and social sciences, where information quickly becomes outdated.

APA Parenthetical References

APA's parenthetical references differ from MLA's as follows: The APA citation includes the publication date, a comma separates each item in the reference, and *p.* or *pp.* precedes the page number. When a subsequent reference to a work follows closely after the initial reference, the date need not be included. Here are specific guidelines:

- If your discussion names the author, do not repeat the name in your parenthetical reference; simply give the date and page number:

```
Researchers de Jager and de Bruyn explain that experimental mice
exposed to an electromagnetic field tended to die earlier than
mice in the control group (1994, p. 224).
```

When two authors of a work are named in the text, their names are connected by *and,* but in a parenthetical reference, their names are connected by an ampersand, &.

- If you cite two or more works in a single reference, list the authors in alphabetical order and separate the citations with semicolons:

```
(Gomez, 1992; Jones, 2001; Leduc, 1996)
```

- If you cite a work with three to six authors, try to name them in your text, to avoid an excessively long parenthetical reference.

```
Franks, Oblesky, Ryan, Jablar, and Perkins (1993) studied the role
of electromagnetic fields in tumor formation.
```

In any subsequent references to this work, name only the first author, followed by *et al.* (Latin abbreviation for "and others").

- If you cite two or more works by the same author published in the same year, assign a letter to each work, alphabetized by title:

```
(Lamont, 1990a, p. 135)
```

```
(Lamont, 1990b, pp. 67-68)
```

Other examples of parenthetical references appear with their corresponding entries in the following discussion of the list of references.

APA References Entries

The APA References list includes each source that you have cited in your document. In preparing the list, type the first line of each entry flush with the left margin. Indent the second and subsequent lines five spaces. Skip one character space after a period, comma, or colon. Double-space within and between entries.

Following are examples of complete citations as they would appear in the References section of your document. Shown immediately below each entry is its corresponding parenthetical reference as it would appear in the text. Note the capitalization, abbreviation, spacing, and punctuation in the sample entries.

APA References entries for books. Any citation for a book should contain all applicable information in the following order: author, date, title, editor or translator, edition, volume number, and facts about publication (city and publisher).

1. Book, Single Author—APA

Kerzin-Fontana, J. B. (2005). *Technology management: A handbook* (3rd ed.) Delmar, NY: American Management Association.

Parenthetical reference: (Kerzin-Fontana, 2005, pp. 3-4)

Use only initials for an author's first and middle name. Capitalize only the first words of a book's title and subtitle and any proper nouns and adjectives. Identify an edition other than the first in parentheses between the title and the period.

2. Book, Two to Five Authors—APA

Aronson, L., Katz, R., & Moustafa, C. (2004). *Toxic waste disposal methods*. New Haven, CT: Yale University Press.

Parenthetical reference: (Aronson, Katz, & Moustafa, 2004)

Use an ampersand (&) before the name of the final author listed in an entry. As an alternative parenthetical reference, name the authors in your text and include date (and page numbers, if appropriate) in parentheses.

3. Book, Six or More Authors—APA

```
Fogle, S. T., et al. (1998). Hyperspace technology. Boston:
    Little, Brown.
```

Parenthetical reference: (Fogle et al., 1998, p. 34)

Et al. is the Latin abbreviation for *et alia,* meaning "and others."

4. Book, Anonymous Author—APA

```
Structured programming. (2005). Boston: Meredith Press.
```

Parenthetical reference: (Structured Programming, 2005, p. 67)

In your list of references, place an anonymous work alphabetically by the first word in its title, ignoring *The, A,* or *An.* In your parenthetical reference, capitalize all key words in a book or article title.

5. Multiple Books, Same Author—APA

```
Chang, J. W. (1997a). Biophysics. Boston: Little, Brown.

Chang, J. W. (1997b). MindQuest. Chicago: Pressler.
```

Parenthetical reference: (Chang, 1997a, 1997b)

Two or more works by the same author not published in the same year are distinguished by their dates alone, without the added letter. They are listed chronologically, earliest to latest.

6. Book, One to Five Editors—APA

```
Morris, A. J., & Pardin-Walker, L. B. (Eds.). (2003). Handbook of
    new information technology. New York: HarperCollins.
```

Parenthetical reference: (Morris & Pardin-Walker, 2003, p. 79)

For more than five editors, name only the first, followed by *et al.*

7. Book, Indirect Source—APA

```
Stubbs, J. (1998). White-collar productivity. Miami: Harris.
```

Parenthetical reference: (as cited in Stubbs, 1998, p. 47)

When your source has cited another source, list only this second source in the References section, but name the original source in the text: "Kline's study (as cited in Stubbs, 1998, p. 47) supports this conclusion."

8. Anthology Selection or Book Chapter—APA

Bowman, J. (1994). Electronic conferencing. In A. Williams (Ed.),

Communication and technology: Today and tomorrow (pp. 123–

142). Denton, TX: Association for Business Communication.

Parenthetical reference: (Bowman, 1994, p. 126)

The page numbers in the complete reference are for the selection cited from the anthology.

APA References entries for periodicals. A citation for an article should give this information (as available), in order: author, publication date, article title (without quotation marks), volume or issue number (or both), and page numbers for the entire article, not just the pages cited.

9. Article, Magazine—APA

DesMarteau, K. (1994, October). Study links sewing machine use to

Alzheimer's disease. Bobbin, 36, 36-38.

Parenthetical reference: (DesMarteau, 1994, p. 36)

If no author is given, provide all other information. Capitalize the first word in an article's title and subtitle, and any proper nouns and adjectives. Capitalize all key words in a periodical title. Italicize the periodical title, volume number, and commas.

10. Article, Journal with New Pagination for Each Issue—APA

Thackman-White, J. R. (2005). Computer-assisted research.

American Library Journal, 51(1), 3-9.

Parenthetical reference: (Thackman-White, 2005, pp. 4-5)

Because each issue in a given year has page numbers that begin at 1, readers need the issue number (in this instance, 1). The 51 denotes the volume number, which is italicized.

11. Article, Journal with Continuous Pagination—APA

Barnstead, M. H. (2004). The writing crisis. Journal of Writing

Theory, 12, 415-433.

Parenthetical reference: (Barnstead, 2004, pp. 415-416)

The 12 denotes the volume number. When page numbers continue from issue to issue for the full year, readers won't need the issue number, because no other issue in that year repeats the same page numbers.

12. Article, Newspaper—APA

> Baranski, V. H. (2005, January 15). Errors in technology
>   assessment. *The Boston Times,* p. 83.
>
> *Parenthetical reference:* (Baranski, 2005, p. 83)

In addition to the year of publication, include the month and day. If the newspaper's name begins with *The,* include it in your citation. Include *p.* or *pp.* before page numbers. For an article on nonconsecutive pages, list each page, separated by a comma.

APA References entries for other sources. Miscellaneous sources range from unsigned encyclopedia entries to conference presentations to government documents. A full citation should give this information (as available): author, publication date, work title (and report or series number), page numbers (if applicable), city, and publisher.

13. Encyclopedia, Dictionary, or Other Alphabetical Reference—APA

> James, R. K. (Ed.). (2001). *The business reference book.* Boston:
>   Business Resources Press.
>
> *Parenthetical reference:* (James, 2001, p. 255)

For an entry that is signed, use the author's name and place the editor's name after the title.

14. Report—APA

> Electrical Power Research Institute. (1994). *Epidemiologic
>   studies of electric utility employees* (Rep. No. RP2964.5).
>   Palo Alto, CA: Author.
>
> *Parenthetical reference:* (Electrical Power Research Institute,
>   [EPRI], 1994, p. 12)

If authors are named, list them first, followed by the publication date. When citing a group author, include the group's abbreviated name in your first parenthetical reference, and use only that abbreviation in any subsequent reference. When the agency or organization is also the publisher, list *Author* in the publisher's slot.

15. Conference Presentation—APA

> Smith, A. A. (1999). Radon concentrations in molded concrete. In
>   A. Hodkins (Ed.), *First British Symposium on Environmental
>   Engineering* (pp. 106-121). London: Harrison Press.
>
> *Parenthetical reference:* (Smith, 1999, p. 109)

In parentheses is the date of publication. The name of the symposium is a proper name and so is capitalized.

For an unpublished presentation, include the presenter's name, year and month, title of the presentation, title of the symposium (italicized), and all available information about the conference or meeting: "Symposium conducted at ..."

16. Interview, Personally Conducted—APA

Parenthetical reference: (G. Nasser, personal interview,
April 2, 2002)

This material is considered a nonrecoverable source and so is cited in the text only, as a parenthetical reference. If you name the respondent in the text, do not repeat the name in the citation.

17. Interview, Published—APA

Jable, C. K. (2000). The future of graphics [interview with James
Lescault]. In K. Prell (Ed.), *Executive views of automation*
(pp. 216-231). Miami: Haber Press, 2001.

Parenthetical reference: (Jable, 2000, pp. 218-223)

Begin with the name of the interviewer, followed by the interview date and title (if available), the designation (in brackets), and the publication information, including the date.

18. Personal Correspondence or Interview—APA

Parenthetical reference: (L. Rogers, personal communication,
May 15, 2001)

This material is considered nonrecoverable and so is cited in the text only, as a parenthetical reference. If you name the person in the text, do not repeat the name in the citation.

19. Brochure or Pamphlet—APA

This material follows the citation format for a book entry (see page 328). After the title of the work, include the designation *Brochure* in brackets.

20. Lecture—APA

Dumont, R. A. (2001, January 15). *Managing natural gas.* Lecture
presented at the University of Massachusetts, Dartmouth.

Parenthetical reference: (Dumont, 2001)

If you name the lecturer in the text, do not repeat the name in the citation.

21. Government Document—APA

Virginia Highway Department. (1997). *Standards for bridge*

   maintenance. Richmond: Author.

Parenthetical reference: (Virginia Highway Department, 1997, p. 49)

If the author is unknown, present the information in this order: name of the issuing agency, publication date, document title, place, and publisher. When the issuing agency is both author and publisher, list *Author* in the publisher slot.

For any congressional document, identify the house of Congress (Senate or House of Representatives) before the date.

U.S. House Armed Services Committee. (2001). *Funding for the military*

   academies. Washington, DC: U.S. Government Printing Office.

Parenthetical reference: (U.S. House, 2001, p. 41)

22. Miscellaneous Items (unpublished manuscripts, dissertations, and so on)—APA

Author (if known). (Date of publication). *Title of work.*

   Sponsoring organization or publisher.

For any work that has group authorship (corporation, committee, and so on), cite the name of the group or agency in place of the author's name.

APA References entries for electronic sources. Any citation for electronic media should allow readers to identify the original source (printed or electronic) and provide an electronic path for retrieving the material.

Begin with the publication information for the printed equivalent. Then, in brackets, name the electronic source ([CD-ROM], [Computer software]), the protocol—the set of standards that ensures compatibility among the different products designed to work together on a particular network (Bitnet, Dialog, FTP, Telnet), and any other items that define a clear path (service provider, database title, access code, retrieval number, site address).

23. Online Database Abstract—APA

Sahl, J. D. (1995). Power lines, viruses, and childhood leukemia.

   Cancer Causes Control, 6(1), 83. Abstract retrieved

   November 7, 2001, from the MEDLINE database.

Parenthetical reference: (Sahl, 1995)

Note that the entry ends with a period. Entries that close with a URL (see examples 29 and 30) have no period at the end.

24. Online Database Article—APA

> Alley, R. A. (2003, January). Ergonomic influences on worker
> satisfaction. *Industrial Psychology, 5*(11), 93-107.
> Retrieved February 10, 2004, from the PsycARTICLES
> database.
>
> *Parenthetical reference:* (Alley, 1995)

25. Computer Software or Software Manual—APA

> Virtual collaboration [Computer software]. (1994). New York:
> HarperCollins.
>
> *Parenthetical reference:* (Virtual, 1994)

For citing a manual, replace the *Computer software* designation in brackets with *Software manual.*

26. CD-ROM Abstract—APA

> Cavanaugh, H. (1995). An EMF study: Good news and bad news
> [CD-ROM]. *Electrical World, 209*(2), 8. Abstract retrieved
> April 7, 2002, from ProQuest File: ABI/INFORM.
>
> *Parenthetical reference:* (Cavanaugh, 1995)

The "8" in the entry denotes the page number of this one-page article.

27. CD-ROM or Internet Reference Work—APA

> Grossman, P., et al. (Eds.). (1997). *Time almanac* [Electronic
> version]. Washington: Compact, 1997.
>
> *Parenthetical reference: (Grossman et al.,* 1997, p. 20)

If the work on CD-ROM or on the Web has a printed equivalent, APA prefers that it be cited in its printed form. If you consulted the work online, write *Electronic version* in brackets after the title.

28. Personal Email—APA

> *Parenthetical reference:* Fred Flynn (personal communication,
> May 10, 2006) provided these statistics.

Instead of being included in the list of references, personal email is cited directly in the text.

29. Web Site—APA

Dumont, R. A. (2005, July 10). An online course in composition.

    Retrieved May 18, 2006, from http://www.umassd.edu/

    englishdepartment.html

Parenthetical reference: (Dumont, 2005)

If the Web address continues from one line to the next, divide it only after a slash.

30. Newsgroup, Discussion List, or Online Forum—APA

Labarge, V. S. (2001, October 20). A cure for computer viruses

    [Msg 2237]. Message posted to http://forums.ntnews.com/

    webin/webz198@.dsg9567

Parenthetical reference: (Labarge, 2001)

APA References List

APA's References section is an alphabetical listing (by author) equivalent to MLA's Works Cited section. Like Works Cited, the reference list includes only works actually cited in the text. Unlike MLA style, APA style calls for only recoverable sources to appear in the reference list. Therefore, personal interviews, email messages, and other unpublished materials are cited in the text only. (For a sample report in APA style, see "Feasibility Analysis of a Career in Technical Marketing," at http://www.ablongman.com/gurak.

CSE and Other Numbered Documentation Styles

In a numbered documentation system, each work is assigned a number sequentially the first time it is cited. This same number is then used for any subsequent reference to that work. Numbered documentation is often used in the physical sciences (astronomy, chemistry, geology, physics) and in the applied sciences (mathematics, medicine, engineering, and computer science).

Particular disciplines have their own preferred documentation styles, described in manuals such as these:

- American Chemical Society, *The ACS Style Guide for Authors and Editors*
- American Institute for Physics, *AIP Style Guide*
- American Medical Association, *Manual of Style*

One widely consulted guide for numerical documentation is *Scientific Style and Format: The CSE Manual for Authors, Editors, and Publishers,* from the

Council of Science Editors. (In addition to its citation-sequence system for documentation, the CSE offers a name-year system that basically duplicates the APA system described on pages 325–335.)

CSE Numbered Citations

In the numbered version of CSE style, a citation in the text appears as a superscript number immediately following the source to which it refers:

> A recent study[1] indicates an elevated leukemia risk among children exposed to certain types of electromagnetic fields. Related studies[2-3] tend to confirm the EMF-cancer hypothesis.

When referring to two or more sources in a single note, separate the numbers by a hyphen if they are in sequence and by commas but no space if they are out of sequence: ([2,6,9]).

The full citation for each source then appears in the numeric listing of references at the end of the document.

References

1. Baron, KL, et al. The electromagnetic spectrum. New York: Pearson; 2005. 476 p.
2. Klingman, JM. Nematode infestation in boreal environments. *J Entymol* 2003;54:475–8.

CSE References Entries

CSE's References section lists each source in the order in which it was first cited. In preparing the list, which should be double-spaced, begin each entry on a new line. Type the number flush with the left margin, followed by a period and a space. Align subsequent lines directly under the first word of line 1.

Following are examples of complete citations as they would appear in the References section for your document.

CSE References entries for books. Any citation for a book should contain all available information in the following order: number assigned to the entry, author or editor, title (and edition), facts about publication (place, publisher, date), and number of pages. Note the capitalization, abbreviation, spacing, and punctuation in the sample entries.

1. Book, Single Author—CSE

1. Kerzin-Fontana JB. Technology management: a handbook. 3rd ed. Delmar, NY; American Management Assoc; 2005. 356 p.

2. Book, Multiple Authors—CSE

2. Aronson L, Katz R, Moustafa C. Toxic waste disposal methods. New Haven: Yale Univ Pr; 2004. 316 p.

3. Book, Anonymous Author—CSE

3. [Anonymous]. Structured programming. Boston: Meredith Pr; 2005. 267 p.

4. Book, One or More Editors—CSE

4. Morris AJ, Pardin-Walker LB, editors. Handbook of new information technology. New York: Harper; 2003. 345 p.

5. Anthology Selection or Book Chapter—CSE

5. Bowman JP. Electronic conferencing. In: Williams A, editor: Communication and technology: today and tomorrow. Denton, TX: Assoc for Business Communication; 1994. p 123-42.

CSE References entries for periodicals. Any citation for an article should contain all available information in the following order: number assigned to the entry, author, article title, periodical title, date (year, month), volume and issue number, and inclusive page numbers for the article. Note the capitalization, abbreviation, spacing, and punctuation in the sample entries.

6. Article, Magazine—CSE

6. DesMarteau K. Study links sewing machine use to Alzheimer's disease. Bobbin 1994 Oct:36-8.

7. Article, Journal with New Pagination Each Issue—CSE

7. Thackman-White JR. Computer-assisted research. Am Library J 2005;51(1):3-9.

8. Article, Journal with Continuous Pagination—CSE

8. Barnstead MH. The writing crisis. J Writing Theory 2004;12:415-33.

9. Article, Newspaper—CSE

9. Baranski VH. Errors in technology assessment. Boston Times 2005 Jan 15;Sect B:3.

10. Article, Online Source—CSE

10. Alley RA. Ergonomic influences on worker satisfaction. Industrial Psychology [article online]. 2003 Jan;5(11). Available from: ftp.pub/journals/industrialpychology/2003 via the INTERNET. Accessed 2004 Feb 10.

Citation for an article published online follows a similar format, with these differences: write *article online* in brackets between the article title and publication date; after "Available from," give the URL followed by a period and your access information.

For more guidelines and examples, consult the *CSE Manual* or go to http://www.wisc.edu/writing/Handbook/DocCSE.html and http://www.lib.ohio-state.edu/guides/cbegd.html.

References

Bizzell, P. (1992). *Academic discourse and critical consciousness.* Pittsburgh: University of Pittsburgh Press.

——————. (1997). Cognition, convention, and certainty: What we need to know about writing. In V. Villanueva (Ed.), *Cross-talk in comp theory: A reader.* Urbana, IL: National Council of Teachers of English.

Blum, D. (1997). Investigative science journalism. In D. Blum & M. Knudson (Eds.), *Field guide for science writers* (pp. 86–93). New York: Oxford.

Brownell, J., & Fitzgerald, M. (1992). Teaching ethics in business communication: The effective/ethical balancing scale. *Bulletin of the Association for Business Communication, 55*(3), 15–18.

Bryan, J. (1992). Down the slippery slope: Ethics and the technical writer as marketer. *Technical Communication Quarterly, 1*(1), 73–88.

Cavazos, E. A., & Morin, G. (1994). *Cyberspace and the law: Your rights and duties in the on-line world.* Cambridge, MA: MIT Press.

Christians, C. G., Tackler, M., Rotzoll, K. B., Brittain-McKee, K., & Woods, R. H., Jr. (2005). Introduction. In C. G., Christians, M., Tackler, K. B., Rotzoll, K., Brittain-McKee, & R. H., Woods Jr. (Eds.), *Media ethics: Cases and moral reasoning* (7th ed., pp. 22–24). Boston: Allyn & Bacon.

Columbia Accident Investigation Board. (2003, August). *Report Volume I.* Washington, DC: Author.

Debs, M. B. (1989). Recent research on collaborative writing in industry. *Technical Communication, 38,* 475–485.

Dragga, S. (1996). "Is this ethical?" A survey of opinion on principles and practices of document design. *Technical Communication, 43*(3), 255–265.

Dumas, J. S., & Redish, J. C. (1994). *A practical guide to usability testing* (2nd ed.). Norwood, NJ: Ablex.

Earthquake hazard analysis for nuclear power plants. (1984, June). *Energy and Technology Review.* p. 8.

Electronic Privacy Information Center (EPIC). (2000). http://www.epic.org

Felker, D. B., Pickering, F., Charrow, V., Holland, V., & Redish, J. (1981). *Guidelines for document designers.* Washington D.C.: American Institutes for Research.

Fink, C. (1988). *Media ethics.* Boston: Allyn & Bacon.

Fortner, B., & Meyer, T. E. (1997). *Number by color: A guide to using color to understand technical data.* New York: Springer-Verlag.

Garfield, E. (1973). What scientific journals can tell us about scientific journals. *IEEE Transactions on Professional Communication, 16,* 200–202.

Gibaldi, J., & Achtert, W. S. (1988). *MLA Handbook for Writers of Research Papers* (3rd ed.). New York: Modern Language Association.

Gouran, D. S., Hirokawa, R. Y., & Martz, A. E. (1986). A critical analysis of factors related to decisional processes involved in the *Challenger* disaster. *Central States Speech Journal, 37*(3), 119–135.

Gross, A., & Walzer, A. (1994). Positivists, postmodernists, Aristotelians, and the *Challenger* disaster. *College English, 56*(4), 420–433.

Hargis, G., Hernandez, A., Hughes, P., & Ramaker, J. (1997). *Developing quality technical information: A handbook for writers and editors.* Upper Saddle River, NJ: Prentice Hall.

Harris, J. (1989). The idea of community in the study of writing. *College Composition and Communication, 40,* 11–22.

Hartley, J. (1985). *Designing instructional text* (2nd ed.). London: Kogan Page.

Helyar, P. S., & Doudnikoff, G. M. (1994). Walking the labyrinth of multimedia law. *Technical Communication, 41*(4), 662–671.

Hill-Duin, A. (1990). Terms and tools: A theory- and research-based approach to collaborative writing. *Bulletin of the Association for Business Communication, 53*(2), 45–50.

Hoft, N. L. (1995). *International technical communication: How to export information about high technology.* New York: Wiley.

Horn, R. E. (1998). *Visual language: Global communication for the 21st century.* Bainbridge, WA: MacroVU.

Horton, W. K. (1990). *Designing and writing online documentation: Help files to hypertext.* New York: Wiley.

——————. (1991). *Illustrating computer documentation: The art of presenting information graphically on paper and online.* New York: Wiley.

Howell, D. (1994, November 12). B-CS renters dish out the dough. *The Eagle* [Bryan, TX], p. A-1.

Hughes, M. (1999). Rigor in usability testing. *Technical Communication, 46*(4), 488–495.

Hulbert, J. E. (1994). Developing collaborative insights and skills. *Bulletin of the Association for Business Communication, 57*(2), 53–56.

Janis, I. L. (1972). *Victims of groupthink: A psychological study of foreign policy decisions and fiascos.* Boston: Houghton-Mifflin.

Japikse, C. (1994). Lasagna in the making. *EPA Journal, 20*(3), 27.

Johannesen, R. L. (1983). *Ethics in human communication* (2nd ed.). Prospect Heights, IL: Waveland Press.

Johnson, R. R. (1997). *User-centered technology: A rhetorical theory for computers and other mundane artifacts.* Albany: State University of New York Press.

Karjala, D. (1999). *What are the issues in copyright term extension—and what happened?* http://www.public.asu.edu/~dkarjala/what.html

Kohl, J. R. (1999). Improving translatability and readability with syntactic cues. *Technical Communication, 46*(2), 149–166.

Kostelnick, C., & Roberts, D. D. (1998). *Designing visible language: Strategies for professional communicators.* Boston: Allyn & Bacon.

Larson, C. U. (1995). *Persuasion: Perception and responsibility* (7th ed.). Belmont, CA: Wadsworth.

Lavin, M. R. (1992). *Business information: How to find it, how to use it* (2nd ed.). Phoenix: Oryx Press.

Lynch, P. J., & Horton, S. (2001). *Web style guide: Basic design principles for creating Web sites.* (2nd ed.). New Haven, CT: Yale University Press.

Matson, E. (1997, October/November). The seven sins of deadly meetings. *Fast Company,* 249–252.

McGuire, G. (1992). Shared minds: A model of collaboration. *Technical Communication, 39,* 467–468.

Miles, T. H. (1989). The memo and "disinformation": Beyond format and style. *Issues in Writing, 2*(1), 42–60.

Morgan, M. (1991). Patterns of composing: Connections between classroom and workplace collaborations. *Technical Communication, 38,* 540–542.

Pace, R. C. (1988). Technical communication, group differentiation, and the decision to launch the space shuttle *Challenger. Journal of Technical Writing and Communication, 18*(3), 207–220.

Patry, W. F. (1985). *The fair use privilege in copyright law.* Washington, DC: Bureau of National Affairs.

Petroski, H. (1996). *Invention by design.* Cambridge, MA: Harvard University Press.

Physicians' Desk Reference (53rd ed.). (1999). Oradell, NJ: Medical Economics.

Plain English Network. (2001, April 16). *Testing your documents.* http://www.plainlanguage. gov/howto/test/htm

Presidential Commission. (1986). *Report to the president on the space shuttle* Challenger *accident.* Vol. 1. Washington, DC: Government Printing Office.

Rosenau, L. (2000, March). Working knowledge: Electricity meters. *Scientific American,* 108.

Rosenfeld, L., & Morville, P. (1998). *Information architecture for the World Wide Web.* Cambridge, MA: O'Reilly.

Rubin, J. (1994). *Handbook of usability testing: How to plan, design, and conduct effective tests.* New York: Wiley.

Ruggiero, V. R. (1998). *The art of thinking: A guide to critical and creative thought.* (5th ed.). New York: Longman.

Schenk, M. T., & Webster, J. K. (1984). *Engineering information resources.* New York: Decker.

Seglin, J. L. (1998, July). Would you lie to save your company? *Inc.,* 53–57.

Strong, W. S. (1993). *The copyright book: A practical guide.* Cambridge, MA: MIT Press.

Tufte, E. R. (1990). *Envisioning information.* Cheshire, CT: Graphics Press.

——————. (1992). *The visual display of quantitative information.* Cheshire, CT: Graphics Press.

Unger, S. H. (1982). *Controlling technology: Ethics and the responsible engineer.* New York: Holt, Rinehart and Winston.

Varchaver, N. (2003, February 17). The perils of e-mail. *Fortune,* 96–102.

Walker, J. R., & Ruszkiewicz, J. (2000). *Writing@online.edu.* New York: Longman.

Wickens, C. D. (1992). *Engineering psychology and human performance* (2nd ed.). New York: HarperCollins.

Wilford, J. N. (1999, April 6). When no one read, who started to write? *New York Times,* pp. D1, D2.

Winsor, D. (1988). Communication failures contributing to the *Challenger* accident: An example for technical communication. *IEEE Transactions on Professional Communication, 31*(3), 101–107.

Yoos, G. (1979). A revision of the concept of ethical appeal. *Philosophy and Rhetoric, 12*(4), 41–58.

ZDNET. (2000). *Intel pill: Is Big Brother inside?* http://www.zdnet.com/zdhelp/stories/main/ 0,5594,2214831,00.html

Credits

Chapter 2

Figure 2.1, Medtronic Kappa™ Generation of Pacing Systems. Reproduced with permission of Medtronic, Inc. Figure 2.2, Black & Decker Instruction Manual, © 1993. Black & Decker (U.S.) Inc. Reprinted by permission. Figure 2.3, Nexium Web site, http://www.purplepill.com. Figure 2.4, *Physicians' Desk Reference* (2006), pp. 644–645.

Chapter 3

Figure 3.3, Reprinted by permission from *IBM ThinkPad 240 User's Reference*, 1/e. © by Lenovo. Figure 3.4, Reprinted by permission from *IBM ThinkPad A20 User's Reference*, 1/e. © by Lenovo.

Chapter 4

Figure 4.1, The Campaign, www.thecampaign.org. Reprinted by permission.

Chapter 5

Figure 5.2, California Institute of Technology, www.caltech.edu. Reprinted by permission. Figure 5.3a, Pesticide Management Education Program at Cornell University, Ithaca, NY. Reprinted by permission. Figure 5b, Courtesy of Nova/WGBH Educational Foundation. Copyright © 2003 WGBH/Boston. Reprinted by permission. Figure 5.4, Reprinted by permission from Microsoft Corporation. Figure 5.5, Reprinted by permission of Microsoft Corporation.

Chapter 6

Figure 6.3, From David Howell, "B-CS Renters Dish Out The Dough." *The Eagle*, 12 Nov. 1994, A-1. Copyright, Bryan-College Station Eagle. Reprinted by permission. Figure 6.4, Reprinted with permission from Society for Technical Communication. Arlington, VA.

Chapter 7

Figure 7.1, Reprinted with permission from Society for Technical Communication. Arlington, VA. Figure 7.2, Reprinted with the permission of the Regents of the University of Minnesota. © 2000 Regents of the University of Minnesota. Figure 7.3, www.paypal.com. These materials have been reproduced with the permission of PayPal, Inc. Copyright © 3006 PayPal, Inc. All rights reserved. Figure 7.4, A privacy statement from the Amazon.com Web site. © 2005 Amazon.com, Inc. All rights reserved. Amazon, Amazon.com and the Amazon.com logo are registered trademarks of Amazon.com, Inc. or its affiliates. Reprinted by permission.

Chapter 8

Figure 8.9, Microsoft Corp. Figure 8.10, From the Washington State Department of Health Web site. www.doh.wa.gov. Figure 8.11, www.thermador.com. Reprinted by permission of BSH Home Appliance Corporation.

Index

Note: Page numbers followed by italicized *f* indicate figures.